FIFTH AVENUE

Architecture and Society
A History of America's Street of Dreams

"*It's impossible not to be entranced by this book. Yet also saddened by it. In faded sepia photographs, a parade of fabulous houses sweeps by. Many are magnificent, others monstrous, a few beautiful. Almost all are gone. With a touching and relentless dedication, Mosette Broderick has pursued the ephemeral glory of Fifth Avenue and reconnected it with the ambitions and follies of the men and women who created it. The result is a book for the shelves of all lovers of New York and its legacy of lost architecture.*"

Andrew Saint, Architectural Historian

"*This is the authoritative account of a fascinating and now almost completely vanished chapter in New York's architectural and social history. Mosette Broderick traces the development of Fifth Avenue northwards from Washington Square, from its modest early brick row houses to the increasingly palatial residences of the Vanderbilts, the Rockefellers, of Jay Gould, Andrew Carnegie and many more, all illustrated with magnificent period photographs and recalling along the way the stories of the many intriguing characters who built them.*"

Timothy Brittain-Catlin, Course Leader, MSt Architecture Apprenticeship Associate Teaching Professor; Director of Studies for Architecture at Homerton college

FIFTH AVENUE

Architecture and Society
A History of America's Street of Dreams

Mosette Broderick

Unicorn Press

IN MEMORY OF THE LATE MARK GIROUARD WHO OPENED ARCHITECTURAL HISTORY TO THE PEOPLE WHO USE THE BUILDINGS.

First published in 2023 by
Unicorn Press
60 Bracondale
Norwich NR1 2BE
UK

tradfordhugh@gmail.com
www.unicornpublishing.org

A CIP record of this book can be obtained from the British Library

ISBN 978 1 739164 02 7

Designed by Karen Wilks
Printed in the UK by TJ Books Limited, Padstow

Frontispiece:
Fifth Avenue and 42nd Street, including a view of the Hotel Bristol.

CONTENTS

As a small child I attended school in an English Georgian-style red brick country house in Oyster Bay, New York. It had been built in 1918 at the tail end of the 'Gilded Age' and was surrounded by spacious grounds. The idea of the school was to continue the entitlement wealthy families felt they had as heirs to an American version of European aristocracy. The house, "Mallows", was briefly owned by the boss of a dry-goods company in Illinois, but the Depression of the 1930s, followed by World War 2, ended its brief period as a country estate and led to its use as a school founded in 1946. As a legacy of the short-lived American aristocracy, the school's founders arranged the curriculum to include solid learning, Latin, sports, a sense of fair play, and the pursuit of high-minded goals. The school trained its students for a life which would evaporate before their formal education ended. The entire set of values melted away.

The students came from families of this world. Inspiration for the high-minded goals of the past came from Mrs. Taggart Whipple, Carol DuBois, John Rousmaniere and Julie Schieflin. Others who understood this history included Anthony K. Baker, Caroline and Christopher Rupp, Joan Williams and Eddie and Steena Auchincloss, Mary de Zulueta Greenebaum. The best exemplar of old American patrician values might well have been Pauline Baker Pitt who long ago corrected me: "It's a boat not a yacht!" Even my professor, Henry Russell Hitchcock, could recite from memory the family trees of notable European aristocrats. With his photographic recall, he could then launch into the American attempts at the same. Many of these families had once owned houses on New York's Fifth Avenue.

This study of the development of New York City through examining Fifth Avenue began in 1980 with a careful reading of the New Building docket books in the New York City Archive. The docket books begin in 1865-66 and perusal of the permits they contain showed that Fifth Avenue led the development of the City northwards. Reading the applications for houses long-lost enabled me to see the City rise visually. Two years spent in the docket books as we battled the pigeons in the Tweed Court house were made possible by the heroic Ken Cobb. Helping with this effort was Robin Sand.

Research through the periodicals of the era in the Avery Library of Columbia University was made richer thanks to material located by Lydia Lachinova.

Life and work interrupted this project, resuming only in the last few years. Steadily encouraging the return has been Herbert Broderick, my husband, who read many iterations of the manuscript. The pandemic and almost eighteen months at home allowed me to work steadily on this book.

Gillian Malpass endured early drafts and encouraged its completion. At a moment of despair, Andrew Saint, a great writer, lived up to his surname. Gillian and Andrew made this venture see the light of day.

Josh Kwassman, graphic designer and computer wiz, set up the laptop and solved all the problems. Geoffrey Tortora, writer and friend, helped by reading through some early chapters.

Akeem Flavors, master of digital work, prepared scans for the book from a weak to a credible state. He is also the epitome of a professional art historian.

José Hernandez, a master map-maker, supplied the images of the Fifth Avenue maps. Daniel Holub of New York University displayed wonderful kindness helping me cope with a very large class during the writing of this book. Audrey Christensen-Tsai, Librarian at the Department of Art History, provided help with images. Randall Say at New York University's Office of the Budget provided great relief this summer, as did Peggy Coon.

The late Christopher S. Gray, a fellow traveler in New York City building history, generously opened his files in his Office of Metropolitan History to me. We spoke so often there while working. We lost him way too early along with his wife, Erin Drake. Park Avenue, a subject he and Erin knew well from farm days forward, will sadly now not be written. Sam Hightower at the Office has been wonderfully helpful, always springing into action in a heat wave on a Saturday.

Sean Khorsandi and Kyle Blaha have been great supporters of this work and made a kind offer to me that I will never forget.

Wendy Doremus, a great friend, provided support and a lovely place to live while completing the text.

Patrick Amsellem is also to be thanked for his support through this project and his willingness to look at every image for a cover picture - a wise and great friend.

Una Chaudhuri, Dean of the Humanities at New York University, has been a gracious supporter of this project.

Mary Rogers went out of her way to provide picture funding from the New York University Center for the Humanities. I am indeed grateful to her.

Friends of the Upper East Side are to be thanked for their gracious support of this project and unfailing humanity.

Hugh Tempest-Radford, a publisher with grace, dignity, wisdom and patience, has managed the project with his Unicorn Press team of Liz Wyse, excellent wordsmith and eagle-eyed copy editor; Karen Wilks, gifted designer and layout genius; Nicola King, clear-thinking and reliable indexer; and Lauren Tanner, industrious Publicity Manager.

To Josephine English Cook, I owe an enormous debt. She took my laptop work and transformed it into a proper manuscript. The picture citations are also a triumph of English's considerable art historical skills. She is adept as scholar, teacher, publishing wiz and human being. She is diplomatic and brilliant. She helped make a silk purse out of a sow's ear.

Mosette Broderick, September 2023

CHAPTER 1
BEFORE FIFTH AVENUE

*"Beyond the Park lay Fifth Avenue—and Fifth Avenue
was where she wanted to be!"*

Edith Wharton, *The Custom of the Country, 1913*[1]

FIFTH AVENUE, NEW YORK CITY, was for a century the address of achievement for wealthy Americans who, over the course of 75 years, moved inexorably northwards along the five miles from Washington Square to 95th Street. The pace became frenetic, the goal a projection of prominence, but the process was always unstable given frequent economic fluctuations. As New York's population doubled in the second half of the 19th century, the northward pull of the Avenue drew the city along with it. As the city grew, each new generation seemed more fabulous than the last, and every generation fled northward.

An address and a house on Fifth Avenue embodied a statement and a claim that a family wished to make. The exterior displayed the wealth and nature of the men, who needed the prestige of a fine address and a matching house, while the interiors became the host to the social machinations that would feed writers such as Edith Wharton and Henry James. Women, gradually shedding the traditional tasks of the home, freed by servants and new mechanical devices, launched an intricate social game. Many women engaged in the encompassing set of social priorities to the point of forcing men to remove fully to an office; up to the mid-19th century, many men had conducted business and held meetings in the home, and some had even made adaptations accordingly. An ambitious businessman, Frederick F. Thompson, had his architects plan heating coils in the front door area of his house to keep messenger boys warm while he composed a reply, although few

This 1876 land map shows the development of Second and Fifth Avenue. The two wide streets were once in competition for future primacy. Fifth Avenue won. Sheet 7: Bounded by McDougall Street, Houston Street, Hancock Street, Bleecker Street, Sixth Avenue, East 20th Street, Avenue A, Delancey Parkway, Bowery and Spring Street, 1867, Plan of New York City, from the Battery to Spuyten Duyvil Creek, J. F. Harrison, survey map.

followed his example. But by the 1870s men worked mostly in offices in lower Manhattan, leaving the house fully to the women.

Knickerbocker New York

In the early days of the nation, Broadway at Bowling Green was the epicenter for a small group of successful merchants, mostly of Dutch ancestry, known as the Knickerbockers, who lived decently if modestly, often moving interchangeably between Albany and Manhattan. The Dutch owned most of the island still from the old "Patroon" days, while some settlers from England had joined with the Dutch and participated in a close-knit society based in lower Manhattan. Old-time Dutch customs carried on even after the language had vanished and many had foresaken the Collegiate Dutch Church for Episcopalian churches like St. Mark's in the Bowery. This section of the young colony was set up by Peter Stuyvesant, Director-General of New Netherland for the Dutch West India Company. Indeed, St. Mark's in the Bowery, a Dutch Reform building linked to the Stuyvesants and on their Farm/Bowery, was sold to the Episcopalian Trinity Corporation for a single dollar in 1799.

Social life among the Knickerbocker families was limited, but distinctive. Christmas was a lesser winter event than New Year's Day, when the ladies dressed up, created alcohol punches, and awaited the calls of the gentlemen who took a cup and went on often to visit dozens of parlors within their group. Santa Claus, gingersnaps, impromptu dancing, and a rather easy conviviality for the young people of this set made this a pleasant life. The unmarried young socialized on the Dutch stoops at the front of the houses in good weather, danced in the small parks, such as Washington Square and City Hall Park, in the evenings and enjoyed a relaxed acquaintance within their circle. Things started to change in the early 19th century, when the blessings of an open and ice-free port and the vast increase of trade after the opening of the Erie Canal in 1825 greatly enriched the merchants of the Port of New York. Many New England merchants, whose harbors froze in the winter, moved to New York, and became a part of the Knickerbocker group. The newly arrived "Yankees" and the settled Dutch families conducted business in a similar manner; they built ships, handled the transfer of goods from ocean-going vessels to coastal and inland boats and vice versa, and ran the frequent European service routes as well as the China trade.

As the mercantile class grew, the Knickerbockers and Yankees moved northwards up Broadway, away from the crowded harbor frontages into modest red brick row houses not dissimilar to those they had occupied before, at locations like Greenwich Street and St. John's Square. Later, they also occupied territory that was once part of the Stuyvesant estate, at addresses such as Bond Street and Lafayette Row. Still the same group, they formed a congenial cluster of some 50 families. The city was expanding, but they were still the important citizens.

Fashionable life at Greenwich Street lasted for only about fifteen years, to be followed by a cluster of homes on Bond Street from about 1830 to 1855 at the latest. By then the new tenements and market at the Bowery to the east were making themselves felt and the shore of the East River had become distinctly working class. Many decently built homes abandoned by the better-off had become boarding houses or tenements; abandoned churches were turned into warehouses. As the buildings were sound, they often lasted 40 years or more before they were replaced.

Avenues of Advance

It was time for the wealthy to move again, but where? By now the matrix of Manhattan's future growth had been fixed by the famous Commissioner's Plan, surveyed by John Randel and adopted by the city in 1811, which set the pattern of avenues and streets at regular intervals that has endured to this day. It took years for Randel's grid, marked out in advance by boundary posts, to command general acceptance. But by 1825 it was clear that the main axes of advance for New York's development of all kinds would be the twelve broad north-south avenues, some 100 feet wide, now gradually opening up with intervals of anything between 610 and 920 feet between them. It remained a question as to which of these avenues would attract fashionable folk and which would succumb to lower-class housing or trade alone.

Two of these generous new avenues, now being hewn out of the solid bedrock of lower Manhattan, looked promising. Towards the East Side, Second Avenue was redolent of the old Dutch connection, and the property at its base was part of a large swathe of land still in the hands of the Stuyvesant family, notably Peter Gerard Stuyvesant (1777–1846). In 1830 there was a particularly smart house at the corner of Bond Street and Second Avenue. The Stuyvesants' plan was to simply continue the existing streets and move north, following the European tradition of leasing, rather than selling, property, but they were too slow. Stuyvesant Square, a park created out of land that they had agreed to donate to the City in 1836, would not be laid out until their new church, St. George's, was completed in 1848.

There were some exceptions to the grid. On St. Mark's Place, an unusual, angled short street between Second Avenue and what was then the "rough" Third Avenue, close to the Knickerbocker enclave around Bond Street, the speculator builder Thomas E. Davis built some smart Federal-style row houses in the 1830s with the financial backing of J. L. and S. Josephs, the New York agents to Nathan M. Rothschild. While the Josephs fell victim to the 1837 financial crash, Davis would survive, build on Staten Island, and later constructed an entire block on Fifth Avenue between 31st and 32nd Streets.

One way or another, Second Avenue was not ready for meaningful development until 1850 and well before then, a better candidate had emerged – Fifth Avenue.

Chapter 2

Washington Square

"Today the art of gardening is practised much more often than any other, in ignorant, impulsive ways, by people who never stop to think that it is an art at all."

Mariana Griswold Van Rensselaer

At the turn of the 19th century, the debate about the future movement of settlement northwards was a matter of much dispute for those with properties on the northern edge of the city. It was unclear how the city would develop.

The line of Fifth Avenue came into existence well before it became one of the great 100-ft north-south axes under the Commissioner's Plan of 1811 for the future development of Manhattan. In 1785, the Common Council of New York City instructed the surveyor Casimir Goerck to make a plan for the division and sale of the common lands north of what became 23rd Street. Goerck proposed a longitudinal axis known as the Middle Road bisecting the center of the island, which was to give access on either side to large subdivisions of land. Little of his plan came into effect, but the line of the Middle Road survived and was taken up in the 1811 Plan as Fifth Avenue. This was now scheduled to begin at Art Street and Greenwich Lane, far south of Goerck's starting point.

The lower sections of this new route, known as Thompson Street, were strategically placed for successful development and soon began to fill up with what were called "second rate genteel houses." John L. and John B. Ireland, of a large landowning family that was related to many older New York families such as the Lawrences and Floyds of Long Island, had purchased the land to the west and built a house for themselves on the northeast of the property, which remained there

Overleaf:
The original main building of the University of the City of New York (later New York University) by Town, Davis & Dakin looms in the rear. To its south is the reformed Dutch church by Minard Lafever. The square appears vastly larger than it is in the image here. The regiment of the merchants of the port appears like toy soldiers while being admired by fashionable women in the middle of the lawn. Seventh Regiment on Review, Washington Square, New York, *Otto Boetticher, 1851.*

for some 80 years. Further north, however, there was a big stumbling block. Across the Avenue's course above the level of 4th Street lay the Potter's Field. This large piece of open ground had begun as the site of some cemeteries owned by downtown churches before a much bigger adjacent area had been bought by the city in 1797 in order to provide a final resting place for New York's poor, including all too many who had died of contagious diseases. It was also occasionally used for public hangings. By 1825 the cemetery was full, and as development crept north, notably along Broadway, there was growing pressure to do away with this unpleasant obstruction to what would otherwise become a fashionable district. The ground was duly leveled over and a new common graveyard designated on the site of present-day Bryant Park.

From Parade Ground to Park

The next steps owed the most to Philip Hone, diarist and Mayor of New York in 1826–27. Hone persuaded the Common Council to relocate the city's military parade ground, hitherto earmarked for a much larger stretch of ground above 23rd Street, on the old Potter's Field site. Parades were fashionable and popular entertainment, and the Washington Military Parade Ground was formally designated in time for Independence Day celebrations in 1826. Duly fenced and landscaped, the field reopened as a park (the city's third and largest) in 1828. Later enlarged to a rectangle, the space soon became known as Washington Square.

Good houses swiftly followed on, beginning with the Federal-style Fourth Street Row, begun on the south side of the square in 1827. A growing interest in building more and better-quality houses led to consideration of the north side of Washington Square, from which Fifth Avenue was to depart. Here the landholdings were divided by a minor watercourse called Minetta Creek, which was soon canalized and marked the approximate line of Fifth Avenue—slightly right of the square's center in terms of its final dimensions.[1]

The key to change here lay with a sizeable piece of farmland that started east of the creek. Stretching in modern terms between Cooper Square, Fifth Avenue, Waverley Place, and 10th Street, this land had been in the ownership of a slightly disreputable sailor, Captain Robert Richard Randall. Like his father before him, Randall was a member of New York's Marine Society, which helped distressed sailors. He had no immediate heirs, so at his death in 1801 he left the farm to provide care for worn-out sailors from the clipper fleets in their final years. His benefaction came to be quaintly known as Sailor's Snug

Harbor. Already in 1801 there had been speculative plans to cover the property's eastern and southern edges in building lots, but they were forced to remain on paper because some greedy Randall family members challenged the will. The case took 29 years to resolve—in favor of Randall's intention—and meanwhile New York City closed in further. The trustees, one of whom was Philip Hone, logically resolved to develop the farm for building on the leasehold system and to create an alternate Sailor's Snug Harbor on Staten Island, where it survives to this day.[2]

Greek Revival

The transformation of an unhappy cemetery into a salubrious European-style green park at its doorstep had vastly increased the value of the Snug Harbor property and its prospects for development, also opening up possibilities for Fifth Avenue beyond. Before that could happen, Washington Square would become the fashionable center of the city for the merchants of the port in the 1830s and 40s, exemplified by the splendid Greek Revival row houses along its northeast side. Unlike the Fourth Street Row opposite, half of them very happily still survive.

As we know, New York City had neither a solid gentry nor great wealth by 1830. In 1831, a group of men from the port, several Presbyterian followers of the merchant Robert Lenox who had come from Scotland to New York, decided to build houses across from the new Washington Square Parade Ground on that long block of 6th Street, which they renamed Waverley Place. These men built a row of what would be the finest Greek Revival houses in the city, which were a story taller than the houses they left near the harbor. Immigration was advancing and their current homes were close to the newly arrived crowds near the harbor, so the merchants chose a fine uptown location even if it required a Broadway stagecoach ride to go downtown to work.

These fourteen parcels along the top of the new parade ground became the most desirable portions of the estate. Facing Waverley Place (at first called 6th Street), they enjoyed a perpetual green view and an extra 25-foot plot at the back for stables. The lessees, working with some difficulty to the directives of Snug Harbor Trustees, were obliged to build a set of houses of high quality to a cohesive design, using the best builders rather than standard operatives, and to complete the building work within two years.

The driver behind the development was a Glaswegian Scot, the merchant trader John Johnston, whose imports included the iconic beverage of the day, Madeira. Johnston's partner, James Boorman, was also involved in Snug Harbor developments along with a third merchant, John Morrison. These figures belonged to a small but cohesive group who lived close to one another, rapidly propelled themselves to the top of New York society, worshiped in the Presbyterian church on Fifth Avenue that opened in 1841, and did much to better civic life in the mid-century. While the houses were in construction, John Johnston took his family to see his Scottish home and then on to the Continent to acquire furnishings for the house. He followed the example of his friends and neighbors, going to the same shops and purchasing identical objects. Johnston bought the same marble topped tables his friends had, four Leghorn white statuary marble fireplace surrounds, alabaster vases, and marble fruits. He purchased two busts, one of Hamilton, the other of Wellington and also bought copies of old master pictures for the house. In Paris, Johnston bought the obligatory mirrors and candle chandeliers expected to be seen in his parlor.[3]

Another Scot by birth, the builder Samuel Thomson, constructed the eastern half of the houses.[4] Thomson's own house in The Row, Number 4, would be given up to rent, and he took his family to his home in Inwood/Fort Washington, building a small Presbyterian church there. A dispute arose halfway through the construction of The Row between house number 6 and 7; we know nothing of the details of the dispute, but one might imagine Thomson was a difficult man.

Instructively, the name of the street was changed to Waverley (later Waverly) Place, in homage to the then-fashionable Waverley novels of Sir Walter Scott. On completion in 1833 the houses, which numbered thirteen altogether rather than the planned fourteen, became known as The Row. They established Washington Square as one of the most elegant residential addresses in New York City. Perhaps not surprisingly, their interiors were virtually identical, with furniture, chandeliers, and marble fireplace surrounds from the same suppliers in Italy and France. Fitting into the existing model was paramount in the small social group of the day—"sameness" was cherished. The merchants of the port socialized together in each other's houses, restricted their employees to members of their household, and upheld a strict code of propriety—the doors of access would soon close if a person was found breaking the code of their household.

The half of these houses that still stand are worth a close look. Set back twelve feet from the bluestone sidewalk behind cast iron fences, one half with anthemion cresting, they constitute one of the nation's most important Greek Revival terrace rows. The finely bonded red brickwork conveys their exceptional quality. A fancy entry door frame in timber atop the stone balustraded marble stoop, stepping forward from the face and flanked by fluted Ionic columns, departs from the New York norm. Behind, round-arched trellises lined in summer with vines overlooked long back gardens.

The convenient "Tea Water" pump of the era before the Croton Distributing Reservoir brought water to the houses and was located just across Waverley Place. It was thought that the pump provided the best water for the beverage of tea—considering the number of bodies in the Square, however, one wonders about the water. The houses had a service as well as a residents' staircase, almost never seen in the city. They also had large gardens to the 100-foot-lot line; beyond the line stables were built on 25 feet of extra land with mews access, which was virtually unknown at that time.

Behind the houses, round-arched trellises, lined in summer with vines, overlooked long back gardens. The spacious gardens encouraged conviviality in the summers, leading to many marriages and consolidating the ties between the merchant families. By the late 1870s a strong camaraderie of widows formed a sustaining bond. The connections seemed genuine and there does not appear to have been rivalry between the widows.

Unfortunately, we do not know who designed the remaining houses of The Row after Thomson departed but its architectural and social significance was not lost in its century. Henry James centers a novel on these houses, Edith Wharton did not ignore the great terrace, and a granddaughter of one of the first house owners, Mariana Alley Griswold, later Mrs. Schuyler Van Rensselaer, became among America's first important art and architecture critics.

To the west of the line of Fifth Avenue, the area from the north frontage of Washington Square, otherwise known as Waverley Place, to as far west as MacDougal Street, was owned by the Rogers family—the three children and heirs of John Rogers, who had shrewdly bought this land in 1796. George P. Rogers, the eldest, was in fact the first person to build on the north side, in 1828, but it was his sister, Mary Rogers, married to the sugar importer William C. Rhinelander, who made rather more impact on the square. In 1839–40 the Rhinelanders built a large and elegant house fronting on Washington Square with a return along the west side of Fifth Avenue. Known as 14 Washington Square North, it was designed by a young English-born cabinet maker named Richard Upjohn, who was in the process of turning himself into an accomplished architect. This house is likely the physical model for Henry James's *Washington Square* abode of Dr. Sloper.[5] The Rhinelander house looked rather less Greek than its neighbors in The Row across the other side of the Avenue, but it had the same marble stoop leading to a column-framed entrance. At the same time, Upjohn was completing the new Episcopal Church of the Ascension at Fifth Avenue and 10th Street not far away—also mainly paid for by the Rhinelanders—while to the west of their mansion he built a second house, 15 Washington Square, in a similar style.

Stories of the growth of New York attracted a number of less well-established British self-identified architects. Some of these men would establish a career—Richard Upjohn, Thomas Thomas, and Griffith Thomas—while others seemed to not get much work and would likely return to England. William Vine, for example, whose sketchbook is at The New-York Historical Society, came to the city and may have done some consulting work designing a fine doorframe.[6]

Love and Commerce

These special houses project the business success, social cohesion and standing of the leaseholders, who worked together to create a terrace row. The back gardens with their summer flowers lining white, grape-covered trellises with round arches at intervals became ideal courting locations—indeed, the inter-marriage among the children of the builders was remarkable. Keeping the businesses in trusted hands, Taylors married Johnstons, Lorrilards married Taylors, Boorman married Taylor and the Griswolds married everyone. As the home was the outward projection for a successful businessman, his family was part of the company in this period and there were a number of marriages made in this older manner, less for love than for keeping the business safe and prosperous. You could always trust the family.

A granddaughter of Saul Alley[9], who owned one of the first houses in the Row, became America's first significant art and architecture critic, who helped establish the careers of H. H. Richardson, McKim, Mead & White, and Augustus Saint Gaudens. Mariana Alley Griswold (1851–1934), was born at 91 Fifth Avenue. Her parents met in the gardens behind the houses in the Row, and she wrote about New York, Fifth Avenue and her neighborhood with great perception.[8] The Griswolds' boats thrived when cotton for sails and wood for hulls was cheap and plentiful, but the new Atlantic cable would regularize boat sailing schedules and the English iron tramp steamers overwhelmed the shipping company.

Mariana Griswold and her family had to remove to Dresden, where one could live comfortably on a small income from renting out New York City properties, when the Civil War upheaval in many merchants' lives forced them to move to Europe[10]. Maybe she met Edith Jones (who became Edith Wharton, the first woman to win a Pulitzer prize) in Dresden—both Edith Jones and Mariana Griswold were unusual in New York's mercantile set because they became writers. Both the Jones and Griswold families lived in Europe after their businesses in New York failed. Mariana Griswold met Schuyler Van Rensselaer, who had attended Harvard Scientific School with the great architect Charles Follen McKim, in Germany and the two were married near Dresden in 1871. When the Griswolds returned to New York, in around 1875, their world had changed. Neither Frank Griswold nor his sister ever managed to accept newcomers and change to the glorious world of their New York City childhood. Indeed, Mariana, widowed early, remained in the family home with her brother; in 1907, Frank would marry a wealthy widow and move uptown. A loft building soon replaced the Griswold residence.

The Gateway to Fifth Avenue

The New York merchants who developed "The Row" fit in around the Washington Parade Ground, but New York was growing and there were not enough lots to accommodate the beginnings of new development. Snug Harbor and the John Rogers' property just to the west of the Square abutted the farm of the old Knickerbockers of modest means, the Brevoorts, which would become the gateway to Fifth Avenue. The Brevoorts were more ordinary than the vaunted Stuyvesants, who owned most of the property on Second Avenue and had a distinguished history. However, the development of their farmland was to prove decisive in the growth of New York's most famous Avenue.

Between 1835 and 1845 the small-scale house builders of single homes who wanted a pleasant residence debated the comparative merits of Fifth and Second Avenue. Both were newly laid out; both were 100 feet wide; which one would become the grand avenue? Of course, Fifth Avenue would win, as the *Evening Post* noted.[11] But why? Perhaps it was the decorative plantings of flowers between the street and the houses that provided the final element to make what had been lowly Middle Road into Fifth Avenue. LaGrange Terrace on Lafayette Row was contemporary with the Row. A speculative venture of nine houses in a terrace, which was an amateur version of some terraces at London's Regent's Park, it was the other great residential address (without the park and as workers from close by Bowery stalls spilled over, LaGrange Terrace had only 33 years in the sun). The houses on Lafayette Row were able to get a permit for fifteen-foot front gardens (The Row had only a twelve-foot front gardens).

Those interested in developing Fifth Avenue immediately petitioned for the fifteen-foot front garden for their proposed houses. In 1844 the special privilege of a front garden was extended on Fifth Avenue to 42nd Street, a concession that surely colors the emergence of Fifth Avenue as the victor in the rivalry of the avenues. The early houses of Fifth Avenue were enhanced by green spaces, with lawns, trees, and plantings. The open spaces around the houses gave them an elegance, which almost granted lower Fifth Avenue a new life in the 1920s. Mariana Van Rensselaer notes the gardens were still an attraction almost 90 years after they were planted. She longed for the old days of gardens and neighborliness among the residents and, conceding that Washington Square and Lower Avenue were all about old families who knew each other, she missed the days when a person's surname established all the information needed to be part of the group. Mrs. Van Rensselaer was not the only person to find lower Fifth Avenue a nostalgic quarter and a few misguided attempts to return to the Lower Avenue took place. In 1919–20 the capitalist Thomas Fortune Ryan bought an old house on 14th Street and the property across the street on Lenox land as he and George F. Baker considered returning to Knickerbocker New York. We will return to this lost cause later along. Sadly, this never happened.

The glory of lower Fifth Avenue is best told by Mariana van Rensselaer's important article in *The Century* in 1893, charmingly illustrated with engravings taken from the paintings of Childe Hassam[12]. Mrs. van Rensselaer's recollections of her life on the Avenue were probably formed as the preparation for the Columbian Centennial event held in October just before the piece appeared. She writes from the vantage point of a life-long resident, rather oblivious to the changes racing toward her childhood home.

Washington Square proved to be the supreme location for the successful merchants of the port. Newly arriving Scottish businessmen joined the established Knickerbocker society in the Square, mingling socially and intermarrying. With its flower-bedecked gardens and neighborly conviviality, it is scarcely surprising that many of its denizens looked on the Greek Revival houses of Washington Square with fond nostalgia, as it became increasingly removed from the northwards thrust and ostentatious dynamism of Fifth Avenue.

CHAPTER 3

TURNING THE CORNER

"They lived in a large house in Washington Square – a quiet corner in a noisy city."

Henry James, *Washington Square*

THE SPECULATIVE BUILDER's red brick row houses along the south side of Washington Square were transformed into something more refined and personal with the first houses built just around the corner from Waverly Place. Here a new material, brownstone, and a version of the Renaissance detailing evident in London's smart new houses and the clubs of Pall Mall, change the flavor of New York's domestic architecture. The first houses on Fifth Avenue were a subtle mixture of different styles and materials, and this diverse architectural eclecticism would return later on in the Avenue's subsequent development.

Despite the obstruction of Potter's Field, Fifth Avenue had been laid out as far north as 13th Street by 1824. The Field's subsequent transformation into Washington Square made it easy for the builders of The Row to turn the corner into the empty Avenue. James Boorman was one of a group of merchants who built this row. He and his partner, also a house builder here, had a corner on the market of the Dundee Linen trade and he was, as were his neighbors, an early importer of steel from Sweden and Russia. He soon (likely in the early 1840s) began building speculative houses at 1–7 Fifth Avenue between the mews of The Row and 8th Street. These modest brick buildings, set in greenery, became home to one of the city's first schools for well-born young girls, and Boorman's sister, Esther Smith, ran the academy before leaving it to a teacher, Lucy Green, who made the school a highly regarded institution. Thus, Fifth Avenue began with an educational institution just behind Boorman's own house and stable.

5 AND 7 FIFTH
AVENUE

*James Boorman
developed nos. 1–7.
Seen here are 5 and 7
Fifth Avenue, built
c. 1830s.*

Opposite, behind William C. Rhinelander's residence at the west
corner of Washington Square and Fifth Avenue, Boorman left an
empty lot intended as a green space that would provide relief from
the urban development. The next buildings to the north, still on
Rhinelander-Rogers land, were three houses that were built on the
Avenue frontage between here and 8th Street. In keeping with the
pattern at the commencement of the Avenue, all of these (nos. 4, 6,
and 8) were individual commissions. The notable example was 8 Fifth
Avenue at the corner of 8th Street, erected as late as the 1850s by John
Taylor Johnston (1820–93), the older son of John Johnston of The
Row fame. The younger Johnston had previously been living with
his family in The Row and started building here only after he married
Frances Colles in 1851. His architect may have been Frederick
Diaper, but contemporary accounts give Diaper's New York City
pupil, Alfred J. Bloor, as the designer. At all events, Diaper's excellent
sense of proportion was evident, particularly in the balance between
front and void on the main façade, showing the house's sophistication
in comparison to its near neighbors. Remarkable too was the facing
stone, a gray Lee Quarry Stone from Massachusetts, which made a
neutral foil for the brick houses of Johnston's friends and family close
by, before bleaching to a lighter color. The Johnston house is the
first house to break away from brick and the Federal/Greek Revival
mode. His house in the new Renaissance row house mode blended
in with the brick when completed, but within his lifetime would be a
standout as it turned almost white, in marked contrast to its dull color
at the time of construction.

Nos. 4, 6, 8 Fifth
Avenue

*The Rhinelander garden
provided a large green
gap in the block before
the rowhouses. The
house at the top of the
block is the John Taylor
Johnston house of Lee
Quarry stone, which
whitened as it aged.*

William Rhinelander
House, northwest
corner of Fifth
Avenue and
Washington Square

*The wide W. C.
Rhinelander House was
home to two generations
of Rhinelanders. The
brick house was the
likely inspiration for
the house of Dr. Sloper
in Henry James's
Washington Square.
The large rear garden
is clearly seen in this
photograph.*

Artistic Patrons

John Taylor Johnston was always interested in the arts. Not long
after completing his Fifth Avenue house, he and his younger brother,
James Boorman Johnston (1822–87), paid for a large three-story brick
studio building on 10th Street near Sixth Avenue in 1857. Intended
as a portal for American artists to meet, create, and sell to potential
clients, it was designed by the Paris-trained architect Richard Morris
Hunt. This was one of the first purpose-built collective set of artists'

studios anywhere in the world, and surely the first devoted to selling art as well as making it.[1]

The elder Johnston son also amassed what was perhaps the best art collection in mid-19th-century America. He and the dry goods entrepreneur A. T. Stewart were the great collectors of serious paintings in the New York of their day. As well as the usual French academic works favored in their era, Johnston bought a great J. M. W. Turner and a most significant Winslow Homer—the latter among many contemporary American pictures acquired by him. Both are now in the Metropolitan Museum, of which Johnston was a founder and the first president. In due course he would turn a stable just behind his 8th Street house into a gallery to contain his art collection, perhaps the third in New York after Samuel Ward's on Bond Street and August Belmont's on 18th Street. A reversal in the 1873 stock market crash forced Johnston to sell some of his best pictures, but he recovered and in 1893 died in his house[2].

The rival art collector of the day, William Tilden Blodgett (1823–75), rose from a varnish business to become an art collector as well as founding figure of the Metropolitan Museum of Art with Johnston. Blodgett used his profits to purchase New York City real estate. He traveled to Europe in 1870 intent upon buying art works for the new museum; like Johnston, he was an untrained American businessman who bought many great works. Blodgett lived a block east of Johnston on University Place.[3]

Setting the Tone
By the time that Johnston Jr. got round to building, the next hunk of land northwards had long come into play. Between 8th Street and 11th Street lay a moderate-sized farm property held by the Brevoort family, which stretched across the line of the Avenue as far east as Broadway. The Brevoorts were landowners on a much smaller scale than the Stuyvesants or the Astors, who already held large sections of land, were becoming, but the first house they built on Fifth Avenue gave a lead to the opulent scale and style of much that was to follow. Hendrik, or Henry, Brevoort I (1747–1841) had been a successful farmer, but his son, Henry Brevoort Jr. (1782–1848), had higher aspirations. A supporter of Washington Irving and married to a South Carolina belle, he liked to see himself as a patron of literature and the arts. At first, he considered building a house in the congenial enclave between Bond Street and Second Avenue. It was said that his elderly father strongly opposed this location and demanded that his son build the inaugural house on Fifth Avenue. Could the old man

see the future, or was he merely planting his son in a nice house as an anchor for developing the rest of the property? At this time, some of the upper lots of the property were sold but not yet built upon.

At any rate, Brevoort junior sought the best architectural office in the city, Town & Davis, and allowed them a budget big enough to build a distinctive and fine version of the Greek Revival. Completed in 1834, the Brevoort house at the west corner of Fifth Avenue and 9th Street was large and free-standing rather than part of a terrace like the houses of The Row, with two street fronts including a bow feature on the longer side, and a lovely entrance with a columned portico *in antis*. Its elegant proportions reflected an understanding of the fine points of architecture. There was also a generous garden. The composition set the scale and tone for the next decade of houses on Fifth Avenue.

Anticipating the social life of the Avenue to come, in 1840 Brevoort hosted what was only the third masked ball to be held in the city. This genre of entertainment had long been popular in European courts, providing conversation for weeks as a wide guest list selected an appropriate costumed image, then managed to get the attire made. The local newspapers, particularly James Gordon Bennett's recently established *New York Herald*, followed the event with gushing reports. To the Brevoorts' embarrassment, the daughter of the British Consul came as Lalla Rookh, the exotic heroine of Thomas Moore's then-fashionable poem of that name, and a South Carolinian youth, obviously invited by Mrs. Brevoort, came dressed as Feramors, Lalla Rookh's minstrel lover in the same poem. The young people fled during the party to get married, presumably against family wishes. The reaction to the elopement was enough to set a ban on masked balls for two generations.

Henry Brevoort Jr. had been a curious and adventurous youth, who had joined John Jacob Astor's American Fur Company. Back in New York and on his own, Brevoort was tempted by Astor's embrace of a fledgling building type, the transient hotel. Building lots just below his inaugural house did not move following the 1837 economic downturn. Could his grand costume ball of 1840 serve to call attention to the properties? In 1845, Brevoort built a hotel across the street from his house at 9–13 Fifth Avenue, a brave venture that required the purchase of three plots on the east side of the Avenue, where the market for houses was still slow, and replacing three speculatively built houses which had become first class boarding houses and rental properties (Henry James's father had brought his family to this house

*Henry Brevoort House.
The magnetism and
the growth of Fifth
Avenue as the favored
boulevard pulled the
city north. The house
was designed by the
best architects of the
day, Town and Davis,
rather than by the usual
builders. The proportions
of the windows are
luxurious compared
to the usual jammed
rowhouse. The door
frame is distinguished as
well. The open garden
set the pattern for the
first houses. The stable
appears behind the
house.*

briefly before he moved them to a house on 14th Street). Brevoort's
own house was a fine structure, but the hotel was banal. The first stage
of the hotel was a bulky and ungraceful commercial structure, built
directly on the street omitting the green of a front garden. Perhaps
the third new hotel in the city of the day, it was enough of a success
to inspire the purchase of a plot just to the north, belonging to a Solas
Wood. Like Astor, Brevoort would name the hotel for himself. The
Brevoort Hotel would expand to the north in 1854.[4]

Henry Brevoort Jr. died in 1848. His son had left Manhattan for
Brooklyn, where his Lefferts bride's family had large properties. His
widow, Laura Carson Brevoort, disposed of some empty lots and
sold her signature house to Henry de Rham, a dry goods and banking
man and old family friend. De Rham kept the house for 80 years—a
perfect encapsulation of early 19th-century grandeur. The house
survived until 1925.[5]

BREVOORT/DE RHAM
HOUSE, 24 FIFTH
AVENUE

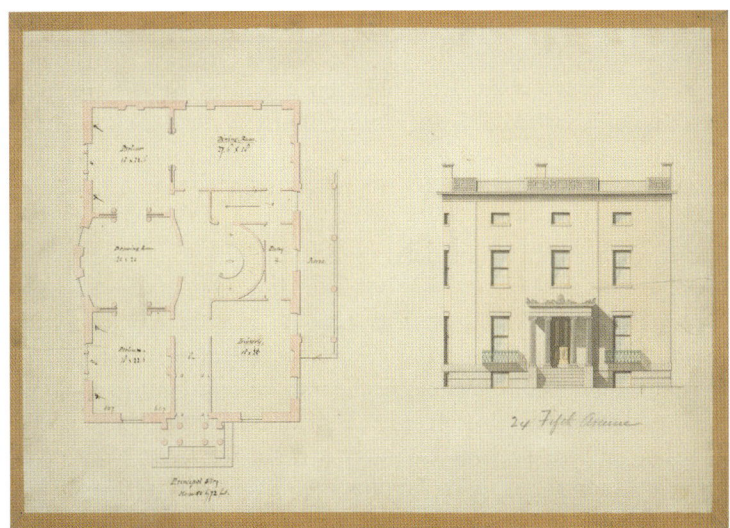

BREVOORT/DE RHAM
HOUSE, 24 FIFTH
AVENUE

*The plan reveals an
unusual central entry
and hall. The house was
built to be distinct from
the speculative houses of
its day.*

DR. EDWARD PARTRIDGE
HOUSE, 19 FIFTH
AVENUE

*The block was part of
the Brevoort property.
The sister of Henry
Brevoort married James
Renwick and was given
this plot of land by her
father. Her son, James
Renwick Jr., declared
himself an architect and
designed this house for
his parents. The essay in
the round arch style with
curved arch moldings
around the door and
windows was unique
on the Avenue. Perhaps
Renwick was making
a gesture to Germany,
where he would travel
to design St. Patrick's
Cathedral. The round
arch was popular in
mid-century German-
speaking cities. After the
Renwicks departed, it
was a boarding house
then leased to Samuel
Clemans. Renwick
family House, 21 Fifth
Avenue (Brevoort
Hotel with Mark Twain
House).*

Some of the lots eventually developed on Brevoort property along streets on either side of the Avenue came under the auspices of Henry Brevoort Jr.'s nephew, James Renwick. Though never formally trained as an architect, Renwick received his first commission in 1843 in the shape of Grace Church, significantly built on Brevoort land not far to the east on Broadway. He would go on to design St. Patrick's Cathedral and the Smithsonian in Washington and numerous other commissions. Probably among Renwick's Brevoort commissions was 21 Fifth Avenue, the interesting house built for his Brevoort mother at the southeast corner with 9th Street in 1851. This corner house was designed in the round-arched or *Rundbogen* style—a rare reference to modern Germany within New York City. Neither Renwick himself nor his father, an engineer and chemist, had any known German connection at that date. A possible source is the first section of the Astor Library just then newly finished on Lafayette Row.

Fashionable Churches

During the two decades after the completion of Henry Brevoort's house, Fifth Avenue south of 14th Street began to come together socially, with the building of a series of large and ambitious houses that it is best to take as far as possible in chronological order. Anchoring them all, at a time when churches were still a crucial factor in strengthening the status of New York's fashionable communities, were two churches close to one another on the west side of the Avenue. Despite Brevoort's efforts to promote the blocks, some fourteen vacant lots persisted between Washington Square and 14th Street.

North of 10th[6] Street rose Richard Upjohn's brownstone Gothic
Church of the Ascension for the Episcopalians (1839–40), an
interesting parallel to his contemporary and more famous Trinity
Church at the end of Wall Street. The congregation had relocated
to Fifth Avenue following a fire at their previous church on Canal
Street. The body of the church extended along 10th Street, while
around the 11th Street corner, Upjohn built a quaint rectory, again
in brownstone, with Tudor hoods over the windows. But the stout
tower of the Ascension Church was quickly outdone by the First
Presbyterian Church (1846), which took up the whole of the next
block north between 11th and 12th Streets. The Presbyterians
too were shifting north for the convenience of their more opulent
worshippers, in their case from Wall Street. Here the architect was
the English-born Joseph C. Wells, who provided a design in a more
archaeological form of Gothic than Upjohn could as yet manage,
with a noble tower based on that of Magdalen College, Oxford. Both
these brownstone churches survive, greatly enriched by donors over
the years.

Fifth Avenue and
11th Street

*The open spaces of
Lower Fifth Avenue
are clearly revealed in
this early image. Part
of the lawn of the First
Presbyterian Church,
Fifth Avenue and 11th
Street.*

The James Lenox family block. James Lenox, a bibliophile, scholar, and recluse, was thought to be the third richest man in New York. He built his own house in a Gothic domestic style and that of his sister Henrietta next door. The crenelated brownstone houses were large and went deeply east. Lenox's library eventually wound up in the New York Public Library.

Just as the Rhinelanders largely paid for the Ascension, so too First Presbyterian relied on the munificence of its vastly wealthy elder, James Lenox (1800–80), who at the same time was building a double mansion, also in the Gothic style, across from the church at 53 Fifth Avenue. A curious entry in the New York City land book notes that the property at 58 Fifth Avenue across the street was owned by the brand-new St. Bartholomew's Episcopal Church. St. Bartholomew's, a broad church in the manner of the day, would instead build on Lafayette Place, likely selling the plot to First Presbyterian in the mid 1840s. The plot went to James Lenox, the son of Robert Lenox, one of those Scottish immigrants who started out as a successful merchant before shifting into real estate as the city grew. Some years after his father died in 1839, James, a bachelor, retired to a reclusive life devoted to learning and philanthropy, moving into his new house the year after the church opened. Occupying the northeast corner with 12th Street, it was one of a pair, designed as a single near-symmetrical composition.

JAMES AND HENRIETTA LENOX HOUSES, FIFTH AVENUE AND 12TH STREET

Architect unknown—could it be James Dakin of Town and Davis, who had built the main building for the University of the City of New York?

FIFTH AVENUE AND 12TH STREET

47, 49, 51 Fifth Avenue on the east Side, three truly wide early houses. Each house was an individual commission. The southern houses were likely those of Harry Audethen John Dallert, and Mrs. Mary A. Fitzgerald. By 1900 the block was no longer private homes.

New York Gothic

Lenox himself enjoyed a 72-foot frontage on Fifth Avenue—the widest yet—and an equally large garden that extended 125 feet along the side street. Next door to the north was the slightly smaller house for his sister Henrietta and Lenox also established houses for his other sisters and their families on corner lots nearby. Lenox kept his family close, though no one else.

60 AND 62 FIFTH
AVENUE

*Two important city
houses on the west side
of Fifth Avenue between
12th and 13th Streets.
No. 60 was built in 1845
for Robert Minturn,
later sold to Marshall O.
Roberts. The house was
built by Thomas Thomas
and son. No. 62 was
built in 1848 for C. N.
Talbert, sold to George
L. Kingsland. The
architect is unknown but
could also be Thomas
Thomas and his son
Griffith.*

Surprisingly, the Lenox house and its neighbor were Gothic, a style seldom used in New York for residential buildings. Perhaps the bookish Lenox, who wrote about Scottish subjects and would have seen himself as a member of New York's Scottish community, was thinking of Sir Walter Scott and the Waverley novels, or perhaps he just hankered after something like an English or Scottish academic building of the time in the Tudor-Gothic idiom. The architect of the austere, rather gloomy composition is unknown. The natural conjecture would be Joseph C. Wells from the church across the street, but the simplicity of the Lenox houses with their hefty brownstone facing blocks seems too severe for him. The crenellations and large window hoods rather resemble the University of the City of New York's original Main Building on the east side of Washington Square, designed by James Dakin, then with Town & Davis, in the 1830s.

As a generous philanthropist and bibliophile, Lenox went on to fund the then Presbyterian Hospital (1868–72) on his uptown farm known today as Lenox Hill, and the nearby Lenox Library (1871–77), built to the designs of Richard Morris Hunt to contain his superb book collection. Both these buildings have gone, but the New York Public Library has the Lenox books and art works in its Research Collection at 42nd Street. Lenox remained a recluse with his library, socializing only with his family on the block, attended by devoted and venerable servants.

French Style

Next, two houses by French-born merchants—the first to bring to the Avenue the French taste, which would soon become dominant. In 1849 Hart M. Shiff, who had been working in New Orleans, bought two lots just above the former Brevoort, now de Rham house, at the southwest corner of Fifth Avenue and 10th Street. He commissioned Detlef Lienau, a recent immigrant from Germany, to build an imposing, free-standing house with a return of 126 feet along 10th Street. It may seem curious that an architect who was born in Denmark, and from a German family, built New York's first French style house, but Lienau had studied in Paris at the École des Beaux-Arts. 32 Fifth Avenue, as the house became, boasted the first mansard roof in New York, perhaps in honor of Shiff's French origins.[7] The Shiff house has a central doorway like the Brevoort house, the interior was equally remarkable, possessing a grand staircase, hot and cold running water, central heating and finishings by the French architect and cabinet maker, Leon Marcotte, with whom Lienau had a brief partnership. Shiff was only able to enjoy his house briefly, as he died in 1851.

Across from Shiff's mansion, another merchant of French birth, Francis Cottenet, also built a fine, but short-lived, house in the 1840s known as 37 Fifth Avenue, at the northeast corner with 10th Street. Cottenet was an importer of French goods, and his daughter had married William Colford Schermerhorn, from New York's ranking Knickerbocker family. Like the Shiff house, this one too was probably designed by Lienau, who was certainly the architect of Cottenet's country villa (1852) at Ardsley on the Hudson, fancifully known as Nuits (amazingly, it still stands), as well as of Schermerhorn's palatial house on West 23rd Street (1860), which is long gone. What is certain is that Lienau designed the replacement to no. 37 with flats in 1871, referred to later in this volume.

Town & Davis with James Dakin. New York University's Old Main Building, Washington Square.

HART M. SHIFF HOUSE,
SOUTHWEST CORNER
OF FIFTH AVENUE AND
10TH STREET

*Perhaps the first house
in New York built
with a mansard roof.
The conceit of a central
entrance and a novel
plan takes us back to the
Brevoort house. Later
the home of the print
collector Amos Eno.*

By the mid-1850s the French mansard roof had come to stay. A notable example of this was 40 Fifth Avenue, the John A. C. Gray house, built immediately north of the Church of the Ascension to designs by the English-born architect and park designer, Calvert Vaux (1857–59). Gray was a banker who may have known Vaux through the Central Park project, then in its early stages. This very distinctive brick and brownstone house had windows on three sides and a florid mansard roof. The interior was assigned to Jacob Wrey Mould, another English immigrant with a complicated background and a variety of interests, who enriched it with strong colors.[8] Vaux featured the house in his book *Villas and Cottages* of 1857. It was leased to Murray Forbes Smith, father of the future Alva Vanderbilt, in about 1859, while later Cyrus McCormick, the inventor of the mechanical reaper who founded the McCormick Harvesting Machine Company, lived there.

JOHN A. C. GRAY HOUSE, WEST SIDE OF FIFTH AVENUE BETWEEN 10TH AND 11TH STREETS

John A. C. Gray, president of the Bank of New York, was a principal figure in the creation of Central Park. He lured Calvert Vaux from the park to Fifth Avenue to build a Victorian Gothic residence for himself and his family. The Gray House and that of Runyon Martin a decade later are the only High Victorian Gothic houses on the boulevard. The house to the North, a traditional red brick row house of the 1850s, is likely the work of the Throop family from Albany, New York. The father was a builder, and the son Alfred Throop, likely designed the house. It seems the upper mansard is later and possibly the work of J. W. Mould.

From all this array of fine mansions along the lower reaches of the Avenue there is just one survivor, no. 47, a broad-faced brownstone house now jammed between apartment buildings. It was erected in 1852–53 for Irad Hawley, president of the Pennsylvania Coal Company, and is today the premises of the Salmagundi Club.

Above 14th Street

Development was much slower to proceed above 14th Street. In 1836 the Snug Harbor trustees and John Rogers Jr. petitioned the Common Council to extend the Avenue from 13th to 23rd Streets, but it was not until about 1851 that this section of the road was fully paved. For some years the only buildings along this stretch of the Avenue were a low pair of houses in an almost suburban setting, on the west side at 18th Street. These had been commissioned in 1843–44 from Henry Brevoort's architects, Town & Davis, by Henry H. Elliott, an iron merchant, and Robert C. Townsend, a dry goods merchant. The two houses were modest in scale but well detailed in the Greek taste, with bay windows on the street front and on both flanks, where there were lawns. Faced with Westchester marble, they were the last recipients of free stone cut at the Sing Sing prison, as a full-scale riot on the part of the city's stonecutters put a stop to any further giveaways. The houses set on their greensward must have made a picturesque appearance on the lonely lands, with empty fields and red cows for neighbors. The next owners of the houses were Samuel P. Avery, still then a print dealer and the woman who would become Countess Leary—she and her brother lived in a number on houses of Fifth Avenue. In the early 1870s the houses were demolished for the concert hall of Chickering Pianos. The pace of change was indeed rapid.[9]

Gradually, however, this part of the Avenue filled up. A conspicuous early example was Augustus Belmont's house back at the corner of 14th Street, which merits a chapter of its own.

Boarding Houses and Apartments

Despite this array of smart houses, it would be a mistake to suppose the lower reaches of Fifth Avenue in the 1840s and '50s were exclusively dominated by private owners. On some portions of the Avenue, boarding houses soon began to emerge, as if by stealth. New York City had a long tradition of genteel boarding in fashionable houses, where two or three boarders within a house paid some $10 a week to live without household responsibility. Take for instance the group near the bottom on the east side, nos. 1–7, on the same frontage as Renwick senior's house, probably built by John Boorman in 1854, which quickly became boarding houses. On the facing block

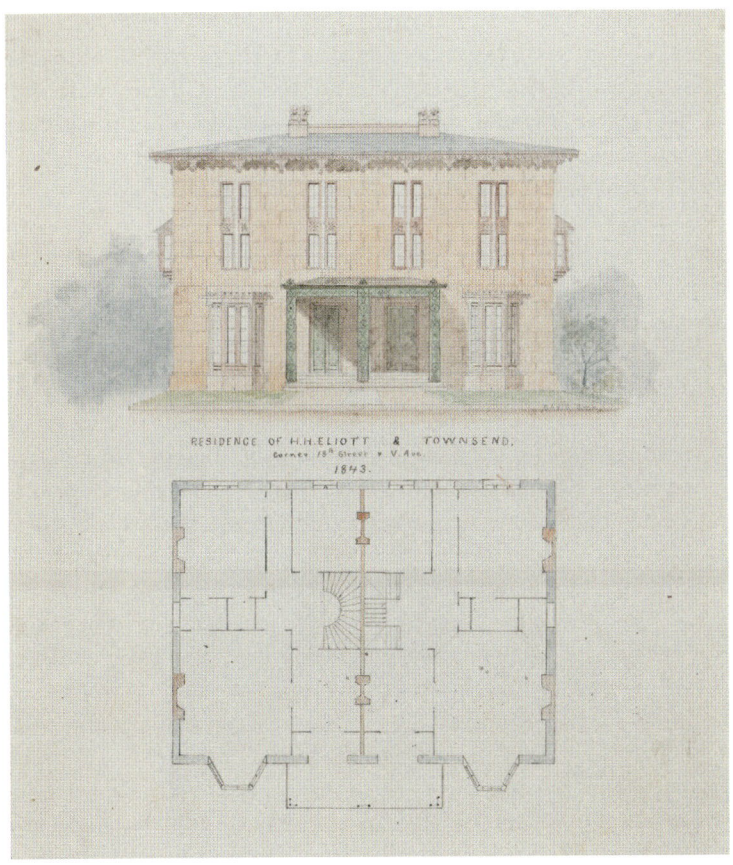

RESIDENCE OF H.H.ELIOTT & TOWNSEND.
Corner 18th Street & V. Ave.
1843.

CORNER OF FIFTH
AVENUE AND 18TH
STREET

Town & Davis designed
a pair of houses with the
entrances in the middle
of the design in 1843–44.
These were the first
houses on Fifth Avenue
above 14th Street. Low
and surrounded by
gardens, the houses went
down for Chickering
Hall in less than two
generations. Residence
of H. H. Elliot & Robert
C. Townsend.

Residence of H. H. Elliot
& Robert C. Townsend,
corner of Fifth Avenue
and 18th Street,
elevations and details of
door and banister posts,
1843.

on the opposite side of the Avenue, the Brevoort estate developed the plots next to the northwest corner of 8th Street as speculative houses, nos. 10, 12, and 14. The rest of the block, in the possession of William Rhinelander, remained empty and added to the green or garden feeling of the lower avenue. But after the real estate bust of 1873, Rhinelander decided to build a hotel, the Berkley.

By then the glory days of individual residences in this section of the Avenue were over, and they were giving way to luxury hotels and prestigious flats. The change was symbolized in 1871, when Francis Cottenet demolished his own house and garden at 37 Fifth Avenue to create the Grosvenor, a block of French flats where Cottenet lived when he was in town. This was New York's first apartment hotel with an exclusive residential mix. Unusually, the apartments were L-shaped and wrapped around a Parisian-style inner courtyard. It is interesting that although Cottenet was French, he selected a London appellation for the new multiple dwelling. Perhaps he thought that an Anglophilic name would attract fellow society figures to the Grosvenor. This domestic pattern will emerge as the apartment and residential hotel takes over from the boarding house for the middle and upper middle class and will be discussed later in the tale.

The march up Fifth Avenue was begun by a diverse group of merchants and businessmen, which included people who were not deeply entrenched members of the traditional Knickerbocker social circle, still located primarily on Second Avenue. The houses were commissioned rather than speculatively built and were constructed in a variety of materials and modes. They established Fifth Avenue as the street of the future for successful people.

CHAPTER 4

BELMONT: THE "KING OF FIFTH AVENUE"

"Within four years, Belmont's name was on the lips of every New Yorker. He was the city's leading investment banker and the hottest thing to hit society—and he was a Jew."

Kenneth L. Fisher

AUGUST BELMONT was a German Jewish immigrant who capitalized on an economic boom, married a beautiful woman from a notable family and owned two fine Fifth Avenue mansions. The couple reached the apex of New York's high society in the mid-19th century.

Belmont started out as August Schonberg, a German of Sephardic Jewish ancestry born at Alzey in the Rhineland. The date of his birth is disputed; it could have been 1813 but more likely was 1816. After his mother's death, young August went to Frankfurt, where he started sweeping floors for the Rothschilds, but he studied languages and mathematics in his spare time, soon came to his employers' notice, and rose to a position of trust in the firm while he was still in his early twenties, which was how he found himself in New York.

August Belmont brought the custom of European meal services with fine table ware, wine served with the meal and a French chef, perhaps the first in New York. He was known to New Yorkers as the "King of Fifth Avenue."

When August Schonberg got off the boat in New York in 1837, he was bound for Cuba to look over Rothschild sugar interests in Havana and intended his visit as just a stop-over. He arrived as a panic struck the New York economy, but Belmont shrewdly guessed that a healthy economic boom would shortly follow the bad patch. His first move was to take on some Rothschild interests in the city, which were in the hands of J. L. and S. Josephs and Co., who were suffering from the panic, and had to be straightened out. The sharp and quick decisions he made gained his employers' respect and allowed him to set up a company combining trading on his own behalf with representing the Rothschilds in Frankfurt. His timing was good. New York's dry

August Belmont in costume for a fancy-dress ball at Delmonico's.

goods merchants were selling to plantation economies and starting to invest in them, heralding a fifteen-year boom in Southern investments – the cotton, sugar, and dyes of the South were products New York could cherish. He opted to remain in New York and, determined to establish himself as a sophisticated European, adopted a French version of his name, August Belmont[1].

A House Fit for a King

Owning a smart house was part of the careful image Belmont now chose to project. Rather than taking a speculatively built house, he decided in the mid-1840s to build at the top of the developing portion of the Avenue, selecting a site at 82 Fifth Avenue, on the northwest corner of Fifth Avenue and 14th St. At around this time the lots on the Avenue were starting to attract buyers who were commissioning special architect-designed houses.[2] There were some fifteen vacant lots available when Belmont purchased his at the northern end, but above 14th Street, nothing was then developed.[3]

To design his house, Belmont selected Frederick Diaper, an English-born architect in his 30s who claimed training in the London office of Robert Smirke. As a German speaker, it is perhaps surprising that Belmont did not try to work with Detlef Lienau or one of the other German-born, professionally trained architects who were starting just then to establish themselves in New York. But Lienau was still young, while Diaper had already built quite extensively, including a house near Albany for William Paterson van Rensselaer. At the same time as he built for Belmont, Diaper was designing another house close by at the corner of Fifth Avenue and 12th Street, for Robert B. Minturn of Grinnell, Minturn & Co., general merchants in a large way of business, notably the whale oil trade. Later Diaper designed the New York Society Library on University Place, the William H. Aspinwall house nearby with its great art collection, and Jay Gould's first house at 578 Fifth on the west side of the Avenue (1869). He also created the Delmonico's restaurant when it moved to 1 East 14th Street at the northeast corner of Fifth Avenue in 1862. Belmont, by going to Diaper, was securing himself a place among the city's élite.

The house at 82 Fifth Avenue was completed by 1847, confirming Belmont as a major player in the politics and financing of New York. To go further, he needed a wife. His choice had been foreshadowed by an obscure episode in 1841, when Belmont opted to uphold the honor of Caroline Slidell Perry, one of the ten children of Commodore Matthew Perry, later famed for the so-called opening of Japan in 1853–54. There is an oft repeated tale, which is untrue. In the story,

Caroline had been the object of an insulting remark and although Belmont did not know exactly what was said, he demanded a duel with the offender, in which he was struck by a bullet in the groin, leaving him with a lifelong limp. In truth, there was a duel, but not over Caroline Perry, whom he probably met later. In due course his relationship with Caroline developed, and after Belmont had converted to the Episcopal faith of his future bride, they married in 1849. The couple went on to have six children.

High Society

Beautiful and elegant, and far more socially fluid and educated than other wealthy wives of the day, Caroline Belmont completed her husband's rise to prominence. "Tiny" Belmont, as she was called, represented the highwater mark for New York society in the middle of the century. Everyone noticed her furs and jewels, and her presence at the opera or an event ensured success. Riding high in society circles, Belmont recognized financial success was closely tied to political

AUGUST BELMONT
HOUSE 109 FIFTH
AVENUE

August Belmont's marriage house. Belmont hopped four blocks to the north and crossed to the east side of the Avenue. Belmont built or renovated a slightly earlier house for his position at the top of New York City life.

109 FIFTH AVENUE

Frederick Diaper, born in England, sent this photo to the Royal Institute of British Architects as a proud sign of his New York success.

favors. He began to take an interest in Democratic politics in the early 1850s and supported James Buchanan in his losing bid for the presidency in 1852. Nevertheless, the successful candidate, Franklin Pierce, appointed him Minister to the Netherlands, leading to the Belmonts spending the years 1854–57 in The Hague.

After Buchanan won his second bid for the presidency, he declined to promote Belmont to a post in Madrid, so his diplomatic career ended, and the couple were obliged to return to New York. With their growing family, they moved further up to 18th Street on the opposite side of the Avenue in 1857, where a large house, 109 Fifth Avenue, had been recently built for John Gihon, a dry goods merchant, who overreached himself and was forced to sell. Belmont sold his house at 82 Fifth Avenue to Henry Van Schaick, a wealthy landowner with properties in the Albany area of New York State. Behind the new house was an empty lot facing 18th Street and the large property allowed Belmont to expand. Meanwhile his connection with the Perrys helped him to gain membership in the exclusive Knickerbocker Club.

It is not clear whether the Belmonts adapted Gihon's house at no. 109 or whether they pulled it down and built a new house from scratch, nor do we know whether Diaper was again involved. Diaper did send a photograph of the house to the RIBA, so it was likely his work. At any rate, the very grand new Belmont residence became an exemplar for understated but elegant design. It was fronted in brick still, not yet brownstone, and boasted two Adamesque porched entries. On the empty lot to the east Belmont built a dedicated art gallery with a separate entry from the side street, which did not double up as a ballroom, unlike some other New York private galleries of the day. It was not the first of its kind, but the sophistication of its French paintings, including some nudes, attracted notice. Already it had been rumored that the bibliophile and collector James Lenox had been quite shocked by Belmont's pictures while he was still at 82 Fifth Avenue across the road from Lenox's house. But although Belmont knew the value of possessing an art collection and his large collection of European pictures was admired, he amassed paintings in much the same way as Mrs. Astor, who had one of the least notable picture collections in New York. He took more pleasure in horses and wine.

Belmont was the man who established wine as part of the American grandee meal and his cellars were famous. But his social success as a host became strained and faltered after he invited "Boss" Tweed, New York's Democratic and legendarily corrupt mayor, to dinner in 1871. He was subsequently shunned by the "gentlemen" of his world for several years.

"Tiny," on the other hand, was always greatly admired and set the standard for society women for the middle years of the century. Persuaded by her husband to wear fresh Worth gowns instead of having the silk in store for a year or two, as was the Knickerbocker norm, Tiny married the Knickerbocker world to new money with grace. But after fresh investment in the railroads in 1869, the West and real estate propelled the economy in New York into a great boom

109 FIFTH AVENUE

No sooner had "Tiny" Belmont died than their double home was gobbled up by Arnold Constable for a post in Ladies Mile.

"Tiny" Belmont was the most admired woman in New York in the mid-century. Caroline Slidell Perry Belmont (Mrs. August Belmont, Sr.).

and a new social era. Many new people tried to enter the world where Caroline Belmont had reigned, and she now retreated from her place at the apex of fashionable society. Perhaps a rumor about an affair reached her ears (her husband did find beautiful women entrancing), but it was more likely that the illness and death in 1875 of her daughter, Jane Pauline ("Jeannie"), preoccupied her.

August and Tiny lived in the house until the end of their lives, in 1890 and 1892 respectively. Their venerable double home was then immediately sold to the old-time store, Arnold Constable & Co., whose Broadway store had moved north in the 1870s. Commercial buildings were already neighboring properties on Fifth Avenue to the Belmonts, and their house went down without a whimper. This once-golden address had become part of "department store alley."

Belmont's spectacular rise to prominence in mid-century New York left a lasting imprint on Fifth Avenue. Despite the religion of his birth, he was made a member of the Knickerbocker Club and he socialized with men who loved horses, racing, wine and women. His stylish and elegant wife was a much-admired fashionable icon, although his credentials as a great American figure were tarnished by his association with Boss Tweed and his political affiliation with the Democratic Party—few men on Fifth Avenue were associated with the Democrats. Ultimately, the relentless march of New York wealth and fashion swept the glittering couple aside and they faded even as the next generation, represented by Belmont's sons, became prominent in financial and social circles – Alva Vanderbilt married a Belmont son, while August Belmont Jr. was a prime mover in the creation of the Interborough Rapid Transit, the first subway in New York.

From Row House to Brownstone

"I have never walked down Fifth Avenue without thinking of money."

Anthony Trollope, North America, 1863

ALTHOUGH LONG GONE, the late 18th- and early 19th-century row house in New York was a formulaic response to the plots of land within walking distance from the port. Once the island was laid out, the lots were 25 feet wide to 100 feet deep (laid out with a chain—they were really 98 feet deep.) Initially, the houses were constructed of timber, which was plentiful and cheap. The exterior brick wall ranged from a few inches to a foot. As the carpentry trade developed, rafters, window frames, and the needed wooden features were standardized. Custom work was rare. Indeed, as the city rose a block a year in the middle of the 19th century, construction elements were placed a block or so just above last year's work. William Ross, an architect who had not long ago arrived from England, wrote in 1835 that New York houses were much better built than their English counterparts.[1] The physical appearance of the London houses was similar, but the New York houses were sturdier. English house models continued to dominate domestic architecture throughout most of 19th century.

The Brownstone

The typical row house persisted, but both the cladding and the style changed in the 1840s. As Fifth Avenue emerged as a prime boulevard, the soft brown sandstone quarried in the region and used effectively at Trinity Church on Wall Street would cover the façade brick work. The house form and frame continued, but now the brownstone veneer ranged from six inches to eighteen inches, depending on the budget for the house. The adoption of brownstones coincided with

4, 5 WASHINGTON
SQUARE NORTH

*The Snug Harbor
Image Collection has
recently been found
and digitized. Looking
east, summer awnings
in place.*

the real growth of the speculative house in Manhattan on the avenues
and side streets.

As brownstone replaced brick, the style of the house detail also
shifted. The houses became taller, the stoop higher. The woodwork
in the finer houses was mahogany, and the door hardware was silver
plated. The stylistic flavor changed to the Italian Palazzo mode, as
seen in the clubs of Pall Mall in London and the speculative houses
being constructed at the time in West London.[2] The row house/
brownstone was an icon of respectability in New York until the early
20th century.

The exterior might be either brownstone or brick, but there was
always a stoop to the side of the house. The house would then open
to a foyer with the double parlor across the hallway. The restrictions
caused by the off-side entry created a formula that was difficult to
depart from despite some efforts to do so. The interiors had no light

in the middle of the row house; in the 1840s the depth from the front to the back garden was some 48 feet, and this would extend as the century progressed. In the first half of the 19th century there were windows in the front and at the back of the house, looking out upon the garden where the summer heat had to be endured. By the second half of the century, upper middle class and wealthy house owners left the city to summer elsewhere, so the back garden could withstand more of a physical intrusion from house extensions.

The parlor floor was the only part of the house where visitors might be entertained. After climbing the stoop steps, a guest would be greeted at the door and ushered into the parlor. In the earlier days, the guest space was within the two parlors with pocket doors between the rooms, so if tea was served, the guests might go to the other parlor, and the pocket doors closed until the tea service could be cleared. The traditional house had a kitchen and family dining room just below the stoop. As entertaining changed and a better dining room to entertain guests became fashionable in the mid-century, a back parlor might become a dining room, or by the end of the century, a large dining room could be attached to the house protruding into the back garden. The private space of a row house began at the single staircase which led to the upper two floors where the family had bedrooms. Servants, if residing in the house, would occupy rooms in the very top of the house.

STATE STREET, Nºˢ 16-19, ABOUT 1864

ENGRAVED FOR THE SOCIETY OF ICONOPHILES, 1907.

The Federal row houses at State Street, drawn here as if 1864. The houses were brick with a modest stoop to the parlor floor. A half floor just below the stoop held the kitchen at the rear and a family dining room just under the street. The houses were three stories with two dormers for each house where the servants lived. The houses had a Federal door surrounding a fan light window. These Federal houses in lower Manhattan are long gone.

Fifth Avenue looking south in an anonymous watercolor. We are at 31st Street. The repetitive brownstones have typical high stoops, flowerbeds, and lawn in front of the houses. The block we see to the right shows how different speculative builders worked side by side in a similar manner and material. The row on the left side seems a single developer, possibly the Josephs who had worked with the Rothschilds in the 1830s.

The brownstone fronted row house also differed from the earlier brick row house in the areas of modern comforts. By the time the brownstone front replaced the brick row house, internal heating with hot-air furnaces had arrived. The old fireplaces on one wall were retained but better comfort could be created with a furnace. The engineering feat of the era was the Croton water system, which brought running water to private houses The arrival of the Croton water created a need for a sewer system. In the 1840s bathrooms and toilets, features of internal convenience which we now take for granted, began to appear in the brownstone houses then being built for the middle and upper classes.[3]

CHAPTER 5

INTERRUPTION TO THE PUSH NORTHWARD

"A larger more handsome building than Buckingham Palace."

The Prince of Wales in *Harper's Weekly,* 1890

As the homogenous streets, now of brownstone-fronted houses, marched northwards, their relentless progress was interrupted by the arrival of the magnificent Fifth Avenue Hotel, which generated its own eddy of traffic and subsidiary businesses, creating a brake on developers and forcing speculative housebuilders to leapfrog the area and move further north.

As the city rose above 23rd Street, the blocks on Fifth Avenue were quickly built up in similar, speculative rows on the standard 25-by-100-foot plots, with a thin brownstone veneer covering the brickwork for the fronts alone and uniform high stoops over basements. Before the era of records, it is almost impossible to know who designed these strings of houses. Mechanical and undistinguished in appearance like stamped-out die-cuts, there were already 340 of them on the Avenue by 1860, not counting the far greater number along the cross streets. So alike were they that in summer only window boxes differentiated each family's home. It was humorously noted that many a man returning at night with perhaps too much alcohol in his system might walk up and ring the silvered doorbell of a neighbor. Interspersed among these houses, however, were some notable exceptions, and it is with these that this chapter is mainly concerned.

Between about 21st and 26th Street, Fifth Avenue crossed farmland that had formerly belonged to the Peters family, the descendants of a freed slave, and subsequently the Horn family. It included a charming farmhouse of framed construction in the old Dutch style with a deep sweeping roof and a veranda, set about 200 yards west of the line of the Avenue, at the intersection of the future 23rd Street. This had probably already become a roadhouse for passing travelers when, in 1841, the Horns sold it to William ("Corporal") Thomson, who renamed it Madison Cottage. Here men riding or racing their thoroughbred horses up the Avenue stopped off for refreshment, while cattle shows were held in the yard behind. There were still a number of such refreshment places along the length of the Avenue as late as the early 20th century. According to an advertisement said to date from 1852, stages left Madison "Cottage" every four minutes during the day. Not long after that the roadhouse property was demolished in favor of a large, tented establishment called Franconi's Hippodrome and filled with exotic animals. This too had failed by 1856.

Clubland

By then the district was undergoing radical change. The most striking sign of a new dignity was not a house but a club, the Union Club, built two blocks south of the Hippodrome site at Fifth Avenue and 21st Street, which was to be the most desirable in the City for a very long time. Clubs were to be a vital part of the life of the Avenue.

UNION CLUB HOUSE, FIFTH AVENUE AND 21ST STREET

View from 21st Street looking south. Griffith Thomas mimics the clubs of London's Pall Mall. The brownstone structure, the first purpose-built club building. There with elaborate window lintels was a signature feature of the architect. The windows go to the floor on the upper stories. A projecting cornice is another signature feature of a Griffith Thomas building.

In the struggle for social acceptance and power, the house was the domain of women, but in the club, men held sway, made business contacts and deals, and plotted. They were also places that encouraged exclusiveness, in due course fostering the antisemitism which took an upswing in the city's clubs after centuries of relative harmony.[1]

In the middle of the 19th century, clubs often took over existing houses as club headquarters. That was no longer good enough for the Union Club, which since its foundation in 1836 as one of the city's three pioneering social clubs had suffered the indignity of occupying three successive homes along different addresses in Broadway. Now the 600 or so exclusively male members—no woman was allowed to pass the threshold—wanted permanence and status. Griffith Thomas was the prolific architect who provided these qualities, deploying the same suave Italianate style as Charles Barry had applied to the clubs of London's Pall Mall. Here was brownstone at its best, only three stories high above ground level yet far overtopping the houses on either side, with tiers of heavy pedimented windows along both flanks, five on one side and three on the other. The front was dignified by a deep open portico behind a row of single Corinthian columns. It was all undeniably impressive, but James Gordon Bennett of the *New York Herald* hated its exclusion of women, writing: "This nursery for old bachelors, and their conspiracies, cannot resist the opposing forces of the ladies, with their genial re-unions of the young and the old of both sexes mingling together in the polka, at whist, at billiards, and over their oysters and champagne for 'medicinal purposes'."

The Fifth Avenue Hotel

The site of Madison Cottage and Franconi's Hippodrome met a more generous and public fate at the hands of the same designer. Amos Richards Eno (1810–98), the initiator, was an old-fashioned Connecticut Yankee who became a model for the fresh type of New York property magnate. Originally a dry goods merchant operating from 74 Broadway, Eno had invested in real estate, riding the elevator of Manhattan's growth. He had taken over the Hart Shiff house at 32 Fifth Avenue for himself, but was looking for new investments. A little further east along 23rd Street, taking its name from the nearby "cottage," Madison Square had been open as a park since 1847. Eno now calculated on the potential of a luxury hotel where the street crossed Fifth Avenue, then the very top of the city.

Begun in 1857 and finished two years later, the Fifth Avenue Hotel was a full block in width. It cost Eno vast sums and during its construction was widely criticized as a folly. Once again, the architect was Griffith

FIFTH AVENUE HOTEL

Thomas, this time assisted by William Washburn. The style was plainer than at the Union Club, but the front was in "marble" rather than the usual brownstone, with shops all along the ground story.

Inside, the hotel boasted all the latest comforts for travelers, not least a so-called "vertical railroad," in other words, one of the first safety elevators made for commercial use, supplied by Otis Tufts of Boston. The interiors were perhaps the most lavish in America at the time. They included a restaurant with very long tables, where residents and their guests could mingle for four meals a day. There was a reading room, a barber shop, and a telegraph connection—all staples of future luxury hotels for a century to come. Brilliantly, Eno brought in Boston's great hotel keeper, Paran Stevens, to run the establishment. This marked the start of the New York career of Stevens and his ambitious second wife Marietta, who was to be a major factor in the next phase of the city's social development.

The Fifth Avenue Hotel was a triumph, achieving wide and immediate recognition. In Britain it was fully covered by *The Builder*, the leading architectural magazine, which estimated that it cost a million dollars—the true bill was likely half that. In October 1860, three years after the opening, the British connection was dramatically renewed

THE DINING-ROOM OF THE FIFTH AVENUE HOTEL, ON MADISON SQUARE.

when the hotel was chosen as the New York base for the first visit to America by Albert Edward, Prince of Wales, the future Edward VII. The city went wild with anticipation and paid the closest attention to every move the nineteen-year-old prince made. Crowds watched his carriage bring him to the hotel, where the management aggrandized rooms for his stay, and followed all the events he attended. Edward was photographed at Matthew Brady's Studio, visited many institutions, and was lionized at a reception at the Academy of Music. A ball held in his honor included all those who possessed the requisite formal attire and array of jewels. This proved to be too inclusive a formula, and the dance floor collapsed from the numbers of people. Prominent New Yorkers vied with one another for invitations to these occasions and strove for positions near the prince.

This visit by the heir to the British throne was the greatest social event in the city since the return farewell tour of General Lafayette decades earlier. The festivities marked the start of a growing fascination in fashionable New York with the manners, customs and aristocracy of Europe, as well as the launch of new figures into New York City's social story. Edward, for his part, was overwhelmed by the pressure of continuous events, and only too happy to relieve it on one occasion by arranging a game of leapfrog in the hall of the Fifth Avenue Hotel.

FIFTH AVENUE HOTEL

The communal dining room with long tables served four meals each day to hotel tenants. Guests or customers were welcome to join the tables at meals.

This was a very different kind of prince from the mature man who liked rich American women and overdone luxury who wealthy and/or social climbing Americans would meet in England later in the story. Despite its whirlwind social success, the Fifth Avenue Hotel and its busy environs caused the northward course of the Avenue to hiccup.

The traffic, commerce, and activity generated by the hotel put off the brownstone dwellers and a break in fashionable development occurred north of the hotel. The best housing leapt above 23rd Street and recommenced at 30th Street as the Avenue neared Astor territory and in due course, manufacturing and loft buildings filled the gap without much resistance. The Fifth Avenue Hotel maintained its reputation into the 1870s; it was here, for instance, that Ulysses S. Grant launched his second presidential campaign. But it was soon in competition with newer hotels at the bottom of Central Park like the Plaza, first opened in 1890. Accordingly, the management

STEREOSCOPIC IMAGE OF FIFTH AVENUE HOTEL, FRONT VIEW, MADISON SQUARE

The awkward site of 23rd Street and Fifth Avenue both stopped row house progress and started a retail trade zone. The large white hotel in a Renaissance style set the standard for the mid-century hostelry.

called in Stanford White of McKim, Mead & White to spruce up the public areas in 1894, providing new ceiling detail and carpets for the hotel lobby. But that was only a reprieve; the hotel closed and was demolished in 1908.

To return to Amos Eno, after his shrewd gamble over the Fifth Avenue Hotel he continued quietly with his real estate investments, purchasing property at what would become Times Square and the Upper West Side. He also started the Second National Bank just a few blocks above the hotel, and his son, John Chester Eno, was made director. When John Chester embezzled four million dollars from the bank and fled to Canada, Amos Eno, as a new patrician, quietly provided the missing money, so assuring the depositors' security. When he died in 1898, he left a collection of fine prints of immense value to The New York Public Library which enhanced the collection.

Avenue Hotel, front view, Madison Square.

Leonard W. Jerome

The Flashiest House of Manhattan.

Leonard Jerome was one the great characters who represent a portion of 19th-century American life. Born on a farm in upstate New York, Jerome was intelligent, but erratic. He started out in the law before acquiring a wife, Clarissa (Clara), and three daughters, moving to the city, and taking up a new career in stockbroking. A natural gambler, Jerome made a great fortune in stocks during the wild days around the 1857 economic collapse.

Jerome was living in Brooklyn at that time, but in 1859 on the strength of his market success he selected a big parcel of empty land one street away from Fifth Avenue at the corner of Madison Avenue and 26th Street and made very grandiose plans for a house, employing the English-born Thomas R. Jackson as architect. The house he designed belonged in spirit to Fifth Avenue, even though it was situated on the next block further east. The first part built was a palatial set of stables, in which red carpet featured on the floors, providing the thoroughbreds with human-level standards of luxury. Above that was the ballroom.

LEONARD W. JEROME
HOUSE, MADISON
AVENUE AT 23RD STREET

Jerome built the flashiest Manhattan house of the mid-19th century not on Fifth, but at Madison Avenue. The brick house with a stone base has multiple window lintels or round arch and other styles. A very elaborate iron porch acted as a status symbol rather than as a place to sit. The great mansard roof placed the house above its surroundings.

The overall result was an enormous, attention-seeking mansion, topped with a mansard roof and dripping with ornate and excessive detail, such as its intricate wrought iron grilles. The wrought iron grilles were once intended to deflect intense sunlight, but for this house, they were probably more of a status symbol. At parties one fountain dispensed perfume, while another shot champagne into the air. The house's sheer bombast and vulgarity confirmed Jerome's position at the forefront of the finance world, if only briefly.

The Jeromes moved into the house in 1859, but lived there only for a few years. In common with other prominent New Yorkers in his set, like William Travers and August Belmont, Leonard Jerome seems to have preferred horses, women, and song to his family. But he was also a devotee of opera, so in 1866–67 Jackson went on to build him a private theater between the Madison Avenue house and stables, where Jerome hosted extravagant meals and sponsored performances by aspiring divas. One such grand evening was held in favor of Mary Frances "Fanny" Ronalds, née Cater, the estranged wife of Pierre Lorillard of the P. Lorillard and Company, snuff and tobacco fortune. Ronalds's beauty and vocal talents (she could sing arias from the great operas) made her the toast of the city at that time. Jerome intended to pay for this lady's extravagantly produced recital only to discover that August Belmont claimed to have paid the bills for the same event. In 1867 Mrs. Ronalds moved to Paris before going on to England as the paramour of Arthur Sullivan, of Gilbert and Sullivan fame, and a close friend of the exiled Napoleon III. In the small circle in which they traveled, "belles" were sometimes jointly shared and financed. Jerome favored singers; he was rumored to be the father of an opera star, Minnie Hauk, but without proof.

By 1867 Clara Jerome had had enough of her husband's fancy horses and flamboyant women and took her three daughters to live in Europe. Like Fanny Ronalds, they lived first in Paris, moving to London after the fall of Napoleon III. Their position in England was always financially precarious so when the middle daughter, Jennie (who had perhaps first attended the school at 1 Fifth Avenue), fell in love with Lord Randolph Churchill and they married in haste, Jerome was expected to finance their lives. But by then he could not afford to do so.   In 1869 he had sold the New York house to the American Jockey Club and returned to Brooklyn, his horses, and the race track he had created in the Bronx. In later years his house passed through the hands of various clubs and it was finally demolished in 1968, just after New York City created the Landmark Preservation Commission.

Jerome and the opening of the Fifth Avenue Hotel shone a spotlight on the surrounding streets, attracting a higher end of prostitution houses and the gambling game of the era, Faro. As a result, Fifth Avenue at 23rd Street became the entertainment center of the city and just below 23rd Street, the popular music world started what would be known as Tin Pan Alley. When Jerome's house eventually became a club, the private nature of this section of the city was lost to commerce. Stores would follow the hotel and the Western Union telegraph company set up a branch across the street. As forms of European-inspired elegance became accepted, superb horses, fine coaches and carriages ferried the wealthy through the city. The carriages and coaches, complete with liveried attendants, were a marker of the status of individuals. Coaching became a ritual of the super-wealthy, a grand new way to display clothing and horsemanship. The assembly and viewing point was the Hotel Brunswick at the North East corner of 26th Street and Fifth Avenue just a few blocks above the hotel. The coaching events would fade as the automobile appeared. Residential brownstones would jump over this nexus of the high life and fashionable entertainment and begin again a few streets further to the north.

CHAPTER 6

THE CONSUMMATE NEW YORK BUILDER

"Griffith Thomas is the most fashionable architect of his generation."

The American Institute of Architects, 1908

AMONG THE COUNTLESS BUILDERS of Manhattan brownstones in the middle decades of the 19th century, one name stands out—that of Griffith Thomas. The most prominent architect in New York City in the mid-19th century, Thomas moved with the tastes of the time and designed in both the Italian Palazzo and the French Empire styles. He was criticized for his use of sheet metal cornices, which were elaborate, but he was generally well regarded. He created the first commercial garment-center buildings of cast iron around Leonard Street, the first purpose-built clubhouse (the Union Club), banks, theaters, popular entertainment buildings called "opera houses," textile factories, premises for insurance companies, Delmonico's on 26th Street, department stores (such as the Arnold Constable Store in the Ladies' Mile district and possibly its brownstone predecessor on Canal Street of 1857), and a single country house in Atlanta, Georgia. Thomas designed several of the fashionable churches of the day, notably Dr. Spring's Church on Fifth Avenue at 37th Street and was also the main architect of Amos Eno's Fifth Avenue Hotel. He even designed cemetery gravestones for his clients. Altogether, Thomas seems to have built several hundred structures within the city, from the 1840s to the depression of the 1870s.

The Master of Brownstone
Griffith Thomas was the great master of the brownstone form. He claimed to have built 200 brownstone houses on Fifth Avenue and that at least three of them adorned every block on Fifth Avenue up

In the foreground is Griffith Thomas's brick Presbyterian Church looking mighty brown. The Church retains its original name from its earliest days, but Thomas could not resist the fashionable brownstone, which he used as much as possible on the building. Fifth Avenue was in the throes of the brownstone front wave. Across the street from the Church is a house built on Fifth Avenue when the course of the Avenue was unclear. By the time the Avenue reached the home of Governor E. D. Morgan, his house sat back from the Avenue. In the winter, the front area was filled with water, which then froze making a skating rink for the popular sport of the era.

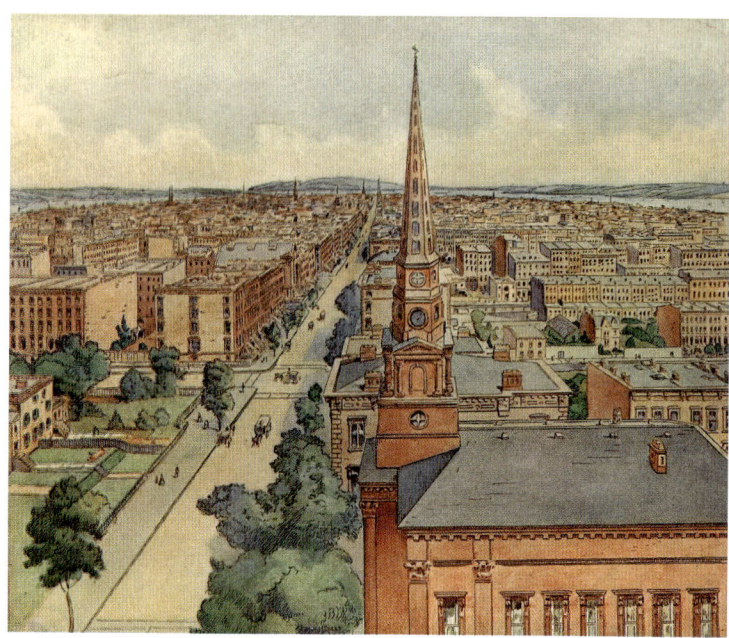

to 42nd Street, beginning in the streets of the 20s. His brownstones were distinguished by elaborate sheet metal cornices and roofs, and his windows in the brownstone fronts usually had a straight projecting lintel over each window. His work included houses for William Backhouse Astor and his wife Caroline Schermerhorn Astor, Marshall O. Roberts, Moses Taylor, and the Astor Estate. For second-tier houses, the Astors employed the builder Peter Kissam, but for major ones they went to Thomas. Thomas's brownstones were especially plentiful around the Fifth Avenue Hotel, but he even supplied brownstones to adventurous clients in the empty streets of the Upper Fifth Avenue, as far up as 83rd Street for the merchant Arnold Constable's families, long before other houses filled in the barren lots.

Thomas of course was far from alone in concentrating on brownstones. From the end of the Civil War to the 1880s, many builders and speculative developers were raising houses in bursts of activity along the empty blocks of what would become midtown. Most of this activity was just off Fifth Avenue, where rows were built to similar designs but varying widths. Often the houses at the row end had frontages of twenty feet across, while those in the middle could measure as little as sixteen or fourteen feet in width. Among the biggest developers of the period were names like Robert Mook, the Jardines, Philip Fitzpatrick, and Charles Duggin with his partner

James Crossman. This great period of building speculative houses for rent ended in the 1880s on Fifth Avenue.

Many architects and builders designed brownstones. The English-born commercial architect favored by Commodore Vanderbilt, John Butler Snook, built the William Henry Vanderbilt house at 40th Street, and it was a double-wide house. Snook also built some narrow, plain brownstones at 105 and 184 Fifth Avenue before the city demanded records—the building permit ledger did not begin until 1865. The clients are not known, but Snook listed these houses in his papers, which were given to the New-York Historical Society.

A Very Private Man

Returning to Griffith Thomas, we know very little about him. Although he worked and lived with the Fifth Avenue set, he did not seem to leave any personal legacy. He was born in Wales (or London) in 1820, the son of a Welsh builder, Thomas Thomas, and came with his father to the United States at a young age, having learned drafting skills and worked with his father until the latter's retirement in about 1855. In those free and flexible days before professional training was valued, the family business evolved from carpentry to architecture. Both father and son had a brownstone on Fifth Avenue, Griffith at no. 92 and his father probably at no. 263.

When his father stepped down, Griffith Thomas sensed a need for a more exuberant approach to reflect the boom in New York City. Sometimes his work could be subtle, resembling the work of Frederick Diaper, as in the Marshall O. Roberts house (107 Fifth Avenue) and W. B. Astor houses. But he could also layer on ornament in a way that New York's great critic, Mariana Van Rensselaer, considered vulgar. His designs seem to use every motif he could manage to convince the builder to include. Did he know his European models first-hand, or did he just see images in the professional press? We do know that he spent the summer of 1870 in the English south coast resort of Brighton.

Griffith Thomas married a woman named Eliza and had three sons. One son joined Thomas at the height of his success, while another moved to Chicago. Thomas himself certainly had enough work to afford to live lavishly in his brownstone at 92 Fifth Avenue. As a "builder's architect," who did not associate much with the architectural societies, he charged the modest fee of only one and a half percent for his commission on the houses at a time when the next generation of architects were pushing for a five percent commission.

In his last years, Thomas suffered a decline. He had started a fine house for himself at 500 Fifth Avenue on the northwest corner of 42nd Street, leasing the site from the Livingston estate, which had been the Siebrecht nursery. Then the economy plunged. Building commissions virtually ceased, and no doubt Thomas was overcommitted financially. In addition, his three sons all died. The grief and the lack of new jobs may have led to his sudden death in 1879 (likely a stroke), just as the economy was rebounding. Thomas was ushered out in a Baptist service and buried rather modestly in the Green-Wood Cemetery in Brooklyn, leaving his widow to contend with his debts and lack of assets. Following this painful collapse, it would seem all the papers were thrown out, leaving no tangible record of the firm.[1]

There was an aftermath. The distinguished ship builder William H. Webb, related by marriage to the Vanderbilts and the Twomblys, had retired in 1869 at the age of 52 to devote the rest of his life to finance and good works. He lived at 515 Fifth Avenue, near the site of Griffith Thomas's intended home at no. 500. Thomas had begun the structure as a private house for himself but when his finances collapsed in around 1875, Webb shared his property, and Thomas changed the detail on the built portion of the house to make it look like an important hotel. As Griffith Thomas's health failed, Webb took over Thomas's unfinished project and had it greatly increased in size to become the Hotel Bristol, an apartment hotel named after its famous equivalent in Paris, which would become a fixture in New York life for decades. *The Record and Guide* described the hotel in 1876 as having suites of rooms and bachelor flats with a communal

Northwest corner of Fifth Avenue and 42nd Street

Siebrecht's Nursery. Griffith Thomas began a house for himself here but the 1873 economic collapse took down Thomas's plan. The planned house was built over to create the now Hotel Bristol.

dining room and a communication system throughout the building. Meals could be delivered to the suites, and the building had both a passenger and a service elevator. The hotel was converted into flats in 1903. One can only wonder if Thomas sensed that the acceptance of the apartment house was growing. Just three blocks away from his property, at 45th Street and Fifth Avenue, he had planned an apartment building for the venerable developer, George Kemp, who had just finished the Buckingham Hotel at 49th Street.[2]

The Legacy of Griffith Thomas

The row house developers of Griffith Thomas's era, who worked in the 1870s and 1880s, flourished, exploiting their building know-how and using money put up by investors to create scores of residences,

Fifth Avenue and the northeast corner of 42nd Street

Demolishing the Hotel Bristol.

Griffith Thomas started
a private home for
himself at 500 Fifth. His
finances dipped in the
1873 depression. The
house was converted
into a hotel with a huge
super structure atop
the almost finished two
stories of Thomas's row
house.

Far left:
FIFTH AVENUE AND
42ND STREET

*Including a view of the
Hotel Bristol. Temple
Emanuel is on the right,
east side of the Avenue.
The E. D. Morgan house
is in the foreground
right.*

which turned a healthy profit in the good years. The next building
opportunity would be the empty land now catching the eye of
builders—the blocks of the upper 30s. Some speculative developers
worked on the Avenue, but most of their activity was just off Fifth
Avenue, where they could build rows from the same design of varying
widths.

As we know, Griffith Thomas oversaw the building of a great number
of houses, as did Robert Mook, the brothers David and John Jardine,
Philip Fitzpatrick, Cornelius O'Reilly, and Charles Duggin, just
before he teamed up with James Crossman.[3] The Astor estate built
many row houses on the properties of the West 30s and 40s, listing
Peter Kissam as builder. Those putting up money often were named
on the permit application and while the sponsors were predominantly
men, occasionally a woman's name appears, probably widows of
the property owners. Although these sponsors were from the old
merchants-o-the port class, many backers about whom we have no
knowledge sponsored houses. The developers included German, Irish

and English surnames. Jewish names began to appear and grow in number as the century progressed.

Many speculative rows were small in number, often intended to be rental houses, and the widths of the frontages could vary. As we know, many on the ends of the row were twenty feet across, but some, in the middle, were sixteen, even only fourteen feet wide. The brownstone fronts were quite similar but the detail around the windows did vary from builder to builder. Some houses had straight lintels above the windows, while others used pediments or round arches—the Jardines seemed to make their window surrounds rather like picture frames. But as images of blocks developed by a specific builder seem not to exist, it is virtually impossible to pin down the detail and tie the houses to a specific speculator. All the speculative brownstones had a high stoop, an asymmetrical entry door which could vary from one builder to another, but to a casual observer, they were repetitive fronts of a material Edith Wharton decried—she had grown up in a brownstone on 23rd Street just off Fifth Avenue and often wrote that it was the most hideous stone ever quarried.

Griffith Thomas personified the spirit of New York enterprise in the mid-century. Without architectural training, he rose from the world of builders, then dominant in New York, to construct scores of brownstones, churches, cast-iron stores and manufacturing buildings, department stores, the first club, and the first big hotel. He was the architect of successful New Yorkers in the mid-century, but he died just at the point when more practiced professionals would take on the building of row houses. We will soon see a generation of younger men, many of whom had traveled abroad and even attended professional training programs, begin to win favor on the upper avenue. Although builders repeated their Fifth Avenue successes in the western portions of the city, new houses were now being individually commissioned or sponsored by high-end architect/developers, keen to exploit plots of land ripe for development on Fifth and Madison Avenues.

CHAPTER 7

SOCIAL ARBITERS AND CLIMBERS

"The only thing I like about rich people is their money."

Nancy Astor

THE KNICKERBOCKER SOCIETY was well established with relatively simple customs and entertainments. As New York began to grow with the arrival of people who had made recent fortunes, whose ways of life were not compatible with the Knickerbocker manners, a complex new social life emerged. Although women were the foot soldiers, the generals were men who made a very complex set of arrangements in order to negotiate the social interface between old and new money. Initially it was the men who moved between the two distinct social groups, although by the 1880s women would take the upper hand when it came to managing the social life of what they perceived to be high society.

A good many of the Prince of Wales's engagements in 1860 had been organized by a curious figure, Isaac Hull Brown (1812–80). Originally a working-class carpenter, Brown rose to become the sexton of James Renwick's fashionable Grace Church, in due course catering to the social ambition and status of the rest of the congregation. Unctuous and blessed with a remarkable memory, yet extremely heavy in person and with a coarse face, Brown (never Mr. Brown) was far from part of the élite, yet he studied the social scene with microscopic precision. He learned and retained detail about the people at Grace Church whom he considered to be prominent, their families, servants, guests, and the like, and knew everyone's secrets. He also devoted his time to cutting out the newer social climbers or "Shoddies," whom he excluded with great precision.

"Snobbish Society's Schoolmaster," a caricature of Ward McAllister as "an ass" telling Uncle Sam he must imitate "an English Snob of the 19th century" or "you will nevah be a gentleman"; Uncle Sam is shown laughing heartily. Ward McAllister set the pace in New York Society in the mid-19th century.

Brown arranged everything. He could supply young men who might dance with girls at balls, but who knew to never renew acquaintance again. He knew the social position of everyone staying in the city's hotels. He could supply carriages for events, linens and dishes for parties, and introductions for guests. He called out for vehicles after a ball and arranged to have people carried to and from social events. He even repaired the floor when it collapsed under the weight of the guests during the Prince's Ball at the Academy of Music. For climbers, Brown, if he was willing, provided the fluidity of ascent but if you failed to meet his standards, total exclusion resulted. Sexton Brown handled all the Grace Church burials with perfect discrimination, but oddly, he himself is buried under a statue of Pythagoras in Green-Wood Cemetery, Brooklyn, the cemetery of choice in the era. However, his social influence did not last; not long after the Prince's Ball, he was cut out by another figure, Samuel Ward McAllister (1827–95), who studied his techniques and used them in a more sophisticated manner.

A Society Swell

Ward McAllister, as he liked to be known, was part of the Savannah-New York connection of the first half of the century. He was related to the banker Samuel Ward, who after his wife's death retired and became something of a fop, building a beautiful house designed by Town and Davis at the corner of Bond Street and Broadway, which contained what was perhaps the first private art gallery in New York. McAllister himself took time to find a sense of direction. As a young man he lived briefly in New York, and it may have been at this time that he attended a ball given by Peter and Sarah Schermerhorn at their house at 6 Great Jones Street and first met the young Caroline Webster Schermerhorn, who was to bring him social cachet and guide him on his social ascent. McAllister then returned to Savannah and began to practice law before following his more ambitious brother and father to the California Gold Rush. He spent two years in the West, then returned to the East when he learned of a wealthy Savannah-born woman living in Madison, New Jersey, Sarah Taintor Gibbons, who possessed valuable income-generating properties. Her father, William T. Gibbons (1794–1852), owned cotton and rice plantations and a valuable harbor property in New Jersey. One suspects that Gibbons did not favor McAllister, who married his daughter in 1853 only after the father's death.

McAllister and his wife promptly departed for an extended trip to Europe. Upon his return, he set himself up in 1859 as a "swell" in Newport, Rhode Island in 1859, then the training ground for success in New York. With his wife's funds, he entertained lavishly on a farm outside Newport, gaining a reputation as a splendid party arranger. McAllister set up the carriages, food, scenic farm animals, and an ample supply of champagne for "frappes." He once even had a dance floor built in the field of the farm, providing musicians to play for a rustic picnic and, as a final touch, arranging for picturesque sheep to be brought to the edge of the property. McAllister's entertainments whiled away the relatively dull days in Newport.

The Civil War interrupted this smooth social ascent. Thus far, McAllister had clearly been living from his late father-in-law's estate, but Gibbons's Savannah plantation was wiped out during the War, and his large residential property at Madison, New Jersey, called "The Forest," had to be put up for sale afterwards. McAllister was now short of capital, living in New York without a proper source of income, only the return on some small rental houses near Fifth Avenue. He moved his family into 16 West 36th Street, a house he rented from the estate of Eugene Livingston. His marriage had probably gone bad, as from then onwards his social career seems to have been a solo performance. His wife does not even get a mention in Society as *I Have Found It*, the somewhat sinister book he published in 1890.

Samuel Ward McAllister, Prince, New York, in The Sketch *106, no. 9 (February 6, 1895): 1.*

McAllister perceived a chance to replace Isaac Brown and was determined to do so – and, thereby, perhaps enhance his purse. He saw an opening to use his self-proclaimed expertise gained in Europe and his connections to "old" New York to set himself up as an arbiter

SAMUEL WARD
MCALLISTER/
LIVINGSTON HOUSE,
16 WEST 36TH STREET

McAllister's wife was wealthy before the Civil War. Money became a problem for McAllister at the end of the war and he rented modest houses off Fifth Avenue.

Caroline Schermerhorn Astor, who self-identified as THE Mrs. Astor, avoided photographers. This is an image at the time of the creation of her social group.

of social importance in the post-bellum city, where money spoke as never before. For a generation, McAllister ruled the roost.

The Mystic Rose

At the outset, his name was not strong enough to attract people, and he had little money. He needed a front person and, with great acumen, he selected the woman he dubbed the Mystic Rose. He had perhaps met Caroline Schermerhorn long ago at the Schermerhorn ball and he certainly knew the family. If there was anything she was not, it was Dante's mystic rose; she was dull, and far from a beauty, described as having a "sallow" complexion. But she came from a solid Knickerbocker family that owned property in Manhattan and she was married to an Astor, so she was "old New York" through and through and with Astor money. She had high social standing, vast wealth, and a name which resonated with those on the rise. She also had no close friends and was in an unhappy marriage from which McAllister's ambitions offered an escape. His coaching of her gave her a far larger role than she would have had on her own.

In 1853 Caroline had married William Backhouse Astor, Jr. at Grace Church. She and her husband both grew up in the same small world of New York City affluence near Bond Street, but the two were ill-suited for a good marriage. Astor, a graduate of Columbia College, was highly intelligent, but deprived of a major position in the family real estate office by primogeniture. Gradually he retreated from New York society, taking to large private yachts, drink, gambling, and women. His wife, on the other hand, loved all things French, maintaining an apartment at 146 Avenue des Champs Elysée, where she spent every spring, as part of a group of Knickerbockers who had established a Parisian subset in the Faubourg Saint-Germain. Though she vowed boats made her quite sea-sick, she crossed the Atlantic every year.[1]

When they married, Caroline and her husband had first lived in a rented row house on Laight Street, and then on 22nd Street, close to her widowed mother. These were temporary arrangements, for in 1854 William Backhouse Astor senior had given his two sons, John and William, large adjacent plots of land he owned along Fifth Avenue between 32nd and 35th Streets—one of many farms the Astors had bought earlier in the century.[2]

William and Caroline were the first to build, erecting their new home at the southwest corner of 34th Street (350 Fifth Avenue) in 1856. It was a big, solid, and stolid brownstone house, originally free on all four sides of windows, a rare conceit for the day, with a lavish garden to the west and south. The architect was Griffith Thomas of Union Club and soon to be Fifth Avenue Hotel fame. Three years later William's older brother John Jacob Astor III and his wife Charlotte built a more French-looking house for their family on the 33rd Street corner, separated by more gardens (338 Fifth Avenue). The Astor sites today occupy opposite ends of the Empire State Building frontage to Fifth Avenue. At the time the two young couples drew fashionable development to the neighborhood, which soon saw smaller brownstones being built on the rest of the Astor holdings here.

The Dancing Years

Balls and dances were the key to McAllister's social strategy, but at first Mrs. Astor, as Caroline came to be called by everyone, had no ballroom in her new house to compete with that of August and Tiny Belmont. In the past, fancy balls had been rare in fashionable New York. The first such occasion on any scale was a late evening ball held in 1830 at the house of G. G. Howland, a principal figure in the port, and attended exclusively by old New Yorkers of the same type. The Schermerhorns had also held balls like the one at which Caroline and McAllister may have met. These elaborately arranged events, with floral displays, bounteous food and silk curtains, enabled florists in the New York area to establish their businesses, building on a reputation for high quality work. New York was emerging from the old days when one firm supplied flowers, hired an orchestra and the like, and now there were several vendors to choose from. The pace of these events picked up after the visit of the Prince of Wales. As these balls grew ever more extravagant in the years after the Civil War, they also became more exclusive. The objective was to parade and display assets and avoid conversation, while keeping others out became part of the exercise and increasingly a sign of having one's finger on the social pulse.

There was certainly a craze for dancing among New Yorkers in the later 19th century. Dance training was a great feature of society; boys met girls from the "proper" caste, and marriages sometimes followed. The leading dance teachers in fashionable circles for almost a century were the Dodworth family of musicians, who brought the "German" to New York in 1844, the standard cotillion event of balls for the next two generations. So successful were Thomas Dodworth's sons, Allen and Harvey, that they were able to purchase a brownstone at 677 Fifth Avenue between 53rd and 54th Streets (more of the block later), which they used until they retired. Formal dance training became a fixture of New York society for a century, ending only in the 1950s when the

This portrait of Mrs. Astor shows her resplendent on her spring visit to Paris. At the time, she still lived in her 34th Street house, although she would soon move uptown to 66th Street.

*John Jacob Astor III's
house was a year old
when this picture was
taken. It sits to the
south of the house of
his brother W. B. Astor
and his wife, Caroline.
The garden between
the two Astor properties
continues the tradition
of garden spaces on
Fifth Avenue. Like the
Hart Shiff house, it
had a central door and
mansard roof.*

*John Jacob Astor III
House during the
funeral procession of
Ulysses S. Grant, looking
south from 34th Street.*

classes were conducted by the ancient Mr. and Mrs. De Rham, who
had lived in the original Brevoort house for almost a century.

While in Europe in the 1850s, McAllister made a study of formal
events, particularly dancing. In London he learned about Almacks, a
club in Pall Mall where dances had been held for a century, organized
and run by women, and he hit on the idea of inventing a New York
version of such events. But ordinary brownstones such as his own
were unsuitable for such events—even the larger ones were too small
for a big reception.

STEREOSCOPIC VIEW OF
34TH STREET AND FIFTH
AVENUE

*34th Street looking
north. J. N. A. Griswold
House on the East side of
Fifth Avenue.*

WILLIAM BACKHOUSE
ASTOR, JR. HOUSE,
FIFTH AVENUE AND
34TH STREET

*William Backhouse Astor
Jr.'s house had windows
on all four sides. The
entry is not at the center,
but slightly to the south
with rooms to either side
of the door. The house
has a traditional stoop.*

The solution was the fashionable restaurant, or later the deluxe hotel incorporating a restaurant or impressive public area. Such places hardly existed before the 1870s, but an entire network of these event spaces rapidly sprang up along Fifth Avenue thereafter. The key venue was Delmonico's, a restaurant started in lower New York in the 1820s by two brothers from Switzerland. Like many New York institutions, Delmonico's was constantly moving northwards to keep up with fashion. It arrived on Fifth Avenue and 14th Street in 1862, occupying the house of Moses Grinell at no. 1 East 14 Street, which was converted into a restaurant, probably by the architect Lienau. It was the first uptown eating establishment and one of the first places where gentlemen and ladies could dine at ease together. Augustus Belmont's original house was sold to Henry Van Shaick, a fixture in Knickerbocker society whose ancestors arrived in New Amsterdam in 1636 making them true patriarchs of the old city, and later became the home of the dry goods merchant William Halsted, before Frederick Diaper converted it into the Knickerbocker Hotel. Delmonico's would stay there until it jumped up to 25th Street in 1876 and then to 44th Street in 1897. But 14th Street was where the McAllister-inspired balls began—on neutral territory and at a commercial establishment. It is likely that McAllister's social machinations were generously rewarded by his beneficiaries, such as Delmonico's and Klunder, the fashionable florist of high society.

The Patriarchs

For the season of 1872, McAllister pulled together a committee called the Patriarchs, to address the problem of too many wishing to attend balls and too few places available. The committee consisted of 24 men, plus McAllister himself. After a debate overseen by McAllister, each of the Patriarchs was to invite five men and four women to select those who would sit at his table for the supper for the Patriarchs Ball, an annual event which set the standard for acceptance in New York society.

The name McAllister invented for the new social organization was resoundingly male. The men thus personally chosen by McAllister were a strange selection, some of them pillars of old New York, others new men of approved character who had risen in the post-Civil War economic boom. He thought about each of them carefully. Most of them lived on or just off Fifth Avenue and many were relatives of the Astors, the richest family in America at the time. The group included the Fifth Avenue resident William Butler Duncan, a banker and broker with Abolitionist relatives who was also connected with the Belmont and the Boss Tweed circle. But Jewish bankers were excluded from the Patriarchs, as were members of the "horsey" set like Augustus Belmont and Leonard Jerome (although another member of that set, the charming, amusing, and kindly William Travers, did get in). For a short time, McAllister's Patriarch system worked well; after a while he doubled their number to 50 and started a second "junior" assembly in 1881, the Family Circle. But its exclusively male committee was the cause of much resentment.

Not everyone jumped aboard the McAllister boat. Some of the old Yankee-Knickerbocker group elected not to play. While willing to attend major events, some acceptable conservatives shunned much of the social menu. These included an "old family" contingent who preferred to have a house on Madison Avenue—men like J. P. Morgan, George F. Baker, Charles T. Barney, and others, like the Roosevelts, Hamilton Fish, and Lewis Rutherfords. Dutch patroon family members circulated on the outer edges of the Patriarchs.

In September 1875 Caroline Astor reacted to the success of the Patriarchs by commissioning Griffith Thomas to add a ballroom to the rear of her house—a perfect cube of 35 feet by 35 feet that cost a large sum, $16,000. She established her own event directly after the new year with the cooperation of Ward McAllister. He would later announce that only 400 people in New York were of the social order to be comfortable in Mrs. Astor's ballroom. Hence the concept of the top of New York Society as the 400.

WILLIAM BACKHOUSE ASTOR, JR. HOUSE, FIFTH AVENUE AND 34TH STREET, SOUTHWEST CORNER

The presence of the Astors on Fifth Avenue brought tenants to the new rows—the row houses to the west of the house are Astor properties. The stoop is unusually wide. The addition of a ballroom to the back (west) of the house was the home to the "400."

By the late 1870s Ward McAllister had created a wonderful place for himself. For many he was the conduit to acceptance in society and women flocked to his door. The public loved to learn the details of the society events and eagerly followed the stories in the newspapers. Reporters were naturally forbidden, but increasingly McAllister supplied copy to the *New York World* in exchange for a fee, while family servants also leaked detail. Some hostesses allowed information to the columnists to flatter their own events.

McAllister now dressed in a version of Parisian *flaneur* clothing. A small, heavy fop, he looked rather like a figure in Beatrix Potter's world of over-dressed animals. How to increase his income must have been much in his mind. The ladies who came to call upon him had daughters and money and were doubtless willing to pay for his influence. He seems also to have supported himself, as Brown had done, by ushering in wealthy newcomers for a subvention and perhaps skimming money off the entertainments. He had financial sidelines too, like the Family Circle Dancing Class for young people in 1881, with balls to be held in the brownstone homes of the patrons (one was held in McAllister's own small, rented home, which must have been a challenge for his increasingly reclusive wife). The Family Circle Dancing Class could accommodate those who might emerge into the upper-class events and give some satisfaction to the mothers paying McAllister to introduce their daughters.

In due course there seems to have been some discontent among New York women, who began to see him as pompous and pretentious, and a counter-movement began, called the New York Assemblies. McAllister was obliged to close the Family Circle and make a Junior Patriarchs, but in 1888 this too was disbanded. Confident hostesses began holding events on "McAllister Nights." Meanwhile word of McAllister's subventions must have come to Caroline Astor's ears, for she began to distance herself from him, while the influential Stuyvesant Fishes also cut him from society in 1889. That year, the city created a huge celebration for the Centennial of Washington's inauguration, with street parades up Fifth Avenue and the house fronts decorated with paper lanterns by Stanford White. A great ball was held, but McAllister was given such a small role that he left town to avoid being shown up as a diminished figure.

Wounded, he put his beliefs into prose, publishing his book, *Society as I Have Known It*, in 1890. His absurd views on the rules of behavior and pomposity only exposed him to ridicule. The Patriarch balls limped on, but McAllister was stripped of his Emperor's attire. He admitted to being a paid reporter of the events for Pulitzer's *World* and tried to invent his own list for the 400. People cut him, as he had cut those who he felt were not important a generation earlier—indeed, in his book McAllister suggested crossing the street to avoid a figure from the past no longer fashionable. McAllister died alone at dinner at the Union Club in 1895 on the night of a ball he did not attend. His cortége down Fifth Avenue passed Mrs. Astor's house, where the shades had been drawn. She had not been a part of his events for some time and had finally seen through his illusion. She did not attend his funeral; few from the earlier days did.

Marietta Stevens's daughter Minnie moved in Edward VII's circle.

Social Climbing

A few American women in the years after the Civil War arrived in New York to play the game according to the rules set by Ward McAllister and his circle. Despite all efforts to break into the New York set, these women were totally rejected, faced with a seeming insurmountable barrier. But it was possible that acquiring a European gloss might bring the wall down and acceptance into a newer version of New York society could be achieved.

The proper brownstone world of good form opened access to those who played by the rules. Someone who never played by anyone else's rules was Marietta Reed Stevens (1827–95), widow of the famous hotelier Paran Stevens.

Born in Lowell, Massachusetts in 1827 as the daughter of a greengrocer, Marietta Reed may have been aspiring to be a teacher when she arrived in Boston and met Paran Stevens (1802–72), possibly when she was working as a house maid. Twenty-five years her elder, Stevens was running two of the top New England hotels, the Revere House Hotel in Boston and the Tremont House in his native Claremont, New Hampshire. He already had a young daughter, Ellen, by his first wife, who died in 1850. By his marriage to the statuesque Marietta he had two children, Mary Fiske Stevens (Minnie), born in 1853, and Harry Leyden Stevens, born in 1859.

As soon as Paran Stevens took on the management of the Fifth Avenue Hotel at Amos Eno's invitation, the couple started to make their mark on New York society. Marietta Stevens took on a house for the family at 244 Fifth Avenue between 27th and 28th Streets a few blocks north of the hotel, on property owned by the Beekman family. This placed her in the midst of respectable brownstone New York, where she would remain for 30 years. Meanwhile her husband, far from confining himself to hotel management, began to invest in real estate in the vicinity. His investments must have made the two Stevenses far richer than running hotels.

Fashionable Hostess

There was another string to their bow. The Stevenses also spent part of their summers in Newport, then emerging as America's most glamorous resort, and held parties at which the star attraction was Marietta's sister, Fanny Reed, who had a fine voice. There is a legendary story about Fanny singing *The Battle Hymn of the Republic* in wartime Newport not long after it was composed in the early 1860s, bringing tears to the eyes of the audience. Soon enough Fanny came to New York with her sister and added glamor to Marietta's Sunday evening musical parties at 244 Fifth Avenue. These declined after Fanny departed for Paris, where she spent the rest of her life as part of the American community. Fanny was friendly in Paris with the actress Mme. Modeska, the great Polish musician Paderewski, and the Hungarian artist Munkácsy, so admired by American collectors at the time, but it is not entirely clear how she supported herself.[3]

Back in New York, Paran Stevens began in the 1860s to buy property and leases in the 37th Street and Fifth Avenue zone, now starting to develop. Around 1870 his ventures grew more ambitious, and he turned to the pre-eminent architect, Richard Morris Hunt, then establishing himself within New York society. Hunt designed a house for Stevens on 36th Street between Fifth and Madison Avenues, and a small commercial building at 1160 Broadway. But the most important of these collaborations was the block of apartments known as the Stevens House.

This was a bigger thing altogether, a grand confection of Second Empire type. Stevens had been in Paris for the 1867 Exposition, when he saw fashionable people living in apartment buildings. New York, he felt, was ready for a grand apartment house on Fifth Avenue, and Hunt, Paris-trained, was the right person to design it, having recently designed an apartment house for Rutherford Stuyvesant on 18th Street, which ushered in the fashion for so-called "French flats." The new venture was much bigger and taller, eight stories high, of which three were in the roof. It faced all along the south side of 27th Street between Broadway and the west side of Fifth Avenue, where its original frontage was a mere 28 feet. The eighteen apartments were served by elevators, and there were grand public rooms finished in luxurious materials, much as in the Fifth Avenue Hotel.

It had hardly been finished when Stevens suddenly died in 1872, leaving

VICTORIA HOTEL

This enormous pile was begun as a high-end apartment house by Paran Stevens. His unexpected death complicated matters. Was New York quite ready for living in a big multiple dwelling? Transformed into a hotel, it was the backbone of Marietta Stevens's finances.

behind him a legacy of disputes with Hunt over the construction of the building, which took years to settle. Marietta was in Europe at the time of her husband's death and, on her return, she found that she had been left property-rich but cash-poor. Nevertheless, she promptly busied herself with making changes to the apartment house, calling in the Boston-based hotel architect, Arthur D. Gilman, who added 34 extra feet on the Fifth Avenue side of the structure, eliminated the individual kitchens, and created a large dining room, thereby making the Stevens House more like a hotel.

The apartment house was Marietta's hope for financial success, but she lacked cash. She now began her life-long pattern of not paying her bills. She paid neither Hunt nor Gilman nor the workmen involved in altering the building and consequently found herself involved in a tissue of litigation, during which she had to endure satirical jibes from Hunt's lawyers over her expensive lifestyle. The lawsuits also involved Paran Stevens's other executor, John Lowell Melcher, who had married her step-daughter Ellen. Tussles over money between Marietta and the Melchers continued for the rest of her life, including an unpleasant courtroom scene. Eventually, amid further litigation and unpaid bills, the apartment house was turned formally into the Victoria Hotel.

Elsewhere, Marietta made what she could of her late husband's investment properties. These included almost a full block on the eastern side of Fifth Avenue between 36th and 37th Streets, on which Stevens held a lease. There were probably restrictions on the lease, as the best Marietta could do in 1878 was have a builder, Arthur Crooks, create six single-story shop fronts in timber with a nursery garden behind. This was the nursery of the first fashionable florist above 23rd Street, Siebrecht & Wadley. The proprietor was a German-trained horticulturalist who studied in Göttingen before emigrating to Hoboken and New Rochelle. He may well have worked with Paran Stevens himself in an earlier Manhattan florist shop before opening on the second site. Known for his interest in exotic plants and flowers, Siebrecht is credited with the introduction of the orchid to New York rooms and lily of the valley in bridal bouquets. The nursery remained on the Stevens site until the 1890s, a notable abnormality in the development pattern of the Avenue.

Marietta had begun to emerge as a major figure in New York society before Paran Stevens died. She lived in a brownstone, she held Sunday receptions with music, she dressed exquisitely, she had a strong personality, and her husband was a recognized figure in commercial circles. She had two young children to incorporate into New York society and also had a toehold in Paris, through her sister Fanny. However, as an ambitious widow she was sometimes snubbed. For instance, Catherine Kernochian, a daughter of Pierre Lorillard the snuff king, remarked that "she had a grandmother," in other words Marietta's grandmother was of no account. Insults like these determined Marietta to beat the grandees at their own game.

Matchmaker and Matriarch

For much of the 1870s Marietta dragged her green-eyed daughter Minnie through France and England, assuring eligible men that a great fortune sat back in New York. One potential suitor even sent an emissary to verify Marietta's claims of wealth. The agent returned with the news that the apartment house was a failure, and there was no sign of the great resources Marietta claimed. Finally, however, in

July 1878 she managed to marry Minnie to a British military man and son of a peer, Colonel Arthur Henry Fitzroy Paget, in a ceremony attended by the now-corpulent Prince of Wales. If the marriage was not as grand as Marietta had wished, it provided her access to New York's haute circles. Even the outstanding hostess of the decade earlier, old New York's "Tiny" Belmont, paid Marietta a call.

Marietta had made it—she was now included in the Patriarch's list. Besides Minnie she had a son, the seemingly charming Harry, who was educated at St. Mark's School, a newly created boys boarding school outside Boston, and in Europe. In 1880, an announcement appeared touting his engagement to Edith Jones—the future Edith Wharton. The young couple seemed happy enough, but there was trouble brewing from Edith's mother, Lucretia Rhinelander Jones, who came from an old New York family and was unwilling to acknowledge Marietta. Old form was important to Mrs. Jones, and she viewed the fact that Marietta had announced the engagement with the Stevens name coming first as bad form. She seems to have terminated the engagement, although Marietta may well have been relieved—Harry was due shortly to receive his share of the estate, but quite likely there was no estate to inherit. In any case, Harry would

CORNER OF FIFTH
AVENUE AND 36TH
STREET

The solidly built-up block between 35th and 36th Streets as it appears today would not indicate that a large greenhouse stood there as recently as the '90s. The brilliant display of colors added a pleasing note to the otherwise dull surroundings, but the rapid growth of business swept away the florist and his riotous colored stock, much to the regret of the afternoon promenaders.

be diagnosed with cancer of the stomach and died in 1885, seemingly on bad terms with his mother at the time of his death. Marietta had a Reed family mausoleum built in the great Mount Auburn Cemetery in Cambridge, Massachusetts. Paran Stevens and Fanny are there but Harry is not—indeed, Harry does not appear in searches for grave sites. Tongues wagged when Harry died; was it from heartbreak over the ending of the engagement? As for Edith, she went on to make an unhappy marriage to Teddy Wharton, of which more later[4]. The social-climbing Mrs. Lemuel Struthers in *The Age of Innocence* is a savage caricature of Marietta.

The breaking off of the engagement did not end Marietta's connection with the Jones family. As we shall see, Edith's aunt Mary Mason Jones had built a grand "marble" mansion on her family property at Fifth Avenue and 57th Street, where she died in 1891. Moving uptown at last, Marietta quickly rented the house from the Jones estate, and there in the following year she entertained the 8th Duke of Marlborough. But this was the last gasp of her glory. In the early months of 1895, the Victoria Hotel failed, and the Stevens estate was declared insolvent. Upon hearing the news, Marietta suffered a massive stroke and died, leaving behind multiple legal issues for her daughter Minnie, by then a fixture in London society circles following The Prince of Wales, to solve.[5]

As set in stone as the code of Knickerbocker New York had been, McAllister started to prise open a place for the representatives of new money of whom he approved. Marietta came at society with a sledgehammer, and she succeeded in breaking the wall and having a last laugh when she moved into Mary Mason Jones's home. Edith Wharton's mother, with her adherence to the old ways and disdain for the new wave of social upstarts, must have been beside herself with rage.[6]

THE GILDED AGE

"Clothes make the man. Naked people have little or no influence on society."
Mark Twain

NEW YORK SOCIETY had long been dominated by the Yankees and Knickerbockers, who followed rigid social protocol with dedication and respected family ties above all. Surely, no one back in lower Fifth Avenue ever imagined how rapidly the city would grow. The number of new arrivals at Castle Clinton, the former Battery, at the foot of the island swelled in virtually every decade, as ever-more capacious boats brought more people to fill laboring jobs. The influx of newcomers had forced the merchants of the port northward, abandoning the well-built houses on Greenwich Street and at St. John's Square, for uptown locations.

Almost matching the number of newcomers were a set of New Yorkers who had amassed some economic and social wealth by the mid-century, who were not from the old Knickerbocker world. Professionals, dry goods merchants, speculators, inventors, and bankers now had capital and an ambition to wedge themselves into the world of the Knickerbockers. This meant breaking the "sameness" of the old order, and the adoption of new customs and practices, much noted by Mark Twain. After all, the famous ball held for Edward, Prince of Wales had allowed anyone with proper dress and jewelry an invitation, a munificent gesture which the old families would come to regret.

The New York gentry would continue to cling to their old ways, while the newcomers would overwhelm them with new customs linked to European affectations and the spending of money.

Peter Marié led the dances and flirted with the young women but never married any. His miniature collection numbered over 300 portraits.

The site of the ensuing battle would be the residential property on Fifth Avenue. The weapons deployed would be young daughters, now debutantes, the collection and commissioning of works of art, and the amassing of fine horses and carriages, wine (following the example of August Belmont), and elaborate meal services. Eating in the family dining room in the half-subterranean floor of a row house was replaced by fine dining rooms above ground and the quest for food that supplied more than merely nutrition. Multi-course menus were symbols of the transformation of the old culture of settled customs into a much more dynamic and aspirational era, which Mark Twain would dub The Gilded Age. Opulence replaced simplicity, affectation replaced acceptability and a new city raced to the north.

Belles of the Gilded Age

The belles of this era, some 300 of them, were painted by artists as "miniatures" for the collection of a merchant of the port, Peter Marié, whose ancestors had gone from France to the French West Indies. Marié was ever described as a gentleman of the old school with courtly manners, always welcome at dinners and to lead dances and was a fixture in New York society, despite his Catholic faith. A bachelor, Marié had all of the society women of his era painted in miniature for the collection, which—along with a great library—graced the house (one of three he occupied, including one on Fifth Avenue) in which he saw no necessity to entertain. As a single man, Marié went to parties and flirted with the women, but never had to reciprocate hospitality. The miniatures were given to The New-York Historical Society, where they remain today. He created a portrait

Patriarchs' Ball invitation, December 21, 1896, admission ticket.

PATRIARCHS' BALL

DECEMBER

THIS TICKET MUST BE

NOT TRANSFERABLE

21ST 1896

SHOWN AT THE DOOR

TO BE RETURNED

IF NOT USED

ADMIT *Miss Justine de Peyster*

INVITED BY MR. *Johnston Livingston*

gallery of the women at the dances of the Patriarchs and the balls of Mrs. Astor. One wonders if there was more to his story.

Dining Out in Style

If Peter Marié entertained, he did so at a restaurant, although New York had few socially acceptable venues. Dining out as a delight began early in the century, but it was restricted to the business areas and male-dominant diners. Indeed, women did not eat out alone without escorts until the end of the 19th century, likely at the Waldorf Astoria Hotel restaurants. Restaurants for men of leisure and groups of male and female diners, such as Delmonico's and Café Martin, first appeared on Fifth Avenue. The well-established, and by now 30-year-old restaurant begun by the Swiss brothers Delmonico in lower Manhattan, was opened at 15th Street and Fifth Avenue in April of 1862, where it stayed until moving uptown to 26th Street and Fifth Avenue (1876–99), and finally ending up at 44th Street and Fifth (1897–1923). If an appropriate restaurant was becoming an alternate location to a home, then society balls could also be held in a commercial establishment. Delmonico's became the fashionable restaurant of the Gilded Age, hosting many balls and Patriarch evenings.

One of the many small portraits of New York's young female society, commissioned by Peter Marié and kept in his house. Young Edith Jones Wharton appears in this group of miniatures.

Nothing was more motivating for the socially ambitious young man or woman than the desire to attend a glittering and fashionable party or a ball. The pressure created a perfect foil for Ward McAllister, the

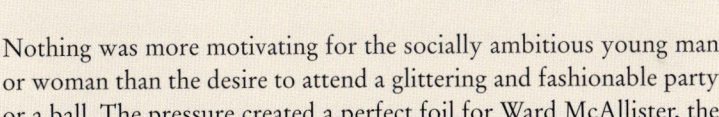

Another miniature from Peter Marié's collection. The Daughters of Robert Minturn, Carl A. Weidner and Fredrika Weidner, 1899, watercolor on ivory.

FIFTH AVENUE AND
26TH STREET

Delmonico's on 26th Street, the fashionable restaurant of the Gilded Age. The building is two lots wide with a street level entry.

Marietta Stevens was described as statuesque. She used a sledgehammer and her daughter to be invited to Alva Vanderbilt's ball. Marietta Stevens, Vanderbilt Ball, March 26, 1883.

arbiter of social taste, whose manipulations were infantile compared to those being made by Marietta Reed Stevens, who crashed through every wall created to keep her out. From 1872 onwards, the Patriarchs Ball would set the standard for acceptance in New York Society, along with the Ball in January in the home of Mrs. Astor.

The competition for a coveted ticket obsessed many women and to gain an invitation was a triumph. To read about the ball in the newspapers was a pleasure experienced by many other women, who were never to be on the list. New York's working class were fascinated to read about the extravagant entertainments with amazing displays of out-of-season flowers, the glow of candles, beautiful people in opulent attire, and the dazzle of jewels. Reading about the glamor provided a distraction from the hard life of the people who worked in New York and newspaper profits were boosted by the stories of the joys of being wealthy.

Delmonico's menu for February 7, 1873.

Society in New York remained focused on internal events, rather than causes or intellectual pursuits. Edith Wharton and Mariana Van Rensselaer were most unusual for breaking away from expected behavior to write. In New York little was required other than money, a suitable family, and the interest in being a part of an increasingly lavish world. Society was therefore easier to penetrate than in cities where men and some women might have had more serious pursuits. The fluidity of New York society was fueled by increasingly costly expenditures.

The Gilded Age was born and thrived, then died on Fifth Avenue. The centrality of New York to this era of social growth was recognized all over the United States as new money raced to Manhattan, often bringing with it marriageable daughters, as Edith Wharton noted in her books. The stories of New York circulating abroad soon led to a wave of impecunious European aristocrats coming to the city in search of a "dollar bride." It would seem the Gilded Age was a honey pot which would attract numerous bees to the streets of Fifth Avenue, observed with some dismay by denizens of the Knickerbocker class, such as Henry James and Edith Wharton. Ultimately, the Gilded Age would eventually suffocate old New York as the city's wealthiest residents strove for acceptance in European high society.

CHAPTER 8

THE INVASION OF RETAIL

"The streets were never so crowded with Christmas shoppers. The interior of Tiffany's shop was jammed full this afternoon. Navigation on Broadway is impeded by the great raft of carriages before Stewart's store."

The Diary of George Templeton Strong, December 22, 1873

THE RESIDENTIAL ENCLAVES on Fifth Avenue below 14th street were largely bypassed by the fashionable drive northwards. Many of them became boarding houses for respectable, but increasingly impecunious, denizens of old New York. Immediately to the north, Fifth Avenue was transformed by the lofts and factories of the garment district, and where clothes were detailed and finished, a retail industry soon followed. Ladies' Mile on Sixth Avenue began on 14th Street and continued to 23rd Street. Benjamin Atman's great department store, originally pioneered on Sixth Avenue before moving to Fifth Avenue, would hoist the ladies' shopping area to Fifth Avenue at 34th Street in the early years of the 20th century. The rapid increase in ready to wear garments fueled the growth of the department store. By the second decade of the 20th century, Fifth Avenue was the premier shopping street in North America.

Remarkably, the lower part of Fifth Avenue remained as originally built and unaffected by the pace of change all the way to the Presbyterian Church on 12th Street. Whether it was because a few house owners of old Yankee/Knickerbocker descent resisted change, or that a few just lived long lives, as did William C. Rhinelander's daughters at the corner of Washington Square, the blocks remained an enclave of New York as it had been before 1850. However, some of the houses became stealth boarding houses or flats which we will discuss in a chapter later along. The gracious and verdant blocks with their patches of green seemed sacred and would stay so for a full century.

*The rowhouses above
the Fifth Avenue Hotel
were quickly converted
to shops on the street
fronts as we can see
in the outstretched
awnings. Marietta
Stevens lived in a row
house here.*

The hotelier Paran Stevens, who leased the Fifth Avenue Hotel, had noticed the transformation of some of the first generation of houses below 14th Street into private hotels, stealth apartment houses, and traditional boarding houses as he ran the hotel. The "sacred" location mattered, especially to those being left behind by the great inflation in the cost of being fashionable in the city. Lower Fifth Avenue was quietly and stealthily becoming a focus of multiple dwellings, as many members of the old Yankee/Knickerbocker New York society found themselves financially challenged by the mid-century. It was costly to keep up with their peers as faster money drove up the cost of a fashionable life. Many of these women, known as "soiled doves," struggled to maintain a position within their former group. The transformation of the older houses into low key and, hopefully, unrecognizable boarding houses and small apartments allowed figures from the earlier city to preserve their sense of importance in the changing social world.

The Garment District

It was in the next blocks to the north, developed in the 1850s and close to the Fifth Avenue Hotel and shopping area around Union Square, that commercial pressure was first felt. Here, many of the houses were homes to widows of the men who had built them, who wanted to remain in their family residence. But, as the widows passed on, their families were obliged to acknowledge the march of the garment manufacturers who supplied stores on Sixth Avenue nearby. It was here, on the blocks between Union Square and the Astor properties in the streets of the Upper 20s, that the so-called "Ladies' Mile" sprang up from the 1860s onwards.

The New York City garment business went back to the days of the cotton brokers in the 1850s, when it was found that it made better economic sense to make up complete garments in the city and ship them south to the plantations than for the enslaved people to sew the pieces together themselves. In the early days, the textile merchants and needle-workers congregated around Leonard Street, but they gradually moved northwards to the district east of Washington Square. That was the start of New York's ready-made garment business. For the time being, fashionable men continued to go to bespoke tailors, while middle-class and wealthy women had dressmakers come to their homes. But slowly the mass garment trade penetrated this market too.

Until well on in the century, the garment trade made do with converted premises. But after about 1890 it began to seek out a new building type, the tall and narrow New York loft building, which offered a multiplicity of spaces for the hundreds of small firms that carried out the finishing details for ready-to-wear items. These developments might occupy the sites of one or two houses and rise to twelve stories. For the most part the resulting lofts were neither well-lit inside nor well designed on the outside. Between about 1890 and 1905 an entire section of the city was rebuilt with these lofts, serving what was fast developing into the largest ready-to-wear industry in the world.

From the 1880s onwards, the principals in the majority of the new garment businesses were escapees from the recent Russian pogroms and the women who did the sewing were for the most part also new Jewish immigrants. The business of the workshops, which were at the mercy of exaggerated economic fluctuations, came to be conducted almost entirely in Yiddish. Some of the garment workers were also

This is likely in the growing loft and fashion trade area between Union Square and Sixth Avenue, around 18th Street.

young Italian women who were also exploited and might be forced to work in locked factory floors, as was exposed at the time of the terrible Triangle Shirtwaist Fire of 1911, when 146 immigrant workers perished. Many owners built up substantial profits which they often plowed into New York City real estate; this would become their main business in the next generation.

Ladies' Mile

The retailing side of the garment trade was closely connected and co-located with the business of manufacturing. The Ladies' Mile made itself apparent soon after the end of the Civil War. It ran northwards from the new huge, iron-fronted A. T. Stewart store on 8th Street at Broadway, encompassing the district where Fifth Avenue and Broadway intersect, and eventually reached as far north as 23rd Street. Among major old-established stores from the SoHo area to take up sites on Broadway was Arnold Constable and Company, which moved up to the corner of 19th Street in 1869. Lord & Taylor and Brooks Brothers followed suit in 1870 when they moved to 20th Street.

At first, Sixth Avenue was the main focus for garment retailing and the retail trade moved to Sixth Avenue as the elevated train route was built. Benjamin Altman, for instance, moved his store here from 43 Third Avenue in 1877, locating himself at 19th Street with a Neo-Grec cast iron front. Over the next few years, he duplicated the facade down to 18th Street, occupying a full block.[1] The year after he moved, in 1878, the Sixth Avenue elevated line began to deliver customers and employees to the large stores. Although Altman made several extensions to his highly successful store, elevated railways tended to degrade property. So, in 1906 he made a bold leap and became the first retailer to relocate a major store on Fifth Avenue, having quietly over the years amassed

Brewster & Co. carriages. The first commercial building on Fifth Avenue, in 1865, was on the west side of the Avenue at 16th Street. Brewster will move up to 42nd Street in what will later be Times Square. Brewster & Co remained on Fifth Avenue at 68th Street in a former row house through World War I.

WINDSOR HOTEL
ON THE EAST SIDE OF
FIFTH AVENUE AT 47TH
STREET

*The land belonged to
E.T. Gerry and William
Field and Son were the
architects.*

*Long-stay hotels were
a new concept for
businessmen needing
to live in Manhattan
for a season. After the
Civil War many came
to New York City with
increasing frequency.
Regional store owners
came to see goods which
they would purchase
for their emporia back
home. Others came in
search of capital and
companies. The Windsor
with its lavish rooms and
public spaces attempted
to create a luxurious
home-like atmosphere
across the street from
Jay Gould's house, and
encouraged guests to
meet one another. The
hotel suffered a horrible
fire on St Patrick's Day
in 1899 with great loss
of life.*

plots between 34th and 35th Streets. There was a hold out on the corner of 34th Street for almost a decade, but eventually Altman would take the entire block, making a fine retail emporium.

By then the wealthy classes of New York had moved much further up the Avenue. The section of Fifth Avenue between 14th and 23rd Street, parallel to the Sixth Avenue Ladies' Mile, had long ago filled up with garment buildings, either in the form of converted brownstones or the new loft type. Once the workshops had taken over, retailing was sure to follow. Mrs. Van Rensselaer remembered that the first fashion business appeared on the southeast corner of 17th Street in 1873 but did not identify the owner. Brewster Carriages was the first company to file a permit for a presence on Fifth Avenue, at 16th Street in 1867. And, in 1870, Carl Pfeiffer, the German-trained architect, filed the first New Building permit for the fashion trade, with a high Victorian Gothic turreted store replacing a row house. A store for a hatter was in the shadow of the Fifth Avenue Hotel, which generated trade and commerce on the residential Avenue around the 23rd Street site.

Further north, some smart houses hung on, but they were increasingly accompanied, or ousted, by fashionable shops such as furriers, perfumers, and hatters. An interesting example is the New York branch of the court dress house run by Kate Reilly in London's West End. Opened in an existing brownstone at 277 Fifth Avenue in 1892, this couturier's shop catered to American women every bit as alert to the fashions worn by the ladies of the British Court as to the styles

*Following the success
of The Windsor, the
Buckingham was the
second long-stay hotel
where guests might meet
and extend their contacts
in the sumptuous public
spaces.*

of Paris. In Edith Wharton's novel *The Buccaneers*, which is set in
the 1870s, she calls the dressmaker Mrs. Connelly, but this is surely a
reflection of Kate Reilly.

Even such a high-class establishment as this contributed to the decline
of residential purity along the Avenue, while some large hotels had
also changed the street's scale. We will see that the large and dour
Windsor Hotel had been built as far north as 47th Street in 1872, to
be replaced in 1901, after a gruesome fire, by the Windsor Arcade,
fronted in elegant Beaux-Arts style and replete with fashionable
shops, offices, and studios. The Windsor Arcade was clearly an
elegant taxpayer awaiting redevelopment after the memory of the fire
faded. Close to the site of the new Altman's department store, the
Waldorf Hotel had arrived in 1893, followed hard on its heels by the
rival Astoria next door (1897). More recently, McKim, Mead & White
had built the very grand Knickerbocker Trust (1902–04)—if hotels
and a bank, why not a high-class department store?

Altman's was soon succeeded by Lord & Taylor, which moved to 424–
434 Fifth Avenue between 38th and 39th Streets in 1914. By then, only
two generations after the houses on this part of the Avenue had been
built, almost no residents remained and Fifth Avenue had become the
street for fashion[2]. The rapid success of ready-made clothing put the
tailors and dress makers out of business, and the new merchandise
required grand signature stores. With extraordinary rapidity the homes
of substantial citizens had ceded to America's palaces of consumerism
and for the next three quarters of a century, the epitome of shopping
in America would be the promenade up Fifth Avenue.

CHAPTER 9

UP THE HILL TO 42ND STREET

*"On the avenue, Fifth Avenue, the photographers will snap us
And you'll find that you're in the rotogravure"*

Song from the film *Easter Parade*

IN THE 1840S NO ONE DREAMED the northward growth of the city would move as quickly as it did.   Much of the land that was going to become the northern reaches of Fifth Avenue was unsettled, raw territory populated by wild animals and squatters using the land for individual purposes. The Minetta Brook ran south near the route of the Avenue and rocky outcroppings were abundant on the east side, though less so on the west side. The 30s were relatively flat but there was a steep hill from 42nd-44th Street that would surely prevent development to the north. Indeed, the new safe water supply for the city was finished between 40th and 42nd Streets in 1842. This big granite Egyptian inspired tank provided sightseers with views of the city below, though the views to the north were blocked by a natural hill just beyond the reservoir. The city's abattoir was nestled below 44th Street but reached by going around the hill; for carriages proceeding north, a special team of "hill horses" had to be employed to get over this small mountain. By the 1840s, a few country houses had appeared, for example a summer house that belonged to the ancestors of John Taylor Johnston, one of the early settlers of The Row. Perched on a hill on the east side on the still-unpaved Avenue, with a great five-pier portico, this house had a view of the Hudson River, surely the Rhine of America. The property was some 40 acres and named Bloomingdale Farm. Johnston's neighbors were temporary wooden shacks, and livestock.[1]

*Residence of Dr.
Samuel P. "Sasparilla"
Townsend.*

A potent example of the morass of confusion which often characterized New York architecture in the 1850s and '60s were the successive houses on the northwest corner of Fifth Avenue and 34th Street, a wide crosstown street that had been heavily developed by the Astor Estate. The original house here was a particularly large and coarse "mansion," built in 1853–55 for Samuel P. Townsend, known for his root beverage and cure-all, Sasparilla.

Sasparilla and Scandal

The Townsend house, with its grand frescoed halls and a Pompeian room, can hardly have been to the liking of the recently married William B. Astor and Caroline Schermerhorn Astor, who built their own house, a restrained brownstone designed by Griffith Thomas, at the answering southwest corner of 34th Street and the Avenue at much the same time, 1855. But they did not have to put up with their neighbor for long. Only four years later, in 1859, the Townsend house was suddenly sold to the founder of a women's school, the Spingler Institute, that had begun on Colonnade Row and then migrated to Union Square. The school's founder, The Rev. Gorham Abbott, turned it into an up-market "college" for young and wealthy women,

A. T. Stewart House,
northwest corner
of Fifth Avenue and
34th Street

A. T. Stewart House,
northwest corner
of Fifth Avenue and
34th Street

*East 34th Street,
looking west. The
J. N. A. Griswold
house is to the right.
We are looking at the
Stewart House and the
speculative row houses
to its west. Stewart's
house was designed
by a local builder
who tried to display
learned detail. The
result is a thick-walled,
awkward arrangement
in Westchester white
stone. The mansard and
huge quoins are part of
a crude attempt to make
an important house
among the brick and
brownstones.*

many of whom lived in the house. However, in the second year of
the "institute" one of the students from the South ran off with a man.
The publicity damaged the reputation of Abbott's school, which in
1866 moved to smaller premises in Park Avenue, but a combination
of the Civil War and scandal had doomed the school. The house was
then sold to the larger-than-life figure of department store fame,
Alexander Turney Stewart and it was thought at first that Stewart
planned to remodel the Townsend house for his wife and himself.
Instead, he quickly demolished the Townsend house and brought in
John Kellum, architect/builder for the notorious New York Mayor
"Boss Tweed."

Department Store Art Patron

Stewart's store on Chambers Street was among the first to offer a multiplicity of wares, making it effectively the first department store in America. Born in Northern Ireland, he came to New York City as a schoolteacher and then had two fortunate breaks. He received a legacy, which he used to buy Belfast linen and import it to New York, opening a shop on Broadway in the early days of commerce in stores within the city as the retail trade moved away from the docks. Even better, he married Cornelia Clinch, a member of the Ireland-Clinch real estate family, who owned property in lower Manhattan. Indeed, she was part of the Knickerbocker group, as was Caroline Schermerhorn Astor, whom she surely knew.

Retail merchants were not acceptable socially, even if the merchant's wife was, and Stewart himself probably did not care to join the social world. The Stewarts did not entertain, and Cornelia Stewart remained rather isolated from social events. So why did he elect to build the largest and showiest house in New York? The answer must be that it was a statement of political presence and ambition. Wealthy from his wife's family real estate and his own such ventures perhaps more than from his stores, Stewart belonged to the fast crowd that summered in Saratoga and indulged in dubious investment practices. He was very active in the city and in political circles and when General Grant became President, he suggested Stewart as Secretary of the Treasury. There was great resistance, and the nomination was quickly retracted.

ASTOR AND A. T. STEWART MANSIONS, FIFTH AVENUE AND 34TH STREET.

THE Mrs. Astor's large house was quickly outclassed by Stewart's stone pile.

All this explains why Stewart asked Tweed's architect to build such a splendid house. Possibly he intended it to become home to a New York City club devoted to the Republican machine, the Manhattan Club, after his and his wife's demise. The Stewarts had two or three children who did not survive infancy, so the house became a vehicle for him to guarantee a civic legacy.

A. T. STEWART HOUSE, FIFTH AVENUE AND 34TH STREET

Looking north on Fifth Avenue.

Mrs. Astor can hardly have been delighted with this grandiose successor to the short-lived Townsend house. If 34th Street was enhanced by the solid Astor house, it was overwhelmed by the Stewart mansion, thickly walled and veneered in Westchester "marble," likely from Stewart's very own quarry there.[2] Caroline Astor is often said to have remarked that she purchased carpets from Stewart's store but would not invite him to walk on them in her house. However, the interior of her neighbor's house was undoubtedly finer, or at least contained better things, than her own. Mrs. Astor owned many paintings, hung in her ballroom for most of the year, but few were distinguished, whereas Stewart's 19th-century art collection—he may well have considered his house as a kind of museum—was among the best of its kind in America. He owned American as well as European works and was really the only collector of American contemporary

MRS. A. T. STEWART'S PICTURE-GALLERY

Stewart's interiors were conspicuously costly. He amassed a notable art collection, including works by American artists as well as expected European painters.

sculpture on Fifth Avenue. Before they moved to 34th Street the Stewarts had lived in the fine De Pau Row just below Washington Square (long gone). Between 1849 and 1861 the Dusseldorf Gallery, which sold many works by American and Italian sculptors of the mid-century, was nearby, at 548 Broadway. The Gallery, which opened to promote paintings of the Dusseldorf school, widened to become an early emporium for art in the city and it was from the Dusseldorf Gallery that Stewart bought Hiram Powers's famous *Greek Slave* in 1859, a version of the one which had been shown to acclaim at the Crystal Palace in London in 1851 and brought over to New York in 1857. He also owned marbles by Thomas Crawford, Richard Rogers, and Harriet Hosmer.

When it came to painting, Stewart bought recent work rather than old masters, relying perhaps on the New York art dealer, wood engraver and a founder of The Metropolitan Museum of Art, Samuel P. Avery, who was an acquaintance. Sometimes he relied on critical reputation for certain French works of art he purchased, but he chose rather better than his contemporaries, including August Belmont, his arch political rival. Stewart bought the much-vaunted *Horse Fair* by Rosa

Bonheur and Ernest Meissonier's important Napoleonic battle scene, *1807, Friedland*, as well as works by Alfred Stevens, William-Adolphe Bouguereau, Jean-Léon Gérôme, Marià Fortuny, and the ever-popular Mihály Munkácsy. Among American painters he acquired fine works by Frederick Church and Alfred Bierstadt. He also had pictures by Daniel Huntington, whose portraits were mandatory for Knickerbocker families, but these may have come from his wife's side. Several of the fine pictures he bought, which were sold at his widow's death, are now prominently displayed in the Metropolitan Museum.

Such purchases of art were exceptional. A generation or two later, consultants, decorative firms, and art dealers filled Fifth Avenue homes with art works, but Stewart chose for himself. He traveled frequently to Europe for items in his store and many of his art purchases followed from buying trips in which he showed the same discrimination—he had a good eye and selected well. Sometimes he went with a member of his wife's family, visiting mills in Manchester, then going over to the continent to look at textiles in the glass-roofed display areas of mills in France and Germany.

Within the 34th Street house Stewart selected the colors and furnishings. The interior walls were said to be lined with Carrara marble and he hired an itinerant Italian painter, Mario Brigaldi, who had worked in Rio de Janeiro and Spain as well as New York, to paint encaustic murals in several rooms. All in all, his mansion was a resounding statement of his achievement and political interests. But the store, which had been the basis of his fortune, did not long survive Stewart's death in 1876, when a Tweed ring figure, who had married into the Clinch family, took it over, and drove it into bankruptcy. As for the Stewart house, it survived only until 1900, when the Knickerbocker Trust resolved to demolish it despite its solidity, just 35 years after its construction. The architect for the new bank building that replaced it was primarily Stanford White of McKim, Mead & White. His wife was a niece of Mrs. Stewart, from whom White had expected a great legacy, but he was disappointed.

Astor Ambitions

The house across from Stewart's mansion, 355 Fifth Avenue at the northeast corner with 34th Street, was once a home to J. N. A. Griswold, one of the leading merchants of the port at its height in the mid-century and part of the same Griswold clan as the family who lived in The Row at Washington Square. His Fifth Avenue brownstone stood on property belonging to the Beekman family and would become a commercial property when the first part of the

Waldorf hotel was built at 33rd Street, extending north through the Astor's garden. The hotel traffic increased when the Astoria portion was soon built, making the new hotel a full block in the 1890s. By the 1890s Benjamin Altman was acquiring properties such as the Griswold house to make way for his future big store between 34th and 35th Streets on the east side of Fifth Avenue. The Griswold house was a hold-out. A lease held by the art dealers, Knoedlers, kept the Griswold house alive until 1912, when Altman demolished it and was finally able to finish that corner of his great store.[3]

Returning to Fifth Avenue, a fine house was between 35th and 36th Streets built for Charlotte Augusta Astor, the wife of the lawyer J. Coleman Drayton and daughter of W. B. and Caroline Schermerhorn Astor in 1882, a year after the Astor estate bought the block, by the young McKim, Mead & White firm. But the marriage fell apart in the 1890s to the horror of her mother, and Charlotte was disinherited by her father. The Astor real estate office had bought the frontage up through 35th Street, which was the old Thompson farm. In the 1880s the Astor Estate Office sold, then subsequently repurchased the block to 35th Street for the Astor children. The Fifth Avenue run of the Astor holdings had stopped at 34th Street until the new section was re-purchased and added in the 1880s and the Colman Drayton house was subsequently built on the new land. Several other houses would be built on the block, including a property for John Caswell that quite quickly became a club building.

Far left:
The J. N. A. Griswold House, forty years after it was built. It remained a hold-out, while Benjamin Altman built his department store on Fifth Avenue between 34th and 35th Streets, leaving the brownstone standing until the lease on Knoedler & Co. ran out. Altman then filled out the site with his beautiful store.

Altman store after the Griswold House had been removed. B. Altman and Co. store when completed.

The Croton Reservoir at the left supplied the growing city with clean water from 1842 until the last years of the century. The Easter Parade, Fifth Avenue looking north from 41st Street.

The Croton Reservoir

Above about 37th Street, Fifth Avenue was affected by the presence of the Croton Reservoir, built on Murray Hill between 1834 and 1842 as the termination of the famous Croton Aqueduct, constructed to bring safe, clean water to the houses of Manhattan, and at a time when it was well beyond the city's northernmost extent. The proximity of the tourists walking on the top of the reservoir and the Civil War riots kept speculators/builders wary of these blocks. Its site, between 40th and 42nd Streets, is now covered by the New York Public Library and Bryant Park. The hills here were steep and as we know required the cooperation of "hill horses" to pull carriages northward.

The observatory rose on the north side of 42nd Street. The first passenger safety elevator took people to the top, where this image was drawn. The Croton Reservoir and the New York Crystal Palace sit below. By 1853 little had been built above 42nd Street.

A Town and Davis house
for W. C. H. Waddell.
The Gothic residence
was unusual in New
York City. Manhattan
changed so quickly that
this country residence
was quickly superseded
by the block-by-block
uptown growth of the
city. William Coventry
Henry Waddell and
Family by Mary
Pillsbury Weston, 1852.
Fifth Avenue was the
location for many who
had free time to make an
afternoon promenade.
With a still walkable
city in the residential
quarters, young girls
walked to soda fountains
holding their skirts
just right for modesty
and to avoid the street
debris and dust. Ladies
displayed their fashion
on their walks, and men
met with each other.
The walk was a social
experience in Fifth
Avenue, and it was to
emerge as the Easter
Parade.[4]

Overleaf:
Fifth Avenue and 42nd
Street in 1845. This
view shows the newly
completed Croton
Reservoir. Chauncey M.
Depew was a Republican
politician and attorney
for Vanderbilt railroad
interests, who was eight
years old when running
water was introduced
to the city. He wrote
a memoir that gives a
startling idea of how
near we still are to a
primitive village. The
Public Library now
occupies this site.

Nevertheless, a few houses were soon built within sight of the reservoir. As early as 1845, New Yorkers who enjoyed a walk on its thick battered Egyptian-style granite walls would have been surprised to see a Gothic-style house covered in a yellow/gray stucco arise amid the sloping wheat fields of Murray Field, at the corner of the Avenue with what was to be 37th Street. It was designed by A. J. Davis for William Coventry Waddell, a former financial adviser to President Martin Van Buren and later marshal of New York. The picturesque house and grounds followed on from Waddell's second marriage to a widow, Charlotte Augusta Southwick, who established an early salon, enthusiastically visited by the English novelist W. M. Thackeray during his 1852 lecture tour of the United States. However, Waddell came a cropper in the financial panic of 1857, so that his house was sold and demolished barely a decade after its construction.

It was replaced by a Presbyterian church, designed by Griffith Thomas for an old New York congregation that had started out on Wall Street in 1767, but now almost all the "gentry" members of the church had moved uptown. Like the Wall Street original, the new building was known as the Brick Church, and in many respects followed the previous design, though in a more pretentious Italianate idiom, with an imposing tower and spire at the north end facing 37th Street. Although the congregation demanded the Brick Church be brick, the taste of the day tended to brownstone, so the church had a brownstone base, trim, and tower. It survived until 1930, at which

The Croton Reservoir became the first trustworthy water supply for the rapidly growing city. The high granite walls shaped in an Egyptoid manner became a major tourist location until a new water source opened in the Central Park. City visitors walked on the top of the wall to see the sites below. The New York Public Library would be built on the site. Looking Southwest from Fifth Avenue and 42nd Street across from the Croton Reservoir, possibly during the 1889 Centennial Parade.

point the neighborhood had changed. In combination with another parish, the Brick Church was rebuilt again, this time in bright red brick, at 91st Street and Park Avenue, where it remains to this day.

A. J. Davis was involved in another early venture in this then-uptown locality. That was at 487–491 Fifth Avenue, immediately opposite the Croton Reservoir at 41st and 42nd Streets, where in 1856 he designed a row of early houses for a speculator, George Higgins. They were pretentiously known as the House of Mansions. Their Gothic style was rare for domestic architecture in the United States, perhaps because it was too "church-like" for Americans, and Gothic was seldom popular in New York. The houses did not appeal and after a fierce sales attempt, they switched purpose to become, in 1860, the home to New Jersey's Rutgers Female Institute, later Douglass College, which stayed on here until 1882.

Across the street from the Brick Church, at the north corner with 37th Street, Edwin D. Morgan built a house, later known as 411 Fifth Avenue, around the time that he was appointed New York State Governor in 1858. Externally, this would become a large but orthodox and discreet brick house, with a smaller house for his son next door along the side street, and a substantial flower garden along the Avenue to its north. Morgan continued to be politically influential after his Civil War governorship ended and he and his wife Eliza mostly entertained politicians, including a reception for President Rutherford Hayes in 1877. He died in 1883, but the house survived until 1914.

Block of dwelling houses on Fifth Avenue, including the A. J. Davis house, opposite the Croton Reservoir.

FOR SALE ON MODERATE TERMS:

THE

Block of Dwelling Houses upon Murray Hi

FIFTH AVENUE, OPPOSITE THE CROTON RESERVOIR.

Croton Reservoir, Fifth Avenue in 1879, looking south.

JOHN D. WENDEL
HOME, 442–444 FIFTH
AVENUE

We see the Wendel
House surrounded by a
back garden and planted
property to its north.

The Austere Wendels

The E. D. Morgan house was not especially pretentious, but a block further north a more imposing mansion in the same Italianate style was built in 1856 at the corner of 39th Street. 442 Fifth Avenue, a corner house faced in brick over a brownstone base, was owned by the Wendel family for 80 years. The Wendel House was well-proportioned, and the detail distinguishes the residence from the usual speculative row houses. There is even a terrace on the south beyond the house wall. It was built for John D. Wendel, the only child of Johann Gottlieb Wendel, early partner of the original John Jacob Astor, and husband of Elizabeth Astor, his half-sister. The Wendels took no interest in display or society, living quietly with their seven children, not one of whom married. After John D. Wendel died in 1876, the family tradition of austerity and frugality continued, and this persisted even after his widow died and their only son, the second Johann Gottlieb Wendel, took over. Each of his five surviving sisters lived in the room of her childhood and the family steadfastly refused electricity, the telephone, and new clothing. Nevertheless, they were very rich and had a fine summer estate up the Hudson. By the time of Johann Gottlieb Jr.'s death in 1912, commercial buildings were transforming the neighborhood. When the business workers left, Ella Wendel, the last of the family, would walk her poodle, Tobey, in the ample garden behind the house. When she died in 1931, the life of the Wendel house came to an end.

Vanderbilt Vanguard

After the Civil War the select band of houses on the Avenue between 34th and 42nd Streets grew in number. On the corner of 38th Street, for instance, the brothers David and John Jardine, recently arrived from Scotland, built what were to be among the earliest of their many row houses in the city. Further north at the southeast corner of 40th Street there arrived 459 Fifth Avenue (1864), the first house of William Henry Vanderbilt, son of the great railroad magnate Cornelius ("Commodore") Vanderbilt. It replaced Croton Cottage, one of the small wooden bars popular with those riding to the north, which had also provided refreshment for those walking atop the thick battered walls of the reservoir. After a difficult early relationship with his demanding father, William Henry had extracted himself from the family farm on Staten Island at the end of the war and joined the railroad business, and his father bought him the Croton Cottage site for $80,000. The family architect, J. B. Snook, built the house, a solid and large, but not especially distinguished, brownstone firmly in the Italianate mode, three main stories high, with three windows wide facing both street fronts. It had a central entrance at the top of a high

WILLIAM H.
VANDERBILT HOUSE,
EAST SIDE OF FIFTH
AVENUE AND 40TH
STREET

*The Vanderbilt family
architect, J. B. Snook,
attempted an upgraded,
large brownstone. Snook
was a master of the soft
sandstone. The house
has a central entry and
a very low stoop. Snook
detailed the window
lintels differently on all
three principal floors and
made the house large
and comfortable inside
the walls.*

stoop, leading to a staircase in the center. After the Commodore's death in 1877, the now immensely wealthy William Henry Vanderbilt would go on to build a great new palazzo at 51st Street and left 459 Fifth Avenue to his son Frederick. We will see the grand Vanderbilt houses, built when William Henry Vanderbilt moved his family north, in the following chapter. The last Vanderbilts moved out of J.B. Snook house around the turn of the century, and the house was finally demolished around 1915 in favor of the Arnold Constable department store, previously at 109–111 Fifth Avenue.

Once beyond the great hill that had shielded Thomas Mook's cattle yards a vestige of times past survived. Ye Old Willow Tavern, sited near an old tree at 44th Street and Fifth Avenue at the southeast corner, provided refreshments for loiterers and passers-by. This last remnant of the 1840s survived until bought out for an office building at the beginning of the 20th century. The draft riots of 1863 had raged through this part of town, burning down the Colored Orphans Asylum that sat between 44th and 45th Streets, though fortunately the children had been evacuated before the fire. With the cattle yards now moved west and the war over, the development community returned to Fifth Avenue.

Jumping three blocks further north, the notorious William M. "Boss" Tweed, riding high in the late 1860s, bought 511 Fifth Avenue, a small brownstone at the southeast corner of 43rd Street, opposite the reservoir. Not many years later he was indicted for corruption, eventually dying in the Ludlow Street Jail. In 1882 Richard T. Wilson, who had been commissary general for the Confederate Army and sold cotton blankets as wool during the Civil War, took on the house and redecorated the interiors. The Wilsons had social pretensions and managed to marry their children off well enough for people to ignore his business record.

Towards a Commercial Future

Finally in this chapter, mention may be made of two later buildings of interest that marked the start of the period when this part of the Avenue, following the pattern of districts further south, ceased to be purely residential and started to go up in scale. Across the street from the Wendel house at 39th Street, the younger members of the family must have been unhappy to see the overweening building of the Union League Club go up in 1881. This was the club's third premises. It had begun as a Civil War breakaway from the venerable Union Club further south on the Avenue by members including Frederick Law Olmsted and George Templeton Strong, who felt that the attitude of the old club was too lukewarm and compromising towards the war aims of the North. It started out in the Union Square district, then moved to the former Jerome mansion on Madison Avenue in 1868. But the members wanted a purpose-built home and held an architectural competition in 1878. The winners were Peabody and Stearns of Boston, whose beefy building with prominent swept gable and tall roof front announced that this part of the Avenue was to become clubland for the foreseeable future.

Further north, at the southeast corner of 42nd Street, on a plot with only a 23-foot frontage to the Avenue, arose in 1882–84 the seven-story American Safe Deposit Company and Columbia Bank Building, a fledgling work in Renaissance taste by the young Charles Follen McKim of McKim, Mead & White. The clients were Ashbel Barney, an entrepreneur with a wide range of business interests, and his son C. T. Barney, a great friend of McKim's. The bank and the safe deposit company occupied different levels in the sandstone base, while the upper parts consisted of high-ceilinged bachelor flats expressed externally by brickwork and terracotta spandrel panels. The commercial building with apartments for single men above did not present a path for Fifth Avenue. Commerce would wait another generation to crawl into the Avenue in the form of an office building—rather sadly for McKim, who would work with Barney on residential properties. McKim would see his early attempt to build a commercial bank demolished in his own lifetime, to be replaced by a house as the great residential parade surged northwards…

The country houses and the City Resevoir far above town, were soon to melt away, the steep hill was leveled and the cattle went west, as this now sanctified Avenue of fashion relentlessly marched north. The Union League subsumed a number of houses into clubs and then created purpose-built clubs in the streets of the 40s, while the Columbia Trust on 42nd Street was built with no idea it would soon be replaced by a brownstone. In the following generation, commercial buildings would replace the residential buildings, completely changing the nature of Fifth Avenue.

CHAPTER 10
MID CENTURY BOOM

"The houses on the 'much vaunted' Fifth Avenue were disappointingly homogenous."

John W. Kennion

THE VALUE OF NEW YORK CITY REAL ESTATE went through an astonishing transformation in the middle of the 19th century and real estate was a miraculous vehicle to make money. Plots of prime land moved from modest sums in 1845 to remarkable amounts in twenty years. A lot on 19th Street between Fifth and Sixth Avenue increased from $1,650 to $18,000 within a single generation, while the plots between 56th and 57th Streets on Fifth Avenue rose from $575 to $30,000 in the same time period. Clearly, the memory of these vast increases remained in the minds of real estate investors for the rest of the century but although there would be some booms again, they were never as immense as in the mid-century. The role of speculative house builders would diminish in the Fifth Avenue area as, gradually, more private commissions would appear. Speculators moved to other parts of the city when large farms were broken up and auctioned off as individual lots or parcels of lots. The hope, always, was that a boom similar to that on Fifth Avenue would make all developers very rich, but the explosion of prices on Fifth Avenue would not be repeated so spectacularly across the rest of Manhattan, which instead followed a steady, positive growth pattern.

The building boom was effected with ease as immigration rose dramatically, ensuring there would always be a large pool of laborers. But in the 1860s John W. Kennion wrote in *The Architects' and Builders' Guide* that the houses on the "much vaunted" Fifth Avenue were disappointingly homogenous:

When he [the spectator] has seen one house he has seen them all. The same everlasting high stoops and gloomy brownstone fronts; the same number of holes punched in precisely the same places and only ringing the changes upon square, circular or segmental heads; the same huge cornices bursting with overpowering consoles and projections, and often looking like whole regiments of petrified buffaloes leaping headlong from the roof. To be sure, what we lack in invention we can cover over by 'ornamentation' and hence we have miles of reiterated and unmeaning rope moldings, filigreed jams, and window heads twisted in all sorts of conceivable contortions; if only, the largest merit being, apparently, which is overlaid with rivalry in amount of so-called ornamentation—in short which costs the most.[1]

From Meat to Real Estate

Safely nestled in the downward side of the 42nd Street hill had been the city's meat slaughtering district. As in all urban areas through history, animals were marched down paths to areas of the city where butchers could render the animals into meat. By the second quarter of the 19th century, the market, particularly for beef, was between 44th and 46th Streets. The proprietor of the slaughterhouse, Thomas Mook, ran the operation until the early 1850s, when he decamped for the fields near the Hudson River. As we know, the Bull's Head Tavern, the center of the operation, would linger there until the 20th century—a rare survivor of the early 19th-century city.[2]

Were the high hills and booming abattoir district of Fifth a strong enough impediment to distract development from the northward march? And was any consideration given to trying Second Avenue again? There were still old families located on that Avenue, and Stuyvesant flats developed both on Stuyvesant land and by the Stuyvesant estate would appear at the end of the Civil War. Perhaps Union Square might create a fashionable enclave? It did not happen. Fifth Avenue had become the accepted mover for the northward trek and development pushed relentlessly on. Indeed, as the developers moved northward, the block above the current work site was almost always used as a storehouse of construction debris. Those living in the most recently constructed block heard explosions as the rock was blasted and witnessed all the chaos of the new block being built.[3]

John H. Sherwood, a developer, bought the former cattle yard property from 44th to 46th Streets on the east side of Fifth Avenue for his own house as well as to build units for others. His own brownstone would later (1875 onward) become the Fifth Avenue Bank and itself

Delmonico's
Restaurant, Fifth
Avenue and 44th
Street

would grow and take over the houses next door. The bank catered to the existing and growing numbers of residents of Fifth Avenue, wealthy men and women from the neighborhood, and was replete with a "Ladies' Window" and home-like fittings for the ladies. There were two high-stooped brownstones on that stretch built in 1866 by John Cornell of the iron business and Manton Marble, a social figure of the day.

The long-standing association with the yards would reverberate in 1890 when Sherwood sold part of his holdings to Delmonico's restaurant (1897) for its large new event space and restaurant designed by the well-born architect, James Brown Lord. Then, a year later, Louis Sherry, a caterer with ambition, opened another large venue for big parties across the street. (1898). The sizable Delmonico's and Sherry's would rival other prominent venues even as hotels vied for big social occasions but ultimately, prohibition would shut the doors of the two event spaces.[4]

HOTEL DELMONICO,
FIFTH AVENUE AND
44TH STREET

Delmonico's menu, 1917.

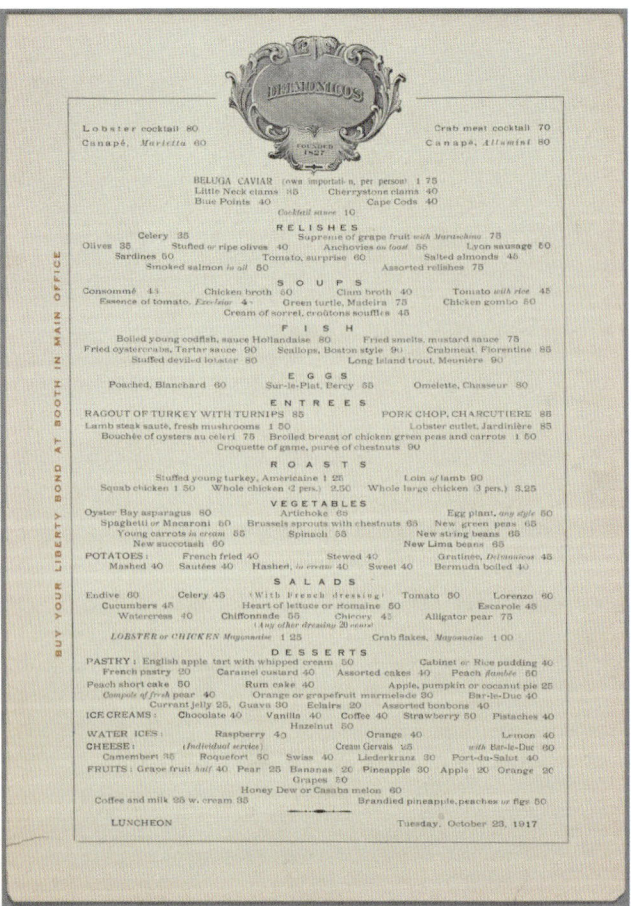

Expelling the Shacks and Goats

John Mason (1773–1839) was a very successful merchant of the port in early 19th-century New York, who formed the Chemical Bank to fund purchases of real estate. Mason bought a large farm in 1825, which meandered over what would become midtown (53rd Street to 64th Streets, Fourth Avenue to Fifth Avenue). The property passed, as we have already discussed, to his three daughters and their heirs. Mary and Rebecca Mason Jones had married Jones men, which explains a connection to Edith Jones (Wharton) while, Sarah (Serena), married a Hamersley. Within two generations, the grandchildren would be immensely rich. The Jones family was connected to the Masons by marriage, so the heirs to the properties included Jones, Hamersleys, Warrens, Goelets, and Gerrys.

Mary Mason Jones was the doyenne of Knickerbocker/Yankee New York. She had moved to a set of three houses on Broadway at Waverley Place, 732–736 Broadway, with her two sisters, from their old houses at 120 Chambers Street (rumor was they had the first indoor bathtub in New York on Chambers Street). Mary, Serena, and Rebecca Mason lived closely to each other, and it was said that they had the three Broadway houses internally linked so that they could host a large party. Both widowed, Mary and Rebecca Jones—along with Caroline Schermerhorn Astor and many others—established themselves in Paris each spring. The glamor of the French Court and stunning work at the Louvre must have been imprinted in the minds of these women. America, and even parts of Westminster in London, favored Parisian-appearing buildings and when they came to build their new homes on Fifth Avenue it was to Paris that they looked for inspiration.

Serena died before the sisters started building, so Mary and Rebecca were left as the heirs to develop this portion of their father's estate. As we know, he had bought land from 54th to 56th Streets, and from 57th to 63rd Streets, from Fifth to Park Avenue (then 4th Avenue). Mary and Rebecca's successive homes reflected the growth of New York City in the mid-century, moving from the old section near the Battery in lower Manhattan, to the Bond Street neighborhood before daringly leaping to the north.

The Jones sisters had once thought that they would stay in Broadway for the rest of their lives. But after returning to New York from Paris in 1868, Mary Mason Jones decided to move away from Broadway as the once fashionable neighborhood was now being penetrated by printing establishments and textile companies. A decision must

*The paving of the
avenues and streets
reached the Mason
property after the
Civil War. The shacks
and small farms
were commonplace
throughout the 19th
century.*

have been made that, if they had to leave their home, they would leap far above the 40s on the Avenue, where their peers were going. By developing the Mason properties in the upper 50s on Fifth Avenue they hoped to avoid confronting commerce again.

The explosion of Fifth Avenue as the vehicle for the northward movement of the city came when Mary Mason Jones built her anchor row between 56th and 57th Streets a generation ahead of block-by-block progress, then occurring in the 40s—the development seemed to move northward a block a year. Surely, this remarkable woman, a part of the leadership of New York's social life, would expect grand surroundings? But Mary Mason Jones built in the howling wilderness surrounded by illegal shacks and wooden bars, goats, and many stray animals.

Just as the Astor homes on 33rd and 34th Streets were anchor buildings for their family estate, the Jones sisters decided to follow suit and build glamorous houses with rental properties. With Paris reverberating in their minds, the Jones sisters went fully French. Mary Mason Jones employed Robert Mook to build her white marble

MARY MASON JONES
HOUSE (LATER THE
RESIDENCE OF MRS.
PARAN STEVENS), FIFTH
AVENUE AND 57TH
STREET, NORTHEAST
CORNER LOOKING
NORTH

*The Buchanan/Mason
farm was ripe for
development after the
streets were laid out.
Mary Mason Jones
and her sister laid out
"anchor" properties to
hasten developments
to their empty land.
Paris was admired by
the social queens of
New York, who spent
the spring in the city.
The white stone corner
house and its auxiliary
individual houses
masked the top of Fifth
Avenue. The elaborate
French design must have
been considered a selling
point to attract the well-
off to the houses.*

MARY MASON JONES
HOUSE, FIFTH AVENUE
AND 57TH STREET,
NORTHEAST CORNER

*Mary Mason Jones
herself lived in the large
corner house. Corpulent,
she sat at her south-
facing windows awaiting
the city to arrive. It
would do so in her
lifetime.*

VIEW ON THE NORTHEAST CORNER OF 5th AV. & 57th ST.

COLFORD JONES BLOCK,
FIFTH AVENUE BETWEEN
55TH AND 56TH STREETS

*Rebecca Mason Jones
built her row to the
south of that for her
sister, using the same
idea to have grand
anchor properties as the
northern edge of the city.
This set of houses is less
spectacular but uses a
Second Empire roof as
Mary Mason Jones did—
just less pronounced.
Mary Mason Jones's
house was a trumpet,
and her sister's, a flute.*

row on Fifth Avenue with a particularly grand, ornate house looking to the south on the corner. She would live in this house for the rest of her life, watching the city crawl towards her. Her house and the row, built in two stages, were the third white stone houses in the city, following the John Taylor Johnson and A. T. Stewart houses. The other houses on the terrace were rented out and although the rentals did not lure the peers of the Jones sisters, Mary was certain of her decision. In the next few years, she would have Robert Mook build houses on much of the Mason property, including on the side streets, in groups of eight and ten houses.

How did Mary Mason Jones's row do? It appears she rented, then sold, the other houses to their speculative builders, and the properties did not fare well. The industrialist and sugar-refiner H. O. Havemeyer would live in no. 743 in 1877 as would, later, Mrs. Adrian Iselin, the wife of an affluent banker and dry goods merchant. But these illustrious residents did not last and it then became a boarding house. The house at 741, next to Mrs. Jones, was occupied by the silk merchant, Cyrus Clark, before he ventured to the West 70s to develop property on Riverside Drive (where he would build a large house for himself) and West End Avenues. Clark shared the surname but no familial relationship with the Clark family developing the area around their big apartment building, The Dakota.

Rebecca Jones selected a more socially prominent architect, Detlef Lienau, to build her row, which is curious, as the sisters had previously done everything together. She took the corner house on Fifth Avenue at 56th Street a block away from her sister. Her houses were brick and stone, and the "Frenchness" resembled the J. J. Astor house on 33rd Street more than Mary Mason Jones's row (one wonders if Lienau built the Astor house). Rebecca's house, 705 Fifth Avenue, hosted the well-known "Rosebud" dinners for young debutantes in 1873. She died in 1878, leaving her fortune to her nephew, Woodbury G. Langdon, who would become a substantial developer in the region.

Edith Wharton would describe her aunt Mary as a corpulent arbiter of New York's social world, even if she chose to not leave her parlor. Society came to her, confronting the rocks, wildlife, shacks, and wooden saloons.[5] Well before Griffith Thomas started to build at 500 Fifth Avenue at 42nd Street, the Jones sisters and a house on 54th Street assured the progress of Fifth Avenue north. When Mary Mason Jones died in her house in 1891 her vision had indeed prevailed, and her pioneering house stood in the midst of a fashionable district.

The Middle of Nowhere

The other large residence in the streets of the 50s was the house built around 1865 for a merchant, William P. Williams, just west of Fifth Avenue. Williams built a large brownstone with windows on all four sides as it was in the "wilderness" and had unobstructed views. A stable block paralleled Fifth Avenue, and a large, planted garden surrounded the house, replete with a small gazebo. Why did Williams build literally in the middle of nowhere? The only neighbors were the Roman Catholic Orphan Asylum and the first Episcopalian Saint Luke's Hospital across the street.

Some twelve years later, a woman who called herself Arabella Worsham bought the house for herself and her seven-year-old son. Arabella ranks with Marietta Stevens and Alva Vanderbilt as the most strong-willed and self-made of ladies—she was a stunning young woman when Collis P. Huntington, of railway fame, spotted her in Richmond, Virginia.

Overleaf:
These properties were still far above the city in the mid-1860s. Looking west from St. Luke's Hospital (right) and the Worsham House (left) with the long blank wall parallel to the Avenue, the Worsham stable on Fifth Avenue and 54th Street, with a view of the Arabella Worsham/ Rockefeller house.

ST. LUKE'S HOSPITAL,
FIFTH AVENUE AND
54TH STREET

*It is encouraging to
see green spaces when
the Episcopal diocese
built their St. Luke's
Hospital, well above
the existing city, c. 1854.
In this period, religious
institutions built their
own hospital facilities.*

*It would move at the
end of the 19th century
again to the north and
empty territory.*

ST. LUKE'S HOSPITAL,
FIFTH AVENUE AND
54TH STREET

WILLIAMS, WORSHAM,
AND JOHN D.
ROCKEFELLER HOUSE,
4 WEST 54TH STREET

*A decade after St. Luke's
Hospital was built, a
single house became its
neighbor across 54th
Street. The unusual
brownstone with a
garden and stable was
fully freestanding.*

Arabella and the married Huntington had an affair, likely resulting in a son, Archer Worsham. Huntington brought Arabella, her widowed mother, and young Archer to New York City, then his home, using the identity of a card dealer, John Worsham, as a cover for Arabella and Archer. Worsham, a married man from Richmond, had conveniently died, so Arabella could now present herself as a respectable widow—and the love of Huntington's life. The remote location of the house was perfect for Collis, as no one was looking out for him in this empty section of the city. Exactly how Arabella managed the funds she had from Huntington is unclear, but he gave her the sum needed to buy and trade properties, including the Williams's house, now 4 West 54th Street. Funds were also provided to decorate the house in what would be perhaps the most complete and stellar example of an Anglo-American, short lived interior mania, the Aesthetic Movement.

WILLIAMS, WORSHAM, AND JOHN D. ROCKEFELLER HOUSE, 4 WEST 54TH STREET

At the death of John D. Rockefeller, this house was pulled down. The photo here must have been taken just before the house was razed for what would become the garden of the Museum of Modern Art.

Arabella lifted the dour interiors of the brownstone to a remarkable height, probably using two firms of the day, George A. Schastey and Pottier & Stymus. They created a festival of exotic rooms: a Moorish Smoking room, Turkish Bath, Japanese bedroom dressing room, and more, all to the height of fashion in 1881. The house predates records but may well have been the design of G. E. Harney.[6]

WORSHAM AND JOHN D. ROCKEFELLER HOUSE, 4 WEST 54TH STREET

Rockefeller added to the house in the half century of residence.

Happily for the family, Mrs. Huntington died, allowing the couple to marry, adopt Archer, now officially Huntington, and move to Collis Huntington's New York house at 38th Street and Park Avenue. The wedding was performed by Henry Ward Beecher in the 54th Street house, which Arabella promptly put on the market; she then began shopping for properties. Arabella began exploring local sites, as did John D. Rockefeller, and somehow, with the assistance of a realtor of the day named George McCready, a complex trade was made, and Rockefeller took on 4 West 54th Street. Rockefeller, a deeply committed Baptist, moved his family into the decorated fantasy of a kept woman with an illegitimate son. 4 West 54th Street would be the family home until the death of Mrs. Rockefeller, when the house closed, never to reopen. The house was demolished in 1938 to become the garden of the Museum of Modern Art.

Row House Building Boom

As we know, the sons of a Scottish architect/builder, David and John Jardine, arrived in New York as the Civil War ended. By 1870, the Jardines were launched into a career as perhaps the most prolific architects in the row house world. Working for developers, the Jardines eventually received commissions from private clients and department store builders in the Ladies' Mile shopping district, including Benjamin Altman who opened his first store on Sixth Avenue. The years before and after the 1873 depression were dominated by Jardine-built houses to the point where they were effectively taking over the practice of Griffith Thomas. By 1871, the Jardines had begun to self-finance some of their rows. Jardine-built brownstones are distinctive and are recognizable by their exceptionally large and framed windows, with window surrounds that are bordered with detail rather like a picture frame.

As always, prominent clergy followed their congregation to new parts of the city. Brick Presbyterian settled uptown on 37th Street, and the residents of the next blocks to be built would soon find themselves represented by the fashionable ecclesiastical institutions of the day. On what had been the Buchanan farm, now Goelet family land, rose that narrow bijou of the Episcopalian faith, The Church of the Heavenly Rest. The Dutch Collegiate Church established a corner on 48th Street, and the German Jewish families created a big and impressive synagogue on 43rd Street, Temple Emanu-El, in the High Victorian style, using a mixture of brownstone, brick and

Left:
MOORISH SMOKING ROOM, WORSHAM AND JOHN D. ROCKEFELLER HOUSE, 4 WEST 54TH STREET

The interiors were commissioned by Arabella Worsham in the Aesthetic taste. Magnificent designs were executed. The Rockefellers retained Arabella's styling.

JABEZ ABEL BOSTWICK HOUSE, 800 FIFTH AVENUE

A set of brothers from Scotland arrived in New York perfectly on time for a massive building boom in the second half of the 19th century. The Jardines would design and execute commercial buildings and department stores, but the high-end brownstone house was their most significant endeavor.

*How quickly Fifth
Avenue blocks changed.
This block was originally
a John B. Snook-
designed brownstone of
1896, rebuilt for a new
owner, John I. Kane, in
the early 20th century.
The rest of the block on
both sides of the Avenue
were early houses by
Charles Duggin, soon
joined by his partner,
James Crossman. The
Duggin & Crossman
House, just to the
north of what is now
the John Innes Kane
House, has an addition
at the roof, but is still
the same house. The
houses to the north have
already been turned into
commercial businesses.
The new Kane house
by McKim, Mead &
White of 1908 seems an
odd return on this block
when, clearly, several
houses were already
converted to commercial
establishments.*

colored stone. The Catholic Diocese was building a new St. Patrick's
Cathedral on land well above the then-city.

Despite these notable ecclesiastical buildings, Fifth Avenue was really
about residences and constant change, with residents moving houses
frequently—people hopped houses at least every twenty years. Other
than those on the Lower Avenue who did remain in their early
Manhattan enclave, moving was continuous and frequent and in every
generation, those who could afford to do so leapt to the new edges of
the city. Those who did not have the capital retreated to boarding in
houses in fashionable areas or moved to a "family style" flat or hotel
(there will be a full discussion of this issue later in the volume).

Staying Put

However, the notorious railroad magnate and financial speculator
Jay Gould, often referred to as the "Scourge of Wall Street," moved
only across the street and then stayed on into the 20th century. Gould
resided at 578 Fifth Avenue on the northwest corner of 47th Street
and had lived there from his famous days of stock manipulation with
the Erie Railroad in 1869. He owned a Frederick Diaper-designed
house, which was very well-built, but elected to go across the Avenue
in 1882 to the northeast corner, where he moved into a Stephen D.
Hatch-designed brownstone, which he bought from former New
York City Mayor George Opdyke. Gould kept the gas lamps on
either side of the stoop, a mayoral honor he did not deserve, after he
purchased the house. Gould hired the highest end interior designers
to decorate the house, calling in the supreme interior design firm
of the day, the Herter Brothers, who were lavishing their skills on
the second William Henry Vanderbilt house, as we shall soon see.
Gould's daughter would remain in the house, making Helen Gould,
Ms. Wendel, Mrs. Louis Hoyt, and two men the only remaining
householders who resisted the siren call to the northern, more palatial

*Jay Gould built a house
then bought the former
mayor's house across the
street. Gould's daughter
lived on in this house,
which is draped in
mourning cloth for the
death and funeral of
President McKinley, shot
at the Buffalo World's
Fair in September of
1901. To the right in
the image is part of the
Windsor Arcade.*

*The unusual brownstone
sat among typical
brownstone rows. The
wide stoop and front
entry are one internal
room south of the party
wall. The mansard roof
was still popular when
the house was built.*

dwelling. The blocks had become so commercial, only these old timers remained in their family houses.

The Fifth Avenue Polka

The ancestors of the Goelet brothers bought land that would become Manhattan's Midtown as the city grew at dizzying speed. The brothers Goelet, with their continuous tradition of naming the boys Robert and Ogden, made a splash in New York and Newport society in the later 1870s. The rise of the brothers was rapid, fueled by the income from many properties. The large rustic property belonging to their eccentric uncle Peter Goelet at 19th Street and Broadway, could be cashed in at his death and developed, as the area now being advanced by large stores. The Goelet brothers also had wives with an inheritance from the Buchanan property on Fifth Avenue and its vicinity in the 40s. Robert and Ogden joined the Fifth Avenue polka at 47th Street across the Avenue from each other with large houses both wider and deeper than most others. Ogden Goelet built a house for his family on the west side of Fifth Avenue. The large residence for the newly wealthy Goelets was substantial and solid. It was not pretty—the commercial architect imposed a mansard roof after the French attic had gone out of fashion. Built by a commercial architect, E. H. Kendall, in 1880, each cost a goodly sum of around $200,000, but the houses were not lovely to behold. [7]

As they moved to the new residences, the Goelets acquired new architects. Robert Goelet became a fast friend of Charles Follen McKim and, soon after, Stanford White, and used them to build the great Southside/Ochre Point, a mansion at the beginning of Cliff Walk in Newport. Robert Goelet's splendid Newport house, appropriate to its era, came in at close to $400,000 still stands today and is held by the family. He would continue with McKim, Mead & White in New York for commercial buildings for the rest of his life, remaining a close friend of Stanford White, and even buying White a membership in the

608 FIFTH AVENUE,
GOELET HOUSE

very snobby, brand new Ristigouche Salmon Fishing Club in Canada. The unspectacular Goelet New York houses, constructed of Philadelphia pressed brick and Belleville, New Jersey brownstone, were said to contain 50 rooms, an indication of their increasing sense of grandeur and rising fortunes. The cabinetry was said to be fine with portions done by Leon Marcotte, the Herter firm (still the original brothers then) and new work by the young Tiffany. The Ogden Goelet house was one of the longest to remain standing, torn down only in 1942, a year before the destruction of the close-by home of Jay Gould.

In Newport, Ogden Goelet selected the then-grander and more socially connected Richard Morris Hunt to design his château, Ochre Court which, though undoubtedly imposing and formal, was a little less well-suited to the summer life of Newport than his brother's Southside mansion. The palace in Newport would become important in the next decade when the desire to marry children to aristocratic families was in full swing. The daughter of Ogden Goelet indeed did wed the Duke of Roxburgh and have, it was said, the only successful of the "Dollar Princess" marriages.

Some of the Goelet land in Manhattan would be turned commercial shortly, as happened when Delmonico's (James Brown Lord, architect) and Sherry's (McKim, Mead & White) opened restaurants and party palaces close by and across the street from each other. Louis Sherry, building on Beekman family land, moved in on the Delmonico patrons with his finely detailed food services. (The legendary horseback dinner hosted by C. K. G. Billings on March 28, 1903 was held in Sherry's. There were 32 horses in a "woodland" setting, and they served a full dinner atop the steeds. The event was one of the nails in the coffin of the Gilded Age). However, the two restaurant and entertainment palaces would thrive until prohibition, which took down both businesses and their buildings.

Robert Goelet, clearly the real estate leader of the brothers, also developed properties in the area around Brick Church. The Goelets had McKim, Mead & White build 404 Fifth Avenue on a row house plot as a second-class commercial building, and around the corner at 3 West 37th Street, a wide brick extension of 404 Fifth Avenue. Although now society men, the Goelets were more than willing to develop commercial properties on Fifth Avenue, where they kept their city homes Undoubtedly, they saw the inevitable rise of commerce on Fifth Avenue, the once-sacred street of houses.[8]

The house on Fifth Avenue still established the position and ambition of its owner. As the street advanced towards the upper 40s and 50s, we see the focus on the house changing from "fitting in" to being distinct. The old days of Knickerbocker norms were being overturned by new additions to New York society. As we saw with Ward McAllister's Patriarch Balls, an opening had been made for some of the new money makers and a grander house would inevitably bring attention to the family of its builder. Increasingly individuality would make the applicant to society noticed. Elizabeth Drexel Lehr, a society figure in the day, wrote an eye-witness account of the Gilded Era in her later years. As she recalled, "When I grew up I watched it [NYC] pass from the era of modest, discreet-looking brick and brownstone houses, each with its high stoop striving to look as much like its neighbor as possible, to the splendors of the great, gaudy palaces which proudly reared their Italian, Gothic, or Oriental structures to house the new millionaires."[9]

CHAPTER 11
VANDERBILT ALLEY

"I have been insane on the subject of money-making all my life."

Cornelius Vanderbilt

THE FORTUNE ASSOCIATED WITH the excessive flowering of Fifth Avenue belonged to the Vanderbilt family. The father Cornelius Vanderbilt and son, William Henry, would create a great family business and corporatize it within two lifetimes. A new generation of Vanderbilts would learn that by spending huge sums of money and pushing hard, they could mow down the world of Mrs. Astor, and the old Knickerbocker/Yankee order. The Vanderbilts went on to shape the "Gilded Age," that thick coating of gold leaf over a stew of many ingredients. Lavish spending replaced the rule-bound world of old New York society and the family-dominated world of their grandmothers' generation. Ward McAllister and Marietta Stevens had established a break with the old order as the beginning of the Gilded Age; now Phase two of New York's Gilded Age evolution had begun.[1]

At the end of the 18th century on the farmland across the harbor from Manhattan on Staten Island, "Commodore" Cornelius Vanderbilt would rise to become a symbolic figure for the mid-19th century in America. Tall, striking in appearance and ruthless in his pursuit of his goals, Vanderbilt would be, at his death, the richest man in the nation. He started out running his own ferry service in New York harbor, expanded into steamboat passenger services, and, from the 1850s onwards, became increasingly invested in America's growing railroad network. His New York Central and Hudson River Railroad was one of the first giant corporations in the history of the United States. The Commodore, ruthless, aggressive, and greedy, had no interest in the fancy world of his social Knickerbocker superiors. He lived in a red brick row house parallel to Washington Square, having moved from Staten Island in 1847, had little interest in a fashionable life beyond his love for fine horses which he shared with Leonard Jerome, William Travers, and August Belmont, fellow aggressive market investors.[2]

Like many businessmen, Commodore Vanderbilt depended upon family as trusted business partners, but he had nine daughters, and three sons, one of whom was stricken by epilepsy. The family had lost the most promising son as a young cadet at West Point. He initially had little respect for his rather bumbling younger son, William Henry, the "dunderheaded" son of a strong and disliked man, described by his father as a "blatherskite," a foolish person who talks too much. When W. H. cheated Cornelius in a deal, he began to look more promising. Needing assistance with his business affairs, the Commodore allowed William Henry to escape from his purgatorial fate, farming on Staten Island, and join his father in Manhattan. William Henry was more interested in what money could buy than was his father, while not eager to be accepted by the merchants of the port, William Henry did not want to be ignored by that group either and was quick to exploit his new Manhattan-based status.[3]

A Vanderbilt on Fifth Avenue

In July of 1863, following the Emancipation Act earlier in the year, serious draft riots had occurred. The violence had a racial and recent immigrant tone. The lower 40s sustained the burning of the Bull's Head Tavern on 44th Street, and looting and burning of the Colored Orphans Asylum, leaving a melancholy and perhaps fearful aura around the site. Despite this recent history, the price tag for the plot across from the Croton Reservoir was remarkably high, $80,000, which put off the speculators. The Commodore, who was now even willing to spring for a home for William Henry, bought the property and William Henry built a large residence clad in a light brownstone, utilizing the skills of the family architect, J. M. Snook (Snook would build the Grand Central Depot shortly thereafter for Commodore Vanderbilt.) The recent horror at the site seemed never reflected upon by the Vanderbilts.

A Vanderbilt had landed on Fifth Avenue. William Henry and his family were very happy in the 40th Street house and even had a family portrait painted showing the next generation, ready to enter the grand world of New York society. The Vanderbilts were the only builders of a mansion on Fifth Avenue at this time who were from New York City; all the excessive-sized houses built in the mid-century were for

The interior of the Vanderbilt residence, with the family getting ready to go out to a major event of the era—the opera in the old Academy of Music. The younger Vanderbilts were starting to move into New York's social scene.

those not hailing from the region. William Henry Vanderbilt, more culturally aware than his father, built the house to show off himself and his family as solid citizens, and attempted to fit himself into the emerging values of the day, perhaps to assure Wall Street that he really was able to handle the railroads after years of his father's dismissive pronouncements.

In 1877, the seemingly immortal Commodore expired. The newspapers had a field day—the revelations about the astounding sum of his net worth was followed by a trial over the will. William Henry had influenced his father to leave the bulk of the estate to him rather than breaking it up and sharing the inheritance equally with his siblings as the Commodore had originally promised to do. The Commodore was a colorful character, and the trial was a festival of amusement to the press and public. As the dirty laundry accusations in the trial became ever more lurid, William Henry decided to halt the proceedings and share more of the estate with his siblings.

Following the settlement, William Henry and his two sons William Kissam and Cornelius Jr., principal beneficiaries of the will, filed building permits for three new houses on the western side of Fifth Avenue, leading to the description of the street as "Vanderbilt Alley." Two daughters of William Henry would soon build in the "Alley," bringing together all the families a short walk apart on the western side of the Avenue.

St. Luke's Hospital, Fifth Avenue and 54th Street.

Fifth Avenue looking north. "Vanderbilt Alley" on the west side of the Avenue.

Marie Louise Kissam Vanderbilt, wife of William Henry, was not eager to leave their 40th Street house. A modest woman, she was distantly related to Peter Kissam, the builder of many Astor rows (the Astor Estate used Kissam for their routine brownstones as we can see on the west side of Fifth Avenue south of 33rd Street and around the corner on the south side of 33rd Street.) Mrs. Vanderbilt may have had no interest in the social world, but her daughters-in-law would feel very differently. The Vanderbilt name, while not an early arrival on the Avenue, would be equated with the idea of palaces on Fifth Avenue and Reginald Vanderbilt would later be the last family resident in a house on Fifth Avenue.[4]

Palaces on Fifth Avenue

The grandchildren of the Commodore would open a crack in the seemingly impenetrable defenses of New York's high society, which dated its pedigree back to the merchants of the port. They had a perfectly nice, long-suffering grandmother (the Commodore put her in the Bloomingdale Asylum so that he could carry on with other women), but Mrs. Catherine Lorillard Kernochan of the Lorillard

Site of the Vanderbilt Twin Houses, from the original painting by J. J. Sawyer. The first Vanderbilt house on Fifth Avenue was built on the corner of 40th Street by W. H. Vanderbilt. The "Commodore," founder of the family fortune, never got farther uptown than Washington Place, where he had a yard spacious enough for a small circus ring, on which to exercise his horses and enable his children to ride. The Commodore was a familiar figure behind a pair of spanking trotters, a taste which was shared by his son, William H., and his grandson, William K. After leaving 40th Street W. H. took possession of the town houses between 51st and 52nd Streets, which, at the time of their erection, were the wonder of the day. Open spaces extended north on both sides of the Avenue almost to the Park. The rapid growth of the Avenue is aptly illustrated in the rural setting of the Beinhauer farm, illustrated below.

snuff family who had put Marietta Stevens down for not having a grandmother, would not be impressed by her humble status.

The upper island above St. Patrick's Cathedral was still rocky and wild with only the Mason Jones and Arabella Worsham, who we met in the last chapter, living in urban houses when William Henry Vanderbilt decided his fantastic wealth must be spent on grander digs for his family. As he looked around, much of the land available for a new house was owned by farms supplying the residential areas below 42nd Street, such as the old Beinhauer farm, then belonging to Isaiah Keyser.

Fifth Avenue brownstones crept northward to the Beinauer Farm, soon to be purchased by William Henry Vanderbilt. St. Patrick's, on the right, was nearing completion.

William Henry bought the entire property between 51st and 52nd Streets, which he would transform from farm to palace in short order. Why did W. H. Vanderbilt elect to move out of his home for another new build? He did not need to establish himself, as had A. T. Stewart, by a building—everyone knew a great deal about him and his family after the well-reported details of the recent trial over his father's will. Perhaps he just thought that as, now, the richest man in America, he ought to inhabit a palace? Or maybe it was revenge for his banishment by his father to a wooden house on a farm in Staten Island long before?

The parade of houses pushing the envelope seems to occur every generation, beginning with the Brevoort house at the base of the Avenue, the A. T. Stewart house at 34th Street, and now the Vanderbilt house—all built above the city, all to establish the identity of the family as prominent in New York City. Both the Stewart and Breevort properties were commissions, not speculative houses. Both were huge and told the cynical city dwellers that these house builders must be taken seriously. Stewart was common and likely too connected to the world of Boss Tweed, but his huge house established him as a powerful figure in the city even if he was pulled from President Grant's proposed cabinet within a day.

Vanderbilt in turn would build the largest house in New York City and establish his imprint on the city in short order. One can only wonder how his siblings felt at the end of a hard-fought trial over their father's will, in which they received small pickings, to see the eloquent statement Vanderbilt was making with his enormous house directly after he had silenced their claims. W. H. Vanderbilt had curried favor with his father by assuring the Commodore a single heir would keep the businesses together, but he would quickly renege on his promise by bringing in J. P. Morgan to create New York Central Railroad and take the company public.

Hiring his family architect, J. B. Snook, and abandoning the thought of a whiter stone or even marble, Vanderbilt set the house in brownstone, which was faster to work with and easier to carve. J. B. Snook had worked for the Vanderbilts for 30 years, completing railroad buildings and stations as well as their houses. Snook's new home for William Henry Vanderbilt on 40th Street had dignified, simple surfaces. However, W. H. Vanderbilt hired the design firm of the Herter Brothers for the new house on 51st/52nd Streets, for what would be the last commission of the two German-born founding brothers, and utilized the expertise of the great Chicago architect,

Charles B. Atwood, who laid out the designs on the walls for Snook's house before returning to the Windy City. If meant to be large and a bit bland on the outside, the house was truly remarkable on the inside. It was the culmination of the work of the Herter Brothers, who supplied much of the furniture and cabinetry for the 58-room house. They took credit for the house, demoting Snook to the position of contractor. There was some coverage of the dispute over the design in the press, but, to be honest, Snook could have done a better design—a simple, old fashioned, brownstone Renaissance palace would have been more dignified.[5]

The house, completed in 1882 was a double one, with the southern half for Mr. and Mrs. Vanderbilt and the northern half for two of his daughters, Margaret and Emily, who had recently married. The huge house was not well reviewed by the press when finished, often being compared to a packing box with incised patterns, employing, it was written, 600 carvers and 60 skilled fine arts workers, as opposed to artisanal and architectural sculptors, to complete the façade.[6] Indeed, the great influx of immigrants to the United States in this period brought many skilled workers to build and decorate the grand new houses. The quality of work was so fine that, when many of the fine houses were demolished in depressingly short order, contemporary workmen were often reduced to tears to destroy the high-quality work they had been tasked to undertake.

VANDERBILT MANSIONS
ON FIFTH AVENUE

The triple house of William Henry Vanderbilt, with a view north on the West side of the Avenue.

*William Henry
Vanderbilt house in
foreground and William
K. Vanderbilt house
across the street.*

A New Grandeur

With the Vanderbilt houses we see the second phase of Fifth Avenue building—houses that are commissioned, not speculatively built, which in many cases express the newfound grandeur of their owners. They represented a revolutionary move away from the usual apogee of success, a brownstone to reflect newly acquired Gilded Age wealth. If the builders of these houses were not part of the old society, they opted to stand out with bigger and showy houses. Their goal was no longer to fit in, but to surpass their peers.

William Henry Vanderbilt knew blatant mansion building would remind the public of the court case and the huge amount he received in the will, so he opted for a brownstone mansion, but tried to fill it with cultural treasure. In the elaborately finished house interior, he included painting done in Paris for the dining room ceiling, a Japanese room (Japonisme was currently at its height), a huge vase from the Demidoff sale of 1880[7] (the second of the pair is in the United Kingdom), and a collection of pictures that call to mind the galleries of the Stewart house. Vanderbilt's purchases, which were on a massive scale, were carried out with Samuel P. Avery, former print maker and now art dealer, whose importance rose after the closing of the Dusseldorf Galleries at the beginning of the Civil War. At this time, there were few dealers in art works and little appetite for the work, but Avery rose to the occasion and helped W. H. Vanderbilt select and fill his house in a very short time, perhaps the culmination of W. H. Vanderbilt's dream of his house as a treasure compound. Vanderbilt bought "homesy-folksy" pictures in the main, including farm scenes, animal pictures, and landscapes, but he had a special attachment to Meissonier, for whom he posed in Paris, and owned some seven pictures by the artist. He amassed six paintings by J. F. Millet, four landscapes by Tryon, two Corots, a Gustave Doré, a Delacroix, and a big Turner.

The Herter firm, who masterminded the interior, were masters of craftsmanship in the High Victorian era and into the next phase, the Aesthetic movement, and made and embellished furniture for W. H. Vanderbilt on a magnificent scale—it seems likely furniture for the W. H. Vanderbilt house was all custom pieces. The Herter Brothers' furniture and décor were original and did not follow specific historic precedent and the rooms might well be considered a high point of aesthetic design, fine workmanship, and quality materials.[8] Certainly W. H. Vanderbilt wanted to assert himself after the years of his father's lack of confidence in him, but perhaps he also found joy in the interiors and objects within the house, safely out of view of the relatives and the public. Every inch of the place boasted some "choice" newly purchased picture or object. The mansion had all the usual grand rooms as well as an "exotic" room which was the latest craze. Arabella Worsham had her special Middle Eastern chamber, W. H. Vanderbilt would commission a Japanese room from the (then) interior decoration firm of the artist John La Farge, the only named decorative artist who is associated with the house. Japonisme was the rage in London and Paris and, to a degree, New York, but no one, including La Farge, had yet been to the island nation opened by "Tiny" Belmont's father, Admiral Perry. Soon Edward Morse would visit and bring back a lantern show and La Farge himself would make the trip. But the W. H. Vanderbilt room was a naïve, but enthusiastic nod to Japan.

One could enter Vanderbilt's house through a two-story cube vestibule in the middle of the block on Fifth Avenue. W. H. Vanderbilt, his wife, and then-young son went through a reduced and hollow version of Ghiberti's *Gates of Paradise* to the south, while his two newly married daughters each had a home on the right.[10] Dead in the middle was a stunning grand malachite vase, over the height of most men, which sat regally in the entry, part of a pair from the Russian Count Demidoff's house above Florence. The elegant entry to the house with its spare décor betrayed the vast amount of treasures within.[11] The over-the-top interiors were quite amazing. The excess seems like badges of wealth on display for a man who previously worked a farm in Staten Island.

The Japanese Room in the William Henry Vanderbilt House

Following the opening of Japan by Admiral Perry, Japanese-themed rooms became fashionable. "The yellows and greens, the red lacquer work, the Miaco lacquer, the Japanese uncut velvet… the cabinets of fantastic shape, and the panels of bronze picked out with gold and silver—all are Japanese."[9] William H. Vanderbilt's Japanese Parlor, northwest corner.

Both A. T. Stewart, the department store king, and W. H. Vanderbilt created huge collections within the thick walls of their homes. In Stewart's day, there was no New York City art museum, while in Vanderbilt's day, the Metropolitan Museum was in its first and rather painting-less years. Could each man have considered the possibility that they might leave their house and collection to the people of New York City? This would have been a heroic legacy but it did not happen.

The Unstoppable Alva

Although New York City had only a small number of settlers directly from France, in the 19th century, Paris was the shining light of education and culture. Those wishing an education in the arts, the medical professions, architecture, and engineering learned the language and traveled to the City of Light. In addition, socially ambitious women and many from the plantations of the South chose to sojourn in France to be near the glamor of Napoleon III and

The entry cubicle featured one of the two great malachite vases once owned by Count Demidoff in Florence. Vanderbilt's door is to the left. Atrium at the William H. Vanderbilt house, with the Demidoff Vase.

his Empress, Eugenie. American women and their belle daughters glittered in the balls of the court and were welcomed in the circle around Napoleon III.

One commission merchant with an ambitious wife, Murray Forbes Smith, came to New York from Mobile in 1859 to attempt to penetrate New York society. Smith likely rented the A. C. Gray house, the early house with a mansard roof by Calvert Vaux (also rented, it would seem, by harvest machine-inventor, Cyrus McCormick). Smith's business ended with the War, and he took his family to Europe. While he worked on his business ties in Liverpool, his wife and daughters went to Paris and Phoebe Smith took her daughters to the Court balls. Rejected in New York, Phoebe Smith joined others trying an end run around the Knickerbockers by affecting Parisian ties. Mademoiselle Coulon ran a boarding school for girls at the edge of Paris in Neuilly-sur-Seine and Mrs. Smith sent her daughter, Alva, to this school. It seems that Marietta Stevens, in Europe for the 1867 Paris fair where

Paran Stevens was a delegate, may have sent her daughter, Minnie, to that same school. It must have appeared that the Paris-acquired charm would open doors in New York, but this proved not to be the case.[12] Smith did not succeed in reclaiming his business and returned to New York, where he descended to opening a house in an unfashionable part of town likely as a boarding house run by his daughter, the unstoppable Alva.

Alva later would insist the boarding house was a sad joke but the New York City address book lists their house as a boarding house run by Alva Smith. Smith declined steadily, and Alva realized she was the key to the family's future. Trading upon some fanciful tales as her mother had before her (Mrs. Smith concocted tales of her social importance), Alva created herself as an available and glamorous young woman in New York's social whirl beginning after the War. Phoebe Smith died in 1871, leaving Alva as the proprietor of the boarding house. This was not to be Alva Smith's future, so she set her sights on the second male heir to the Vanderbilt fortune, William Kissam Vanderbilt.

W. K. Vanderbilt was the first Vanderbilt to put a toe into the privileges of wealth (William Henry's efforts seem to have been much more inward-looking). He had been sent to school in Switzerland, and was a charming and cordial man, ripe for the picking. At a ball in White Sulfur Springs the powerful and irrepressible Alva Smith, who was not a great beauty, laid a trap for him with a clever dress she made from an old curtain, detailed with sprigs of yellow goldenrod from the local countryside, and danced with W. K. Vanderbilt. Alva saved her family when she married W. K. Vanderbilt in 1875, although it would become apparent over the next two decades that the pair were totally ill-suited.[13]

The Vanderbilts were still on the outside of the mercantile social group and little noticed at the time. When the old Commodore finally died, his male heirs were ready to step up—and so was Alva. Always an admirer of things French, Alva was fully aware of the massive restoration work on the old Château de Pierrefonds in progress from 1858 when she was following the French court (Napoleon understood the role of buildings to enhance his power; however, it did not work out quite so well for him). Alva looked to France for inspiration for her new home in Manhattan, and was inspired by Henri-Eugene-Philippe-Louis duc d'Aumale, the fourth son of King Louis Philippe, who restored Chantilly, a potent symbol of French history, and also as a bid for building as prestige and self-image. The magnificent French house of the 1560s had been razed in the French Revolution. Long a

favored destination of British aristocrats, the rebuilding of the lost château, which had been turned into a stone quarry in 1799, started in 1876. The recreation of Chantilly took seven years and was in progress just as America emerged from the economic depression of 1873–79. The Bourbon descendant tried to improve the area after the Franco-Prussian war with thoroughbred horse racing, a delight to the British and American wealthy. The old town had been a capital of a special type of lace; now the Jockey Club seemed a sounder bet. Americans began to travel the 40 miles from Paris to Chantilly for horse racing and gardens (there was an English and a Chinese garden laid out in the later 18th and early 19th centuries), while the restoration effort and outfitting of Chantilly were much noted by Americans visiting France and the American press.[14]

Chantilly lace, horse racing, and the rebuilding of a lost château. Americans flocked to Chantilly. Château de Chantilly, view taken from the parterre, second half of the 19th century.

What was there about a medieval French building that acted as the inspiration for a New York City house? A French-style château was briefly considered at 70th Street and Fifth Avenue in 1870 by "Big" Jim Fisk, who asked French-trained American architect, Richard Morris Hunt, to design a château, which was never built. Fisk, a notorious figure in New York City, grew up in Brattleboro, Vermont and knew Richard Morris Hunt's family there in their youth. Fisk had been involved in the Erie Railroad stock debacle with Jay Gould and must have decided to upstage Gould in his mid-century brownstone on Fifth Avenue. Two years later Fisk ended up in a shoot-out over the glamor woman of the era, Josie Mansfield. Fisk was killed by Edward S. Stokes in the Grand Central Hotel in 1872 and the French corner house never happened. Did Alva know of Hunt's 1870 design? It seems likely Hunt would have shown it to her and she seized upon the idea for a "petite Château" to propel her into society. The success in creating a fairy tale fantasy of the old days at Chantilly, as exploited by the French Court in the late 1860s, must have seemed viable to Alva. Across 52nd Street from her father-in-law, Alva and W. K. Vanderbilt built a château on the blue stone sidewalk of Fifth Avenue with the help of Richard Morris Hunt, who was probably selected by Alva. The inspiration was likely Chantilly, which W. K. Vanderbilt would have known, as he was a great follower of horse racing, and Alva, of course, was comfortable with all things French.

Although one or two Americans had flirted with training at the Parisian Ecole, such as the little-known figures, Alfred H. Throop and Sidney Stratton, the first to enter and succeed in the profession was Richard Morris Hunt. The French Academy of the Fine Arts was considered the premier training ground for the arts professions and only slowly recognized Americans, due in part to the language barrier. Few Americans were fluent in French, making a Parisian sojourn unworkable. Hunt remained at the Ecole and after completion, went to work for Hector-Martin Lefuel in Paris before returning to the United States in 1855. Clearly Hunt traveled in architecture circles in Paris and could well have known the work at Chantilly in the 1870s alongside the architect there, Honoré Daumet, who had trained some American architects including Charles Follen McKim. Certainly, when traveling later with his wife, Hunt was recognized at the racetrack and given hospitality by the then-aging duc d'Aumale. Hunt's wife kept a diary which notes this encounter and reports that they were traveling with the Vanderbilts. [15]

Hunt's first decade in New York was anything but smooth. His first townhouses were a pair for a Theodore Rossiter and his father-in-law Dr. E. Parmly, who refused to give Hunt his fee. Hunt had to sue the owner, which would fuel his life-long devotion to making architecture a sound profession in America. Hunt's fortunes improved when he married Catherine Howland, daughter of one of the families of mercantile New York. Catherine's inheritance enabled Hunt to rise above the practicing architects in New York, who were forced to take any and all jobs, as Griffith Thomas and so many others had been forced by economic necessity to do. Hunt could now afford to await some choice commissions.

How did Hunt and Alva bond to build the "petit château"? Hunt moved in Knickerbocker circles, Alva did not. But she commissioned Hunt to build her first country house, "Idle Hour" in Islip, Long Island, in 1878, just as the court case over the Commmodore's will was settled. Indeed, Alva may have been the first to commission houses in the Vanderbilt family. She selected a site near a fishing club on the Connectiquot River, then considered a fashionable weekend retreat (August Belmont had a racing site close by there as well). Alva and W. K. Vanderbilt asked Hunt to build an enormous wooden house rather in the manner of the newer Norman villas of the French industrialists. The region around the house they called "Idle Hour" did attract some other aspirants to New York society in the late 1870s and early 1880s before falling from favor. The Vanderbilts would soon manage to join Newport society, leaving Idle Hour to occasional use. The house burnt down at the end of the century and was rebuilt by Hunt's sons. [16]

Hunt and Alva established a close, if sometimes contentious relationship, which would last through his lifetime and that of his sons who would take over the practice. Hunt must have found Alva a

JACQUES COEUR HOUSE, BOURGES, FRANCE.

One of several inspirations for the New York house of William K. Vanderbilt.

challenge as did most people, but for her, he dared not take a chance and found the close inspiration we noted in Jacques Coeur's house in Bourges. Perhaps Alva even knew this urban château. Alva began the trend for French châteaux in America, which was followed by others but not by her sisters-in-law. The four daughters of W. H. Vanderbilt had their houses just north of Alva's site designed and built by the men who had created their parents' home. Only her nephew, George Vanderbilt, would ask Hunt to design a château. Alva's architectural knowledge was not well founded when the house was being built. She did not fully understand the difference in the designs favored by the various French kings, but she did educate herself quickly. Her use of houses as a principal expression of her good taste earned her a nomination for an American Institute of Architects award, but she declined the honor. Ultimately, and maybe oddly, Alva would switch from architecture to the cause of women's suffrage.

Following the court case and the subsequent house building frenzy, New Yorkers began to notice the younger Vanderbilts. Hunt's design executed in gray Indiana limestone, was stunning. Newspaper accounts claimed the great French Norman stone from Caen was used throughout, but Caen stone was imported and used as a veneer only on the interiors. The blue roof tiles were met with fine copper ridge cresting. Recessed slightly from the broad sidewalk, the house rose with its great blocks of stone, a handsome insertion in the street-facing wall. The impact of the new house, completed in 1883, can be directly seen when compared to the regular brownstones that abut it on the northern half of the block. The house was wider and deeper than most neighboring residences, with the primary entry in the middle of the Fifth Avenue façade marked by a thin, ornate tourelle. The house surface was richly carved along the bay windows, dormers, and turrets by a number of new immigrants who knew how to dress stone. Figures for the numbers of workmen at the W. H. Vanderbilt and W. K. Vanderbilt houses are reported, likely fancifully, as in the hundreds. The skilled work of this era, which was undertaken by new immigrants to the United States, especially Italians, set a new standard for New York City, ensuring New York was no longer seen an architectural stepchild of Europe.

Wider, deeper, and taller than the surrounding brownstones, the "*petit château*" had a great reception in the city. The house itself, not the opening party, really put the Vanderbilts on the society map. The then-young architect, Charles Follen McKim, just starting his practice as the house was being built, claimed a walk past the house in the evening reassured him that all was well (amazingly, the house would be demolished in Alva's lifetime).[17] The W. K. Vanderbilts had three children, Consuelo, followed by two boys, William K. V. Jr. and Harold, who would all grow up in this castle during the assault on society waged by their mother. The house was built for a social assault, not to be a comfortable home for the family. The house would be the site of many glittering parties, when the three children would hide in the musicians' gallery in the double-height banquet room and watch the spectacle of the balls below. Consuelo remembered crawling up the steps to her room in the dark and felt a rather gothic novel-esque type of fear every evening going to her bedroom[18].

Consuelo's childhood stories reveal the only times when she and her mother were truly happy was late spring, May and June, when they lived in Paris. It was indeed a ritual of many New York grandees, such as Mrs. Astor and many in her set, to spend spring in Paris. In the Parisian shops, as the house was being built, Consuelo remembered Alva buying pictures and antiques. Three major pictures, by Gainsborough, Reynolds, and Rembrandt, were acquired for her and her husband's early collection a few years after the opening of the house (1884–85). She patronized Charles John Wertheimer, who with his brother sold old master pictures in London. *The Toilette of Venus* painted in 1751 by Francois Boucher would arrive from the dealer's sale in 1895, just as the marriage was hitting the rocks.[19] (the painting was given to the Metropolitan Museum). The house interiors were laid out by Hunt for Alva's campaign on society; Hunt, in the new manner of the era, gave out each principal room to a different firm. The interior design companies were, as we know, new in post-Civil War America. Perhaps to keep family squabbles at bay, most new decorative commissions would distribute each firm a room. W. H. Vanderbilt's Herter Brothers did some of the house, while the early-to New York City French firm of Leon Marcotte, who worked for Hart Schiff, also did a room. Two new Parisian firms, Allard & Fils and Gilbert Cuel, also enriched special rooms. Allard and Cuel were to become favored artisans as the more palatial houses were finished.

As in other houses of the day, witness Arabella Worsham and Alva's father-in-law, there was an "exotic" room, here of "Moorish" design by Marcotte, distinguished in function for billiards. Pictures of North Africa and the Middle East alongside a billiards table were then a popular men's fantasy. Women, on the other hand, liked the concept of French interiors. Rooms of the varying "Louis" modes seem to have been inserted in every upscale house in the last twenty years of the 19th century. Alva opted for Louis XV with work done by Allard, who she would continue to use, and Cuel, whom W. K. Vanderbilt would insist

Alva Vanderbilt dressed for her March 1883 ball. Most of the guests were also photographed in costume.

upon for the interior of The Metropolitan Club a decade later.

Alva likely enhanced public anticipation of her new house with tales of gold faucets and all the Caen stone. The center of her battle plan was a huge banquet hall, where she would stage her assault on those who had not accepted her. To do this, she counted upon her childhood chum from Mobile, Consuelo Yznaga, daughter of a Cuban owner of a small plantation, Ravenswood. The Yznaga family flirted with the social whirl in New York, Newport, and New Jersey. The name of the Yznaga daughter, Consuelo, was likely an attempt to create a sophisticated aura for the child and came from the popular novel by Georges Sand, published in 1842–43 and translated into English by 1850. The financial ups and downs of the Yznagas were an issue, but a son, Fernando, succeeded, saving his sister in her later years with a fine inheritance after she had endured economic ruin for decades. There were several Yznaga children, indeed Alva's sister would have an unhappy marriage to brother Fernando. Alva bonded with Consuelo (she named her own daughter after her friend) and, in the end, her marriage was ruined by this friend.

A Costume Ball

Worn-out aristocratic European families in need of fresh money and blood were beginning a 50-year voyage west to find a "Dollar Princess." The eldest son of the English Duke of Manchester, George Montagu, was a true failure. Not good at anything, he sailed to America, fell ill, and was befriended by the Yznagas, who saw his social potential and nursed him back to health. Consuelo Yznaga was attracted to the youth, and her mother, seeing the prospects of a title, managed to marry them off rapidly in New York City in 1876 at Grace Church. The couple had a son, William, in the next year and twin daughters in 1878, but even after the title passed to George, the now-Duke had no means of support, and nor did Consuelo, who became a fixture of entertainment in the court of the Prince of Wales and mistress to many. The wealth needed to support Consuelo and her family did not materialize. Her unhappy life is captured in Edith Wharton's *The Buccaneers*. Consuelo smoked cigars, played the banjo, and sang songs of the southern slaves to the great amusement of the frivolous court of the Prince of Wales, but her life was a tragic one until the early 20th century, when her brother left her his estate.

Consuelo resided in England with her children, while her husband resumed his low life habits. Consuelo and her son came to see Alva and Willie's new home, staying in the château for the winter of 1883. With a British aristocrat in residence and a new house, New York was palpitating to view, Alva planned a ball—a costume ball![20] The

Victorian court in England had once again taken up hosting costume balls and many would follow in America. Justified as a boon to dressmakers and costume makers, florists and such, these parties were insane expenditures usually with a goal in mind—Alva's aim was to force herself in the world of the Astors and McAllisters. Indeed, many succeeded in accomplishing the result the party was meant to create.

The tale of Alva's ball is much told. It was to begin, as these events did, late at night with supper in the wee hours of the morning; some 1,200 invitations were rumored to have been sent out. A fever arose in the city— clearly this would be a magical affair, and the guests would get to walk into the château. The dances of earlier balls had been staged with lavish costumes, but this event topped its predecessors. For the Hobbyhorse Quadrille, the dancers wore costumes of real horsehair. For another quadrille, the young women dressed with an electric light, a new amenity, in their hair with a long line attaching the dancers to the source. This was probably rather dangerous, if novel.

As the young women rehearsed, Alva took note that a member of the quadrille was Carrie Astor, daughter of *The* Mrs. Astor, who had not acknowledged the Vanderbilts. Versions of this famous tale abound. Did Alva use Carrie Astor as a tool to gain a calling card from Carrie's mother? Rather than disappoint a child, Caroline Astor rode up to the château and dropped her calling card onto the silver salver and an invitation to the ball was said to quickly arrive on 34th Street.

Alva Vanderbilt's in-laws, Cornelius and Alice Vanderbilt II at the Ball.

DINING ROOM AT THE WILLIAM K. VANDERBILT HOUSE, 660 FIFTH AVENUE

The great hall used in big events such as the 1883 costume ball. Some of the paintings arrived later.

Consuelo Vanderbilt as a girl. The stairs to her room in her parents' house seemed dark and foreboding to her.

Despite the gossip about frigid relations between Mrs. Astor and Alva, they may have been exaggerated, as reports noted Mrs. Astor and Mrs. Vanderbilt in an animated conversation at the ball. The long-planned event had brought Alva and the younger Vanderbilts fully into New York Society—the house had accomplished everything the plan intended and the Vanderbilts began to receive invitations to the Patriarch's balls. The very night of the ball, in the flower-bedecked house under white calcium light, the Knickerbockers admitted defeat to the newcomers with seemingly unlimited purses.

At the time of the great ball, the treasures for the house had not yet been purchased. As Alva's daughter noted, Alva would buy objects for the New York house on her springtime visits to Paris.

After the great ball, Alva's interest in the New York house slowly faded. She and her husband had now gained admission to Newport, and she set herself another massive building campaign there for Marble House (1888–92), a gift from her husband, hiding it behind wooden walls to generate local curiosity. Alva would later buy a great collection of medieval objects for the Newport house on her annual springtime visits to Paris (this collection is now in Sarasota, Florida). The remarkable mansion, for brief use in summer on a typical small plot of property, was to be the weapon for the next Alva assault upon society—the marriage of her daughter to a titled nobleman. Alva had groomed Consuelo, positioning her in a metal brace every morning to create both perfect posture and a long, swan-like neck. While in a steel corset, Consuelo studied French and German. She was educated to be a trophy wife, replete with a many-million-dollar dowry.

The Dollar Princess

The Newport house had been presented as a gift from W. K. Vanderbilt to Alva, but, in truth, their marriage was dissolving. Consuelo noted her parents were never compatible, which was certainly the truth. What had happened? Alva had met O. P. H. Belmont, the horse-loving son of August, on a long cruise. Her marriage was long over and now Alva did the unthinkable, and sought a divorce, a scandalous step. W. K. Vanderbilt allowed himself to seemingly stage a weekend with a woman in a hotel in England to give Alva the divorce she wished. But the real story may have been a long affair between Consuelo Yznaga and W. K. Vanderbilt, which could even have started during her winter in New York in 1883. W. K. Vanderbilt remained devoted to Consuelo Yznaga through the century, bringing the bodies of Consuelo's daughters back to England on his yacht after they both died of consumption in Italy, for burial.

As Alva would claim, she had the first divorce in New York society but would this harm her campaign for a son-in-law? Inconveniently for Alva, her daughter, as she neared marriage age, had already found a suitable young man in her set. Equally inconveniently, the husband of her mother's selection, the 9th Duke of Marlborough, also had his own love interest. Never allowing these facts to stop her, Alva made the marriage happen. Divorce and a reluctant bride and groom notwithstanding, New York became obsessed with the Duke of Marlborough marrying a Vanderbilt daughter. Every detail of the trousseau, wedding gifts, and flower arrangements was leaked to the newspapers. Hordes appeared at the wedding, while ranks of policemen lined Fifth Avenue around the church. The Vanderbilts did not appear; Alva did not invite them. As Consuelo sobbed before the ceremony, W. K. Vanderbilt presented the 9th Duke with what he really wanted, a huge dowry, probably amounting to $3 million in railroad stock, to save his family palace of Blenheim.[21] The previous duke had made a second marriage to a young New York widow, who was known for sponsoring the organ in the long hall at Blenheim, the central heating, and other improvements. So, the precedent was set. Consuelo crossed the Atlantic for a perfectly unhappy marriage. She

Perhaps the most watched wedding in the Gilded Age. Young Consuelo Vanderbilt married the 9th Duke of Marlborough. The wedding caught newspaper readers' imagination in a day when the lives of the wealthy were a great escape from reality.

Alva Vanderbilt prepared her daughter to marry grandly—she would marry the 9th Duke of Marlborough. This was the ultimate bad marriage. Portrait of the 9th Duke of Marlborough with his family, including Consuelo Vanderbilt.

John Singer Sargent, 1905.

Opposite:
William Kissam Vanderbilt, Jr. House, 666 Fifth Avenue

The William K. Vanderbilt, Jr. House by McKim, Mead & White in construction. The brownstone row is being demolished.

produced the "heir and the spare" and, after a principal role in the Coronation of Edward VII, she escaped Blenheim. When she met the French World War I hero, Colonel Jacques Balsan, whom she wished to marry, his family refused, as she was a divorcee. She had to make a case for an annulment of her marriage to the 9th Duke, and her mother told all, confessing to the ambition and cruelty she had used to arrange a marriage more about herself than her daughter.

In the following years, Alva, as Mrs. Belmont, would become a prime mover in women's suffrage and both Alva and Consuelo joined political causes, abandoning the New York house. The young W. K. Vanderbilt Jr., when he married Virginia Fair of the famous California Comstock Lode family, quickly became a part of the

WILLIAM KISSAM
VANDERBILT HOUSE,
660 FIFTH AVENUE,
52ND STREET AT THE
NORTHWEST CORNER OF
FIFTH AVENUE

*The W. K. Vanderbilt
House on the north
corner. It stands in
stark contrast to the
established brownstones
of the day. W. K.
Vanderbilt Jr. would tear
down the brownstones
to build a version of his
parents' house.*

*Alva Vanderbilt's petit
château.*

social set of Newport and New York. W. K. Vanderbilt Jr. bought the brownstones to the north of his childhood home at the time of his marriage in 1899 and had Stanford White, not Hunt's sons, create an appropriate double half for the house, creating a full block of homage to the château at Bourges at 666 Fifth Avenue. W. K. Vanderbilt Jr. and his wife now had their own château,[22] but despite the new château at 666 Fifth Avenue, Alva's *petit château* and its era had passed.[23]

A Brick Renaissance Château

The third great palace was the last to be started, but only by a brief time. W. K. Vanderbilt was a bon vivant who loved the pleasures of his life, but his older brother, the first male son of W. H. Vanderbilt, was the exact opposite. Hard working, serious, bereft of vices, Cornelius VanderbiltJr. was the principal heir to the W. H. Vanderbilt fortune and railroads. Cornelius Vanderbilt went to work in the banking room of the Kissam firm at the age of sixteen. The Kissams were a big Knickerbocker family, indeed, as we know, his mother, wife of W. H. Vanderbilt, was a Kissam and the Astor estate used a builder, Peter Kissam, for much of their routine work. Cornelius Vanderbilt taught Sunday School at St. Bartholomew's on 46th Street and Madison Avenue and he met Alice Claypoole Gwynne there, whom he would marry in early 1867. The Commodore brought his grandson Cornelius into the business (as was the custom of the old man) that very year and left Cornelius Vanderbilt the largest legacy after W. H. Vanderbilt.

Now exceedingly rich, Cornelius kept working right up to his early demise. Cornelius commissioned his own architect, George Browne Post, a student of Richard Morris Hunt and a man who would be the father of the New York City skyscraper. Post had a strong connection to the Gwynne family from Cleveland days. On a large 125-by-125-foot corner plot at the northwest corner of 57th Street, Post designed a big house for Cornelius and his family. Half the Fifth Avenue frontage comprised five brownstones, which already stood (on the north corner at 58th Street was the large house of the Tiffany and Co president; between was a Lorillard house). Cleverly, and following A. T. Stewart, the entry was on the 57th Street side of the house, allowing the family and visitors the chance to see the brick and stone house only. Post's house, French Renaissance in design, was primarily brick rather than the brownstone of Cornelius's parents' house and the limestone of the house of his brother. Cornelius's mansion relied less on carvers and artisan workmen than did the other two houses.[24] As the house design progressed, Cornelius Vanderbilt agonized about the size of the rooms Post was detailing. Vanderbilt seems to have

Cornelius Vanderbilt
House, northwest
corner of Fifth
Avenue and 57th
Street

*The Cornelius
Vanderbilt house on
the Fifth Avenue side.
The brownstone to
the north would soon
be demolished for an
immense expansion of
the house to 58th Street.*

consulted with the soon-to-be architect Ernest Flagg, then about
to go to Paris, perhaps with some backing from Vanderbilt, but the
Flagg scheme was not used.

Interiors in this house were done by an assembly of American artists.
Rather than using them for the exterior, Cornelius brought in the best
younger artists in the city to decorate the rooms, including Augustus
Saint-Gaudens, David Maitland Armstrong, and John La Farge (not
quite so young) to create sculpture for the interior. These men, whose
work was magnificent, were already known as "artists," not artisans,
and were American, not new immigrants. There was a "Moorish"
parlor here as well, maintaining the special room penchant of the day.
 The interiors tended to be dark and heavy, which led to a rethinking
of the house some twelve years later when Cornelius and his wife
brought Post back to double the size of the house, extending it
through the long block to 58th Street and the small park there where

General Sherman rode his golden horse. Post ended the house on the
north with a grand porte-cochère, driveway, and greenery. The entry,
with panels by the sculptor, Karl Bitter, was for grand events; entry to
the house on ordinary days was still on 57th Street. The north portal
was walled by a magnificent metal fence designed by Post in the
English country house fashion (and now at 106th Street and Central
Park). As demonstrated by the then-Lenox Library and the Villard/
Reid houses, there was some still empty space in New York City's
relentless grid. Henry A. La Farge wrote about the Vanderbilt houses
where his grandfather had worked in a long article.[25] John Donnelly[26],
a stone carver, took credit for much carving on the houses and claimed
that the exteriors were done by mainly British carvers, not French
men as Alva Vanderbilt liked to claim.[27]

The now enormous house was reworked by Post. The great Saint-
Gaudens fireplace and inlaid wooden panels were moved to a second-

floor new billiard room. The work of the American artists was retained in the new house, although some of the La Farge glass was taken to the new house the Vanderbilts were building in Newport after a fire destroyed the house Cornelius had just purchased from Pierre Lorillard, The Breakers. If there was a rivalry between Alva and Mrs. Cornelius Vanderbilt, it was subdued; if there had been a battle, Alva had won it long before. She was now THE Mrs. Vanderbilt, even if not for much longer. Alice Vanderbilt decided to have a proper ballroom, distinct from the rooms of the old house, in the expanded house and turned to the favored Parisian firm of Alva and W. K. Vanderbilt, Allard & Fils. But the days for those splendid fêtes were ending. The Cornelius Vanderbilts held two balls in the new house before Cornelius himself had a massive stroke, which would take his life before the century ended.

Cornelius was genuinely generous to causes he respected. In his view, important paintings that were put on public view were a valid way to improve the lives of the under classes. He purchased Rosa Bonheur's *Horse Fair* from the Stewart art sale and donated it to the new Metropolitan Museum of Art. Indeed, both Vanderbilt brothers

THE CORNELIUS VANDERBILT HOUSE, VIEW FROM THE NORTH

Cornelius Vanderbilt consulted and hired the emerging fine arts world in New York City. Although decorators were retained, Vanderbilt brought in the great young artists Augustus Saint-Gaudens, John La Farge, and David Maitland Armstrong to add features to his rooms. Cornelius Vanderbilt's fireplace by Augustus Saint-Gaudens, mantelpiece by David Maitland Armstrong.

were important donors and trustees of the new museum. The fine Turner painting of Venice Cornelius bought from the Earl of Dudley was also given to the Museum.[28]

The Vanderbilt houses are the summation and the finale of the house as establisher of social acceptance. These remarkable works of many arts would go down in a generation. The Vanderbilts did not see the threat of the tall commercial buildings quietly sneaking uptown and creating shadows for their magnificent houses and gardens. Ultimately, commerce won—but would that the *petit château* had been saved.

CHAPTER 12

THE HOUSES OF THE 50S

"The man who is to do good work in our country must not only be a good man, but also emphatically a man."

Theodore Roosevelt

OTHER DEVELOPERS BESIDE THE VANDERBILTS were drawn to 50th Street and its environs, as demonstrated by the erection of the new Roman Catholic Cathedral, just above 50th Street, which was nearing completion by 1879. At the beginning of the 19th century, as the Catholic population began to grow in New York, the new Archdiocese of the City had bought a patch of land far above paved roads. The rural property had no direct use and went through several stages, including consideration as a cemetery. Even earlier, this part of the country property, which was then over three miles above the city, became the site of the famed Elgin Botanical Gardens founded by Dr. David Hosack (1769–1835), the famous physician to Alexander Hamilton following the notorious duel of 1804. Neither the Archdiocese nor Dr. Hosack could imagine that the City would reach their properties in two generations.

Conventional coverage always states that the Vanderbilt mansions were built on empty land at the northern edge of the city, but some other developers had already claimed houses by the early 1870s. Just below 50th Street, John Snook built a big house on the western corner of 49th Street in 1868 for Martin E. Greene at a huge cost of $50,000. The house would be rebuilt in 1904 for John I. Kane by McKim, Mead & White. Next door were two brownstones built on spec in 1870 by Charles Duggin, who completed another pair on the other side of the Avenue. Duggin, now with a new partner, James Crossman, also constructed a big brownstone for Charles C. O'Conner at

The hilly terrain of what would become Central Park. View looking southward from the Arsenal at Fifth Avenue and 64th Street, including in the background the Deaf and Dumb Asylum (now becoming Columbia College), St. Luke's Hospital, and the dome of the New York Crystal Palace just before the fire, June 1858.

607 Fifth Avenue in 1869, next to two spec houses. All three brownstones look similar, but the house built for O'Conner stood out because a bigger budget was available. The architect used for higher-end Astor projects, Charles W. Clinton, built several houses on the west side between 50th and 51st Streets on land owned by Columbia College, which they had received in a trade with New York State in 1855; they decided to have it developed for income when they were able to acquire the old Deaf and Dumb Asylum just to the east at Madison Avenue, which would become the campus for the college.

The houses on the prime Fifth Avenue portion of the Columbia block were commissioned from Clinton, working for several clients, in 1873 and were substantial. Walter S. Gurnee took the corner with a huge plot, extending 35 feet on the Avenue and 117 feet deep, and built

a mansard-roofed home for an estimate of $150,000. After Gurnee's
death in 1903, as we know, Benjamin Altman leased the house and
had his 34th Street new department store architects, Trowbridge &
Livingston, build a gallery behind the house for Altman's magnificent
painting collection. Just to the north of the Gurnee house, Clinton
built two houses for A. H. Rathbone, then one for John H. Power,
Daniel P. Morgan (in 1880 this house was leased by Darius Ogden
Mills, and the interiors were created by the Herter Brothers working
just up the street for W. H. Vanderbilt), and Samuel D. Babcock. All of
these wide houses filled the block five years before W. H. Vanderbilt
eyed the farm site. So Vanderbilt had a fancy set of neighbors just
across 51st Street. Unlike Mary Mason Jones when she built her row,
this was not the howling wilderness when the Vanderbilts built.

NORTHWEST CORNER OF
FIFTH AVENUE AND 51ST
STREET

*Walter S. Gurnee House,
Charles W. Clinton
architect, 1873. Gurnee/
Altman house is the one
with the horse vehicle in
front of it.*

NORTHWEST CORNER OF
51ST STREET.

*The painting gallery
extension on Benjamin
Altman's house.
Altman's great collection
was given to the young
Metropolitan Museum of
Art at Altman's death.*

An Undesirable Neighbor

Perhaps an obstacle to the sale the Beinauer farm, the property William Henry Vanderbilt wished to purchase for his new triple house, was not just its uptown location. There was a notorious neighbor on the eastern side of Fifth Avenue at 52nd Street—Charles and Ann Lohman (known as Mme Restell) had built a grand brownstone between 1857 and 1860, designed by Robert Mook, who was working with Mary Mason Jones. Few would consider living next door or even across the street from Mme Restell. Ann Trow, later Mrs. Charles R. Lohman, had immigrated from Britain and established herself firmly as New

York and, via the mails, the nation's leading solver of unwanted pregnancies. A dispenser of liquids and tablets, "Mme. Restell" ran a business providing physical abortions, with a special dedication to the city's wealthy citizens. As Mme. Restell's business flourished, the Lohmans had enough money to build a large corner brownstone on the northeast crossing at 52nd Street directly after the Civil War. It is likely the plot they purchased was 100 feet on Fifth Avenue which, after the house, left 75 feet for sale, but no one was interested in the property. The plots purchased just east of the corner house were turned into stable use (Mme Restell herself had a lavish stable on 52nd Street). To position herself in New York, Mme Restell added all the extra decoration she could manage to create an ambience she would have felt was on a par with that of her clients in the city. But the economy had declined into depression by 1873, and the thought of living next to a notorious abortionist who took in boarding patients in her house put off the sales of neighboring lots.

In 1875, Mrs. Lohman retained the architect/developers in the area, Duggin & Crossman, to design an apartment house on her rather unsalable Fifth Avenue plot. It would seem the couple were having financial disagreements and Mme. Restell paid herself for the new building, the Osborne. The Osborne appeared to be two wide (37.5 feet) brownstones—the story of the brownstones as stealth apartment houses will be told later. It is interesting that Duggin & Crossman, who were the builders of the highest end work in the blocks of the 50s, would build for Mme. Restell. The new apartment house might be a very early example of the creation of that purpose-built building type in New York, rather than rehabilitation of the row house as an apartment building. Knowing the spin they would need to use, the Lohmans made thoughtful arrangements. The Osborne would need clever features to attract tenants, so the architects supplied a steam elevator, possibly making this the first apartment house built with an elevator, indeed not one but two, including a back elevator for furniture. The apartments were nine rooms long, and the placement of the units was carefully considered, with kitchens at the rear of the layout. There was a small square courtyard within the building with a glass roof for light in the middle of the building. The apartment house was even named the Osborne—likely after the retreat of Queen Victoria and her consort—to make it distinct from the Lohmans. Mme. Restell's reputation was still too pungent for prospective tenants, although by 1880 the census shows ten households in the building, although the building lost tenants quickly and rents were lowered as a result.

In a rather sneaky raid, Anthony Comstock, an anti-vice activist in the city, trapped Mme. Restell, who had been widowed a year earlier, and took her to court for what would likely be a prison sentence. Ann Lohman went to her stately bathtub in her house and, on April Fool's Day, committed suicide by slitting her throat. (A new book by Jennifer Wright speculates the Mme Restell faked her death.) So much for renters for the Osborne. In a few years the Osborne would be combined with the brownstone house by the Lohman heirs and transformed into the Langham, a transient hotel, which took the name, most likely, from a grand hotel in London only a few years old. The Osborne apartments had not been successful and were eventually demolished in 1900. But the death of Mme. Restell on April 1st gave a green light to the sale of the Beinauer Farm, which W. H. Vanderbilt then rushed to purchase. The abortionist was no longer a poison to the block.

A Dancing Academy

On the east side of Fifth Avenue just to the north, at 677 Fifth Avenue, were two brownstones built by John Correja in 1867. Correja seems to have been active in this area, constructing a signature brownstone marked by a slight porch at the doorframe. The house became a dancing academy, run by the Dodsworth brothers. As we know, dancing was the acceptable form of social gatherings and dancing school a way to present young children to their peers. The Dodsworths were the most important dancing gurus of the century in New York, who introduced the German Cotillion to America in 1844, which would become the standard square dance for the mid-century. The Dodsworth dancing classes, held at the Dodsworth Academy, would remain a point of distinction for New York society for a century. Established families only were permitted into the afternoon sessions for children, beginning at ten years of age (the de Rham family who bought Brevoort's house, the first residence on Fifth Avenue, would preside over this upper-class dance discipline through the 1950s). Soon, the Dodsworths would acquire all the houses through the corner of 685 Fifth Avenue, with the dancing school in one likely 681, which may have been the E.W. Coles house, a big brownstone built by Griffith Thomas in 1872. In 1872, the Dodsworths closed the classes and leased the big skylit interior to the future Metropolitan Museum for the first display of paintings. This was the first glimmer of life at the embryonic Metropolitan Museum with a show in the former dancing master's now empty house of some 174 pictures from the collection of William T. Blodgett, which brought many art-loving New Yorkers to the house. The Metropolitan Museum's lease would expire and the Dodsworths would return to the house with its elaborate dance room until 1879 before the Academy moved south.

Creeping Northward

Across 54th Street on the north corner, William Rockefeller built a house in 1876 and about eight years later, his brother John acquired Arabella Worsham's house just west on 54th Street. William Rockefeller, often described in the day as the "nice" Rockefeller, commissioned a full new house from Stephen Decatur Hatch (the Buildings Department filing listed the cost to be $75,000), a prominent architect perhaps better known for his commercial work. Hatch was building a set of three brownstones on the corner of 53rd Street at the time for F. Amidon, which might have been a point of intersection. Rockefeller would stay in the house for the rest of his life, expanding to 10 East 54th Street in the early 20th century.[2]

These blocks would also become home to several Jewish bankers and attorneys. The prominent lawyer Samuel Untermeyer purchased one of two high-stooped sets of brownstones from H. J. Brooks that had been built mid-block between 55th and 56th Streets, along with an identical brownstone for C. Brooks (they were probably brothers). These houses were built early in 1866 before the neighborhood emerged as "smart." Untermeyer bought the existing house in the now fashionable area. Some of the most successful German Jewish men bought existing houses in the best streets as there was less that could be done to keep an unwanted new neighbor out. Society was willing to work with the German Jewish bankers and lawyers but reluctant to live near them.

Close by at 836 Fifth was Isidor Wormser, race car enthusiast, and a member of the Guggenheim family who rented a unit in the Mary Mason Jones row. Benjamin Altman leased the Gurnee house on 51st Street. Joseph Seligman (1819–88) landed on 56th Street just west of Fifth Avenue and became a banker and prominent funder of Civil War bonds. At the end of the century Adolph Lewisohn, banker, copper mine owner and philanthropist appeared, as did Arthur Lehman, banker and art collector at 31 West 56th Street. Although possibly in business together, German Jewish men were excluded from the top of New York society, where social integration was slow. Wishing to live on Fifth Avenue would involve purchasing an existing house, perhaps in a slightly "worn" area, or beating the rush by building uptown before others, and building in the middle of the block. In London, where Jewish German and South African industrialists waged campaigns for acceptance, they fared a bit better with Edward's court, much to the dislike of the green-eyed Minnie Stevens, daughter of Marietta Stevens and now Lady Paget, who complained of Edward's acceptance of the Jewish wealthy into his court.

COLLIS P. HUNTINGTON HOUSE

Soon after Collis P. Huntington married Arabella Worsham, he commissioned Vanderbilt's architect, G. B. Post, to build a massive granite house for himself and young Archer. The house was built for permanence. As typical for Fifth Avenue, it went down in less than two generations. Perhaps G. B. Post was more important as a skyscraper designer than a residential architect.

Upon the transfer of their house to Rockefeller, Arabella Worsham and Collis P. Huntington commissioned George B. Post, late of Cornelius Vanderbilt house fame, to build a huge and heavy mansion on the southeast corner of 57th Street—perhaps Post's finest work was not in the residential vein. The house, with its multiple mixed architectural signals, was much like George B. Post's tower for Pulitzer's World newspaper, one of New York City's first skyscrapers, which was distinguished by its dome, inspired by St Paul's Cathedral—a stew of far too many forms not blended well together. The five-story granite house that faced 162 feet east on 57th Street was a leaden announcement of Huntington's arrival in New York society. Indeed, tales were told about Huntington promising to pay Ward McAllister to get him invitations to events, but McAllister was not able to oblige.

After Huntington's death in 1900, Arabella spent time in Pasadena, California, where she helped create the Huntington Museum and Library. Collis Huntington did present the Metropolitan Museum with some great paintings (the 57th Street house, perhaps the only failure of Arabella's career as patron of the arts, had very elaborate interiors. All the major decorators of the day contributed to the rooms).[3] The house would be replaced by a "taxpayer," a building whose only function was to secure the property taxes on the site for a decade, then the current Tiffany store after World War II.

In the early years of the 1870s the western corner of 57th Street was developed just opposite Mary Mason Jones's block. Not very long after Mrs. Jones settled in, J. B. Snook built a house for William A. Bigelow. A rather expensive house at $85,000 in 1871 dollars, it was joined by two speculative builder efforts on the block. When Cornelius Vanderbilt decided he wanted his house there he bought out the first three houses and demolished the seven-year-old brownstones to accommodate his first house.

EAST SIDE OF FIFTH AVENUE FROM 57TH TO 56TH STREETS

Speculative built "twin houses" to be rented out by the Vanderbilts to protect their houses across the street from a commercial invasion.

STEVENS/WHITNEY
HOUSE ON THE
SOUTHEAST CORNER
OF FIFTH AVENUE AND
57TH STREET

High Victorian Style

On the southern corner Adele, the widow of the politician Frederick Stevens, built a big house with a 57th Street entry at 2 West 57th Street. Mrs. Stevens built a very interesting break from the brownstone with a late version of High Victorian style house designed by G. E. Harney—the High Victorian domestic mode was little used in a city of spec-built houses. The details of the house involved the use of multiple materials. Mrs. Stevens, who was having Harney build a commercial building at Wall Street at the same time, spent some $150,000 on the house, making it a rare costly house commissioned in the economic downturn of the mid 1870s. It might have been the first New York City house to have interior fittings imported from European rooms, soon to be a commonplace practice. Adele Stevens was one of the first to recognize the European aristocracy as an asset to New York's pressurized social scene. The American attachment to the edges of the aristocracy would grow dramatically in the last quarter of the 19th century and fitting houses with real pieces of sold-off furniture and fittings from the nobility would increase as more members of New York's high society spent time abroad. Mrs.

Stevens's house had a large ballroom and a dedicated art gallery (three drawings for the interiors seem to have been donated to The Metropolitan Museum by John R. Lamantia in 1970).[4] The widow Stevens herself then met a French nobleman and packed up to move to France, putting up the house for sale.

William Collins Whitney, who hailed from Massachusetts, traced his family line going back to the earliest settlers. Son of the Collector of the Port of Boston, Whitney had a dignified upbringing but modest family wealth. He attended Yale in the Civil War years, where he met the businessman Oliver Payne of Ohio and banker Charles T. Barney of Cleveland and New York. Whitney married Payne's sister, Flora, and Barney married Whitney's sister, Lily. The Yale trio became close friends and moved in a social circle that embraced the young Stanford White. Soon after their marriage, Whitney and Flora moved to Washington, D.C., where he was appointed Secretary of the Navy during President Cleveland's first term. Washington was a dull place in those days, but Whitney and Flora were a charming, wealthy couple, and created great entertainments. When Whitney saw the limited potential of his rise in D.C., he headed back to New York.

William C. Whitney with his wife Flora accepted a lavish gift from her brother, Oliver Payne, now immensely wealthy after his oil interests had been acquired by John D. Rockefeller's Standard Oil company, and bought the Stevens house, which became the Whitney home for two decades. Oliver Payne, a bachelor, felt his beloved sister and her husband deserved a big house to launch a New York career, and lavished gifts upon Flora. Some years later, the family would split. Payne and Whitney had been room-mates at Yale; by 1900, they were mortal enemies.

Rather like the back gardens in The Row in the early years of the 19th century, marriages were made in the siloed social set. Indeed, an across-the-street marriage would occur when a Whitney son married a Vanderbilt daughter named Gertrude. She became a sculptor and art patron and was the creator of the Whitney Museum. However, as with so many similar mutually advantageous social matches, the marriage was not a happy one. Neighborhood, church, and dancing classes allowed for the next generation to emerge as the parents wished but did not assure a pleasant life after the wedding.

Finishing off the neighborhood was another house designed by the architect George B. Post, who was well connected socially as well as in business circles through his brother, an important figure in the New

York Produce Exchange. His design of a house for W. J. Hutchinson in 1880 at 4 West 58th Street, played into the style of the Cornelius Vanderbilt house, then in construction a half block away. When the second half of the Cornelius Vanderbilt house was completed a decade later, next door, Hutchinson's wife had just sold their house to the businessman Charles Crocker of San Francisco, who gave it to his daughter as a wedding gift. Hattie Crocker married the lawyer and businessman Charles B. Alexander. Later the Alexanders would buy the Fisk house at 6 West 58th Street and expand their house to the west. The resemblance of the Hutchinson/Alexander house to the Cornelius Vanderbilt house cannot be ignored and, to the casual observer, the two houses appeared rather as one. Later events in the Alexander house included marriages of Roosevelts, Aldrichs, and Sheldon Whitehouse, grandfather of a current United States Senator.

Roosevelt Row

Just around the corner from Adele Stevens and, later, the Whitneys, were the Roosevelt brothers, in a triple set of houses "of principled design." The Roosevelt family, of old Dutch stock, owned very

successful businesses, especially a plate glass firm that provided the glazing for many of the new buildings going up in the city and region. In the mid-century the Roosevelts had lived close to each other around Union Square and 20th Street, in new brownstones built in the repetitive style of the day. The Roosevelt interiors were also typical of the day—nothing was very special or splendid and the emphasis was on family.[5]

Rare image of the Roosevelt family houses. Paget-Whitney wedding at the Stevens/Whitney House, on the southeast corner of Fifth Avenue and 57th Street, with a view of the Roosevelt houses at 4, 6, and 8 57th Street.

But New York was changing. By 1870 commerce was reaching to the area above Union Square, and Lord & Taylor was building a new retail emporium just a half block from the house of Theodore Roosevelt Sr., the father of the future President. When the patriarch of the family, Cornelius Van Schaak Roosevelt died in his house in Union Square, Theodore Sr. inherited a substantial sum. The approaching store, loss of his father, and a comfortable fortune inspired Theodore and his brother to move uptown to the center of fashionable New York. As always, the neighborhood where they lived had reached its twenty-year life span. They had to leave.

The Roosevelt brothers called upon Russell Sturgis, an abolitionist and educator, to build their new houses in the fashionable part of the city. Theodore Roosevelt, Sr. (1831–78), a high-minded leader in the New York world of social causes, hired Sturgis, from principle, not familiarity with Fifth Avenue houses. The elder Roosevelt moved to the new blocks of society, but he had his architect and interior artists create a house that stood for Roosevelt's values, not the wealth his family gained in their plate glass business. Roosevelt stood with one foot in the wealthy Knickerbocker enclave, but apart from it in the statement his house made.

The Roosevelt interiors were distinct from the norm.

Theodore Roosevelt was not a typical Dutch Patroon descendant of his day. Unlike the other houses of this era and location, the decorative work was given to Frank Furness, the Philadelphia architect, and his furniture maker, Daniel Pabst, who created the parlor floor and staircase at great expense. They did no other work on a house in New York City. Furness's father was a leader in the abolition movement and clearly Roosevelt was making a statement about his core value in a location where few others would have such views. He and his family were very consciously driven to do good works and he was active in many charities, personally as well as financially, yet he did like to be a part of the social scene where few others had any true commitment to good causes. As a result, the Roosevelts attended the events of the day but also struck a big position on many good causes. The new houses being built on 57th Street were designed by Russell Sturgis, a man known for his abolitionist stance and high-minded behavior, who was

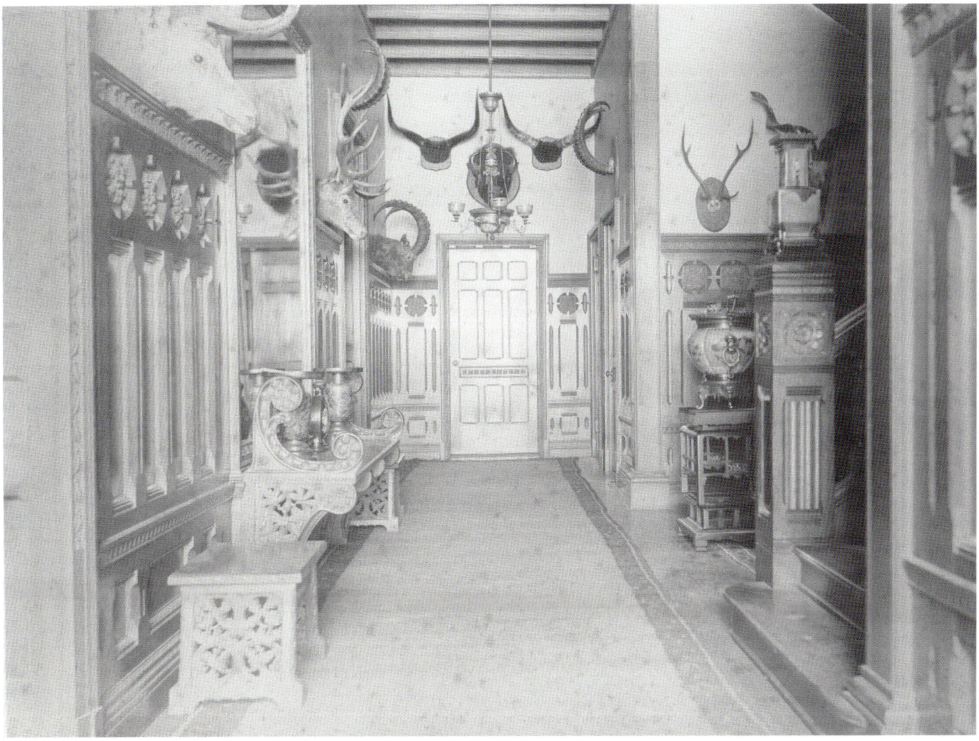

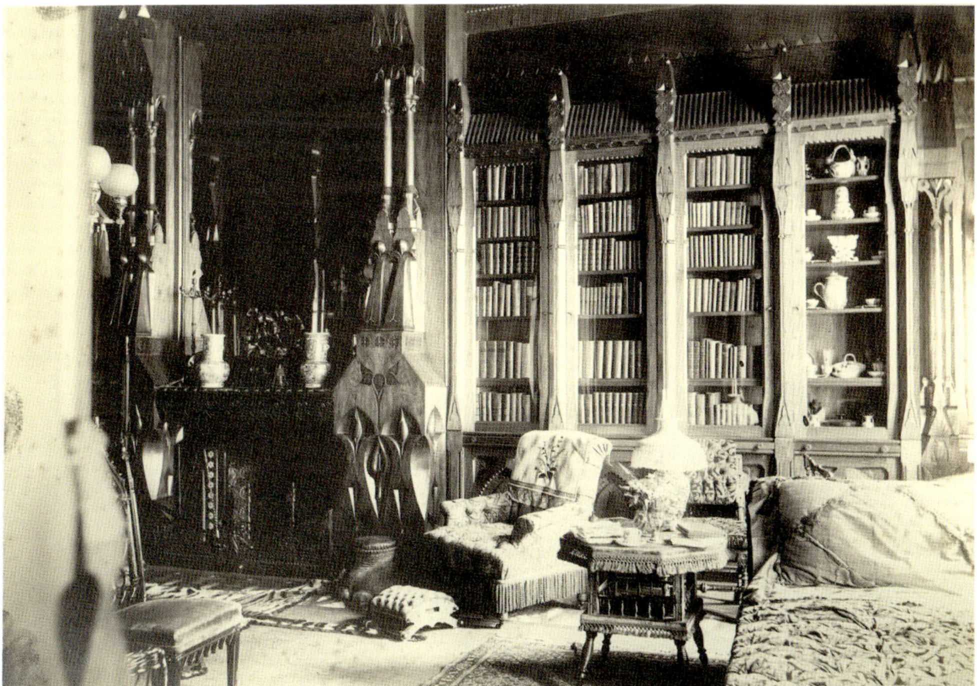

not a builder of the other houses on Fifth Avenue. The Roosevelts joined the society march but their house stood out as different, as did their behavior. Even the interior, plain and modest, as had been decreed by Theodore Roosevelt's mother-in-law some two decades earlier, was now entirely new and totally different from any other house in the neighborhood. The Roosevelts would charge Frank Furness and Daniel Pabst to make substantial furnishings for their houses in the high-minded images of the day (some of the furniture is in the country house of Theodore Roosevelt in Oyster Bay Cove, New York. The house, Sagamore Hill, is open to the public). The Roosevelts could survey all the important events in New York society from their house; the young Theodore Roosevelt remarked that the family could see everything that happened on this grand boulevard from the viewpoint of their house.[6]

The houses, nos. 4, 6, and 8 West 57th Street, were part of a block of wildly clashing styles on this major cross street. 57th Street was a rather remarkable block, occupied by Jewish families as well as patricians. Adolph Lewisohn, the civic minded banker, lived across the street at 9 West 57th Street in a house designed by Arnold Brunner—there was a Blashfield mural painted over the fireplace *c.* 1909.[7]

The grand houses of the 50s, built at the end of the 19th century, would face an even shorter life span than was typical of the day. The combination of the Plaza hotels, which we will explore in the next chapter, and the office buildings that appeared a decade later just east of Fifth Avenue, spelt their doom and the area became commercial very quickly.

CHAPTER 13
PLAZA PLAYERS

"Joseph M. Wells was one of the most learned young men in literature and art whom I have ever met, and a most original thinker."

William R. Mead, Partner, McKim, Mead & White

THE 1858 PLAN FOR "GREENSWARD" created a cut in the grid at 58th Street, which came to be known as the Plaza. This patch of land on the western side of Fifth Avenue just below what is now Central Park was once a beloved skating spot for mid-century New Yorkers, attracting younger ones outfitted boldly to skate and meet on freezing winter's days. On the western edge of 58th to 59th Streets would rise a Victorian styled apartment house constructed to be part of an early cooperative scheme, just as the Cornelius Vanderbilt and Hutchinson houses were being built. The combination of these two very grand houses, close by the new Central Park, and this empty indention of the Plaza from the Avenue, made this new apartment building seem alluring. A builder, a rather unsavory developer, Jared Bradley Flagg, hoped that a multiple-dwelling building close by the Park would be profitable and aimed to recover his building costs quickly by selling, not renting, the units. But Flagg's reputation and the perception of high prices felled the venture.[1]

Flagg was forced to sell the property for $850,000, the same price he had originally paid for it, to retailer John Charles Anderson who then surprisingly died in Paris in 1881. Anderson was himself a character with a possible murder in his history. He was a tobacconist who opened a shop on lower Broadway and hired a beautiful shop assistant—indeed, Anderson was thought to have come up with the innovative idea of having pretty women as shop workers. When Anderson's very own shop assistant, Mary Rogers, was found

Overleaf:
Plaza Hotel by McKim Mead & White

THE P. NEWMANN CO.

murdered, he was suspected of the crime, but it was noted that the politicians in Tammany Hall concealed the relevant witness statement Anderson wrote about the murder of his shop girl and Anderson was not publicly accused. Anderson's heirs, including a married daughter, Laura Anderson Appleton, a contentious woman who may well have owned properties in blocks just west of Fifth Avenue which figure in the land acquisition stories of the new club house buildings, were all caught up in the drama, a sleazy story that made Anderson notorious.

Apartment Speculators

The empty space at 58th Street, a plaza, would not be landscaped or home to fine public sculpture for a decade but was still an appropriate setting to display a new apartment house.[2] When the heirs of the Anderson estate wanted to develop the site, they turned to George W. Da Cuhna, a Portuguese-born architect. He was a pioneering early apartment house developer and architect, who had thought Gramercy Park looked appropriate for an apartment building rather than brownstones. Da Cuhna built the Gramercy Flats building in 1880 (extant, amazingly, on the southeast corner of Gramercy Park). In this boiling mélange of builders, developers, and varied financial backers, the property at 58th to 59th Streets highlights the confusion. It was a festival of newcomers to the world of speculative building, all trying to make a quick fortune with an opportune location just west of Fifth Avenue, at a time when there was no big development money and the apartment house concept was only just becoming established.

At the Anderson site, however, there was an almost immediate clash with Da Cunha, who was replaced by the German-American architect Carl Pfeiffer. Pfeiffer found the project unsavory and also fled the building with a statement to the real estate newspaper denying his part in the design of the building. The Anderson estate gave the apartment house development over to John C. Pfyfe and James Campbell, small-scale contractors in the city who had just marched into the apartment house building market. They advanced $489,000 of their own money and borrowed $790,000 from The New York Life Insurance Company, one of the first big investors in apartment blocks, to finance the acquisition. Apartment building was a new concept as Pfyfe and Campbell strove to build at the Plaza. They likely used Pfeiffer's lower floor design, then capped it with a very heavy, tall, ugly mansard roof. By 1888, the money had run out. Pfyfe & Campbell had failed, and New York Life took over as holder of the second mortgage—at this time mortgages were now entering the corporate portfolio, replacing investments from well-off individuals.

Fine Hotels

The insurance company put up the money to have McKim, Mead & White work over the ungainly building. McKim, Mead & White had a fine working relationship with New York Life, having built a number of office buildings and investment properties for them. New York Life had asked the young firm of architects to design headquarters and office buildings for them in the Midwest and liked their work, including that of the young chief designer, Joseph Morrill Wells, who would work on the interiors of what was now the Plaza Hotel. McKim, Mead & White removed the absurd mansard, added some terracotta detail to the exterior, and did up the interiors. New York Life had changed the purpose to that of a fine hotel—the Plaza Hotel. Indeed, there was local demand for a hotel, which the new building fulfilled.

The Plaza interiors were the masterpiece of the young Joseph M. Wells, chief designer of the firm. Wells made a glamorous dining room topped by a glass dome with stained glass panels, views to the park, and a mosaic floor with a central lion as the hotel's symbol in the floor, while commissioning much fine mahogany woodwork. But Wells was pushing himself too hard and New York Life was rushing the job and trying to keep expenses down. There was no heat in the building and Wells, who was running around guiding the workmen in the cold, caught pneumonia, which killed him a few weeks later.[3]

The Hotel opened on October 1, 1890, as one of the city's more important venues. The new Waldorf Astoria would clearly be the more glamorous establishment in a few years, but the Plaza did attract many to its 400 rooms. However, just fifteen years later, New York Life sold the hotel to a professional hotelier, who hired Henry Janeway Hardenbergh to replace the building. Hardenbergh, who began his career as a designer of apartment buildings in the late 1870s, was now a specialist architect of Edwardian hotels. He was called in to create the seventeen-story hotel that replaced the old Plaza in two years and that still stands today.

While the Plaza Hotel was as far north as Central Park, the Supreme Court Judge P. Henry Dugro bought most of the block across the street on the East Side of Fifth Avenue. He commissioned the architect R.S. Townsend to build the Savoy Hotel at the Plaza which opened in 1892. Dugro could not get the land south of his building, on which were the local 'saloons' for the neighborhood workers and cab men. Dugro did the hotel up to his best fantasies, creating a rather garishly opulent set of guest spaces. The hotel would attract long-term guests up to its demolition in 1927 for a bigger hotel with the same name.

Collateral Development

In 1902, as Civil War heroes were dying off, the great American sculptor, Augustus Saint-Gaudens, was asked to immortalize Union General William Tecumseh Sherman in gilded bronze and the great equestrian work sits on a base by Charles Follen McKim. Both McKim and Saint-Gaudens came from families immersed in the Union cause. Across the Avenue from the Sherman monument the area around the Plaza would attract apartment and hotel builders. The beginning of the development on the East Side would start with Alfred Zucker, who had immigrated to the United States in 1883 from Silesia. He established himself first as a row house designer in the area of Harlem known as the Harlem Flats, then as a master of the loft building on lower Fifth Avenue. In 1895, on land he leased from Mrs. Eldridge Gerry, whose house was just up the street (this was part of her family's Livingston property which we will meet in the next chapter). He built a commercial building with apartments named for his hometown, Bolkenhain, in Prussia, with two apartments per floor in a six-story building. James J. Hill and Isaac Guggenheim were tenants, paying some $8,000 annually. The building would be demolished in 1926 for the second Savoy Plaza hotel by the later firm of McKim, Mead & White, also now abolished.[4] Residential hotels and apartment buildings would soon follow at this plaza.

The area around the Plaza remained active with transient and residential hotel guests through the 1950s. Often, the widows of important families moved into the hotels around the Plaza for their later years: for example, the matriarch of the Straus family, who owned Macy's department store, lived in the penthouse at the Hardenbergh Plaza for her final years. The penthouse was the fictional home of the character, Eloise, from Kay Thompson's book of the same name, published in 1969. The Plaza was also the location for the debutante ball, continuing to host it even as the concept of the event faded out in the 1960s. Years later after the Trump organization briefly owned the property, the movie *Home Alone* was shot there.

As large new apartment buildings began to take over this northern midtown area, in the 20th century, the distinctive character of the neighborhood was lost. The glamorous hotels of the turn of the century, with their wealthy guests, balls, chauffeur driven cars, exotic restaurants and cocktail bars, no longer dominated the neighborhood. Grand retail and jewelry emporia clung to the the plaza location. Elegant services gave way to modern, well-serviced apartments with views of the park and the corporate offices of General Motors and Apple.

CHAPTER 14

FIFTH AVENUE GOES TO HALF

"The difficult immediately, the impossible takes a few minutes longer."

Waldorf Astoria Hotel motto

As the City surged northward, all streets in Manhattan, and, perhaps, especially Fifth Avenue, must have looked like a set of teeth after a boxing match. Empty lots sat among the finished houses and some plots were tied up in disputes. Some earlier, less elaborate houses were pulled down to be replaced with new residences and others were re-fronted.[1] As Fifth Avenue continued to extend north of the Plaza, developers and plot purchasers confronted a newly finished Central Park. While the Park provided an optimal view for those houses on the East Side of Fifth Avenue, the number of house plots available declined to half. There were now no plots on what would become the west side of Fifth Avenue for the rest of this tale. The park, an obstacle as well as an enrichment, did not impede the northward push. The typically sized plots rocketed in price in the early 1870s, only to collapse in the economic downturn of 1873. By the end of the decade, the prices would rise again and continue to do so for two generations.

New York's new Central Park had been created in the middle years of the 19th century. The picturesque rolling landscape, all man-made, promised a verdant view for those contemplating the purchase of house building plots on the other side of the Avenue. At the end of the Civil War, the traditional New York City plot was 25 feet across and 100 feet deep. The plots were reasonably priced in 1865 when the Park was not yet finished. Runyon W. Martin bought one of the plots and called upon Jacob Wrey Mould, the English-trained architect and

Runyon W. Martin Jr. House, 816 Fifth Avenue between 62nd and 63rd Streets

The first, if modest, house on Fifth Avenue across from the new Central Park. The High Victorian Gothic design was the work of Central Park's structures architect, Jacob Wrey Mould. The house was mid-block. The surrounding buildings are well to the south, displaying how empty the site was in the 1860s.

opera expert, to design the first house across from the park and Mould created a house in his High Victorian Gothic style. Martin would have known Mould, as he was a member of All Soul's Unitarian Church, which Mould designed when he arrived in New York. Martin was also a member of the Central Park Commission, so he would have known Mould's wonderful work there on the monuments of the park. Martin had selected a mid-block site for his house that was likely the least costly plot, but the location proved unfortunate. The narrow house with its polychromatic façade, was a very rare example of strident High Victorian style of the mid-century, and looked striking in that empty setting. However, a strong windstorm proved the isolated brick house vulnerable and virtually destroyed the lonely structure.

Filling the Gaps

There was a commercial interlude at the base of the new park. A scattering of modest structures and businesses lined the east side of Fifth Avenue between 59th and 60th Streets; this block hosted a liquor saloon, stable with office—all wooden shanties with Park & Tilford's 1883 Grocery Store six stories tall, a plumber and gas fitter, a

FIFTH AVENUE FROM
62ND TO 63RD STREETS

*Stylistic variation begins
in earnest as houses are
built across from the
park.*

flower store, tailor, and liquor saloon. The next block at 60th and 61st
Streets had a one-story shanty, used as a soda-water and cigar store,
while the balance of the block was vacant. The next block stretched
above 61st Street and had seven vacant plots including the new Jabez
Bostwick house.

From 63rd to 64th Streets was the Progress Club on the northeast
corner and a saloon shanty on the southeast corner of 64th Street.
The rest was vacant—five empty lots on the 64th Street block, six on
the next block. All the remaining blocks had vacant plots beside the
built sites up to the Lenox Library, which was a full block at 70th
Street, and the entire block to its north was empty. The northeast
corner of 72nd Street was a waiting room for the Fifth Avenue Stage
Lines, a soda water and cigar store and the rest of the block of seven
lots was empty. 75th through 76th Streets were totally empty, while
76th to 77th Streets had a saloon on the northeast corner, and the
rest of the block was vacant. 78th through 79th Streets had only the
Cook house, while 79th through 80th Streets had the Brokaw house
property and two lots were empty. On the next block, Louis Stern,

one of the brothers who built a small store into a major department store, bought a plot between 80th and 81st Street and had built a house in the center of the block surrounded by seven empty lots. This building in the center of an empty block suited Jewish men who perhaps wanted the cachet of the address, but not the animosity of neighbors. Not a single block was fully developed. 87th through 88th Streets were entirely empty, and the block above had only a wooden frame house. The Fifth Avenue Riding Academy took part of the block from 90th to 91st Streets before Carnegie bought it for his house a few years later. The vision we have of cohesive blocks would not happen until the early 20th century.

73RD STREET, FIFTH AVENUE

Empty blocks with wooden barricades, Fifth Avenue. Rather like a human with poor dental care, there were solids and voids of the built and not yet constructed. The voids were often locations for wooden fences richly adorned in advertising signage.

Edith Wharton detested the chocolate-colored houses of New York.

The Gerry House

The Mason Estate owned the plots on Fifth Avenue directly above 58th Street. When a portion of the legally disputed over the Mason Estate was settled in 1891, the empty lots were sold to J. J. Astor for the double house he would build with his mother, Caroline Schermerhorn Astor. As the block of lots was released, the other lots would become the Metropolitan Club. E. T. Gerry took the top six lots for his future R. M. Hunt-designed house.

Louisa Livingston Gerry was a descendant of the patrician Livingstons, who married in 1867 to another descendant of an 18th-century family, Elbridge T. Gerry. Gerry's ancestors had a notable history from signing the Declaration of Independence to this day,[2] while Gerry himself founded two groups that fought against cruelty to animals and children. As his mother was part of the Goelet family, there was enormous wealth in the newly-grown city where the once humble Goelet properties were now highly valued.

The couple, educated, genteel, and determined to be known for high-minded causes, asked R.M. Hunt to build a house on a plot at the southeast corner of 61st Street, a large lot at 100 by 100 and 40 feet, which was selected for a house paid for by his wife, Louisa Livingston Gerry, in 1892. Originally it was expected to cost only $200,000, but clearly the house cost greatly increased as Mr. Gerry required a library for his books. Gerry asked for the then-unheard-of participation in the design of the kitchen and other rooms by soliciting suggestions from the staff. The Gerrys created a house that kept them on the same architectural page as the Vanderbilts but allowed them the time to live a more useful life, rising above the ephemeral issues of the day. Rather than raid Europe for furnishings, the Gerrys asked furniture importers and makers, Carlhian & Beaumetz, to create fine replicas based on museum pieces in French collections (one suspects there may be more to this story—likely the Carlhian pieces were cheaper and sturdier). The house, with its thoughtful fittings, was demolished for a hotel 32 years after it was built, soon after Gerry's death. The blocks would remain a major district for hotels for the next century.[3]

Hamersley Houses

As we know, several old-time New York City families purchased farmland miles above the city in the early 19th century, thinking to the distant future. The most notable accumulator of these odd parcels of land was the original J. J. Astor. Following his lead, perhaps, were the Goelets and the Hamersleys, Livingstons, Enos, Kemps, and Bonners. We know the old Thomas Buchanan farm was bought by John Mason (1773–1839) in the 1820s. Mason built a wooden house on the property at what would have been 55th Street and Madison Avenue but ignored the rest of the property for the remainder of his life. The Mason descendants owned property in the center of Manhattan in what would become the streets of the 50s. We have seen how the rapid growth of the urban fabric surprised the Astor and Goelet heirs.

The Hamersleys found themselves rich from a farm purchased only a half century earlier, owning property on a street named for them near Laight Street in lower Manhattan (the street was subsequently de-mapped). The lower Manhattan properties were home to Mary Mason Jones, her sister, Rebecca Colford Jones, and perhaps Edith

Jones (her father was part of the Mason inheritance of property). Hamersley Street is long gone, but their uptown farm came into development after the Civil War. Colonel James W. Hamersley's heir was the sickly Louis Carré Hamersley, whose life was enhanced by the new fortune. Wan, but lucky, in 1882 he married the beautiful Lily Price, a young woman from Troy, New York, of incomparable appearance, ever dressed in white. While Lily was not from an elevated social or financial background, she did fascinate her suitors. She and Louis lived at 257 Fifth Avenue in a brownstone exactly like 255 next door, which belonged to Louis Hamersley's uncle and his family. Lily felt herself equipped and ready to enter New York society aided by Louis's fortune, and the couple planned a married life that departed from 28th Street for a plot on 55th Street and Fifth Avenue on the Mason properties. Lily and Louis hired John B. Snook to build their new house—perhaps Snook was the architect of the 28th Street brownstone row (built about 1860, their house is too early for records), which could explain their attachment to the by now out-of-date architect. Indeed, the brownstone row between 28th and 29th Streets might well also have been part of the Mason downtown lands. It would seem Louis and Lily were unable to have children, as there is evidence that Lily consulted a physician with a specialty in women's health issues. In 1883, Louis Hamersley fell ill and died young (his death occurred shortly after that of his father), and a long legal battle ensued. Lily inherited the value of the income on the estate, but a Hamersley male heir would receive the properties, and this happened some twenty years later when a cousin had a male baby in Newport, Rhode Island. The house at 257 Fifth Avenue was leased to Judge Smith, soon-to-be father-in-law to Stanford White. Judge Smith's wife was a Clinch—a family of John Mason's era who also owned property in lower Manhattan.

Lily Hamersley, after the death of her first husband may have decided to live on, or at least keep a place, in New York, and on Hamersley land at the northeast corner of 60th Street she had A. B. Ogden build an inexpensive house in 1886. The house was likely pulled down shortly after, when it became certain that Lily was to stay on in England, and the Metropolitan Club would soon replace the house (Lily Price was the property owner when the club was built). E. T. Gerry was next door with his Livingston wife.

This was the era when impoverished European aristocrats were attempting to maintain large properties despite decreasing property revenues and were compelled to cross the Atlantic in search of a wealthy bride. One of the leaders of the pack was the disgraced

800 FIFTH AVENUE

The houses of the years after the Civil War were built in many styles. The quality of the design ranged from as exuberant as the Bostwick House with a heavy entrance cut on French detail and mansard roofs to the usual brownstone. The design by the early speculative builders was often quite awkward. The houses would become more "digested" as the decade progressed. Jabez Abel Bostwick House and later houses for two children. D. & J. Jardine architects.

and divorced 8th Duke of Marlborough (George Charles Spencer-Churchill), who had been named in a case of marital infidelity and was outside the fashionable circuit. Lily passed muster and sailed for England where she became his second wife in 1888. He was in desperate need of money for the repairs and restoration of his home Blenheim, and Lily's wealth looked like the perfect solution, but she was not foolish and, although Blenheim did get a new roof, some winter heating, and a grand organ from her generosity, she never deeded over her worth to her husband, as was the expected custom.

Lily married a third time, to Lord William Beresford. All three of her husbands died young. Lily died in 1909 having lived in Deepdene (Thomas Hope's exquisite house, but much changed), a property she ran near Dorking, Surrey. The marriage of her stepson, the 9th Duke of Marlborough (known as Sunny to his family), was partially the work of Lily, who had attempted to lure Sunny to Gertrude Vanderbilt. Instead, Sunny married Gertrude's unwilling cousin, Consuelo.

Lily's now nearly eight-million-dollar estate returned to New York to the son of James Hooker Hamersley, Louis Gordon Hamersley. James Hooker Hamersley married and had a brownstone remodeled, transforming the old house into a white granite palace, 1030 Fifth Avenue, on the northeast corner of 84th Street, which was completed in 1897. The architect was William B. Tuthill of Carnegie Hall fame. Hamersley's son, heir to the Hamersley fortune, lived on in the house until 1923, when he asked James Carpenter, the architect who was overturning the height restrictions on Fifth Avenue along with the sumptuous apartment designer, Rosario Candela, to replace the house with a magnificent apartment house. Hamersley installed himself atop it with a 23-room penthouse.[4]

Fanciful Turrets

Just across 61st Street was a group of houses built for Jabez Abel Bostwick and his children. Bostwick came from an ordinary background but grew wealthy when he joined the oil business and worked with Rockefeller. On the corner in 1877, Bostwick had the Jardines build a rather fanciful turreted house for New York City, then coming out of the building slump of 1873, which was costly at $100,000. After Bostwick's children grew up, Bostwick brought back the Jardines to build two similar row houses next door in 1889, but utilizing different materials, for a modest $35,000 each.

The Bostwick house was replaced in the 1920s by Mrs. Rockefeller Dodge, who had R. S. Shapter build a house she would rarely use.

When the house was up for sale, there were plans for it to be replaced by an apartment building by J. E. R. Carpenter, who would become "Mr. Apartment House" on Fifth Avenue. The proposal for a 12-story building was stopped by the Fifth Avenue Association height regulation of 75 feet.[5] The issue of the height regulation made it to the Supreme Court in 1922, when Mrs. Dodge solved this particular case by purchasing the property, and building a house, rather than allowing an apartment house on the site.

Proceeding northward, we pass the two Roosevelt family houses to the southeast corner of 62nd Street for the Josephine Schmid house of 1894 by Hunt. Josephine Schmid was the widow of a very successful brewer, one of several beer company magnates who moved into wealthy neighborhoods in the mid-century. Most stayed in their social

JOSEPHINE SCHMID
HOUSE, ON THE
SOUTHEAST CORNER
OF FIFTH AVENUE AND
62ND STREET

*R. M. Hunt's Schmid
House commands the
block in its imitations of
Alva Vanderbilt's home.*

circle, but once a widow, Josephine Schmid wanted to move up from the family house just east of Fifth Avenue. She started buying land after taking advantage of the inheritance her surviving daughter had received. Josephine Schmid spent $92,599 on that corner plot, calling in the king of Gilded Age architects, Hunt, for an Alva-influenced château, even if its main façade went east on the street, sacrificing the Fifth Avenue entrance to a door on the long side of the house. The corner turret was a chance for a distinctive and recognizable identity on Fifth Avenue. The Hunt château was filled with furnishings likely seen by Josephine in newspaper accounts that featured all the "treasures" within society houses.

By 1908, her daughter had come to the realization that her very own mother had cheated her out of her full inheritance, so she sued, and a settlement was reached. In 1909, Josephine traveled to Europe, meeting and marrying Don Giovanni del Drago. Although Josephine insisted that she was now Princess Del Drago, her hubris was plain to see—her new husband was the fourth son of a living man with that title. The Gilded Age socialite Mamie Fish (Mrs. Hamilton Fish), the woman who turned the newspapers away from reporting every detail of the lives of the wealthy towards every detail of the lives of celebrities, had some fun with Josephine's princess pretensions. The brewer's wife had never been accepted, even with her new "title." Mamie Fish held a party announcing a guest at the party to be a visiting European prince from Corsica, but the Prince, named as del Drago, turned out to be a monkey dressed in full formal clothing. The obvious insult sent the del Dragos back to Europe and the house would be demolished soon thereafter for the current Knickerbocker Club.[6]

From 62nd to 65th Street

Continuing northward were brownstones of an early date by the Jardines (1869, Thomas Keech speculative developer), re-fronted in the 1890s, and two more row houses by Samuel Adams Warner also of 1870.[7] This run of early speculative houses was undoubtedly due to the construction of the Runyon W. Martin house by Mould, which had been so damaged in the storm. The Martin house would be re-fronted by Robert Henderson Robertson, a well-connected society architect, and became home to Elbridge T. Gerry's son, Robert Livingston Gerry. A racehorse enthusiast, he went on to build a stable down 62nd Street from the design of Alfred Zucker, the German polytechnic-trained architect who would build the Progress Club up the street and had built the early apartment house we passed earlier named the Bolkenhain, on the East Side of Fifth Avenue opposite the Grand Army Plaza.

Finally, protecting the exposed Martin house, a tad late after the storm did its damage on the north side, came a house created for Charles Tracy Barney in 1883, again by Robert Henderson Robertson. The rather small corner house with its two square lozenges above the second story must have had a meaning; one seems to be a lion head (perhaps symbolizing his support for the Zoological Society of New York), the other, possibly a cross. This is indeed odd as Barney also had a new house on West 55th Street by McKim, Mead & White, which had just been finished. Barney also had a studio beyond the house on 55th Street for artists, which he subsidized. Was this house part of a Barney good will effort? Barney is much caught up in the Gilded Era as, among other positions, he was president of the Knickerbocker Trust Bank, which brought on the 1907 economic debacle. As we know, Barney was married to W. C. Whitney's sister, Lily, and was involved in many businesses and projects with his brother-in-law. Barney never resided on Fifth Avenue, moving to the family house on Park Avenue, a big house he would have elaborately renovated by McKim, Mead & White. Like his brother-in-law, Barney lived to the height of the era, but flew too close to the sun. Devastated by the Knickerbocker he committed suicide immediately after the bank failed.

Nestled in among the houses on the upper Avenue was the Progress Club, built in 1888 to host successful Jewish men who were rarely allowed in the upper tier clubs. The large new club house designed by Zucker, was almost square with 92 feet fronting on Fifth Avenue. The club, with the interior features of the new purpose-built club houses on and near Fifth Avenue, may have been separate, but it was surely equal.

Mrs Catherine Lorillard Kernochan, an heir to the Lorillard snuff and tobacco business, may be remembered as the originator of the remark to Mrs. Paran Stevens about the need to have a grandmother of respectable pedigree to be able to penetrate society. Just above the Progress Club, she built a new house designed by Henry F. Kilburn in 1894, who would also build the house next door for William V. Brokaw, who co-owned a successful children's clothing store with his brother. On the corner of 64th Street was the Edward J. Berwind house of 1893 by W. C. Mellon, which faces the side street.[8]

The block between 64th and 65th Streets was mainly speculative brownstones by the Jardines, built between 1870 and 1871. Isidor Wormser, a banker, who came from an Alsatian family and had settled first in Sacramento, bought the center house. Wormser participated in the Vanderbilt automobile races on Long Island with his Mercedes and was a member of Temple Emanu-El. He was related to the Seligmans through marriage. Wormser left the house as it was, perhaps preferring a low profile on these very social blocks. Just to his north, Sophia A. Sherman, wife of the businessman William Watts Sherman, tore down two brownstones for her double-wide house at the corner of 65th Street. The patrons of H. H. Richardson, now dead, the Watts Shermans hired William Russell to build their new house.[9]

The Astors Move North

The Astor houses of the second half of the 1850s at 33rd and 34th Streets on the corners of Fifth Avenue were solidly built to last— surely no one would imagine the city racing northward as quickly as it did. John Jacob Astor and his Charleston-born wife, Augusta, were carrying the mantle of the best of Knickerbocker society. Well-intentioned, charitable, and interested in culture, these Astors carried on the expected interests of the wealthy in the era. Friendly with Richard Morris Hunt and his family, these Astors lived ideal—but short—lives. They would be gone by the end of the century, leaving the house and the position of chief Astor to their son, who did not share the behavior of his parents, but instead departed for England and a future important life there.

Aunt Caroline, on the other corner, was a rather leaden bore, but she got on well with her in-laws. She was, by the time of their death, *The* Mrs. Astor, even if her husband was a second son. William Backhouse Astor, her yacht-centered partner, was a clever and well-educated youth and we know that, as his path and his bride's ways parted, he took to his boat, alcohol, and women. Caroline became the stone-faced queen of society in association with Ward McAllister. Would the pressures on their marriage have been different if W. B. Astor had not needed to escape? He would die rather young in Paris, leaving his fortune to his children and little to his widow. However, Schermerhorn properties were rapidly gaining value, so Caroline may have been almost as wealthy as the other landed families in the city, or as the more recently wealthy. Would Caroline have left her house if her nephew had not decided to build a hotel, the Waldorf, on his 33rd Street half of the block?

Both Caroline Astor and her house on 34th Street were the apogee of New York Society in the middle of the 19th century, but the shadow and bulk of the hotel would ultimately force Caroline to leave the house. Without her now-dead husband and the out of fashion and deceased McAllister, she chose to listen to her son. He convinced

his mother to speak with Alva's architect, R. M. Hunt, at dinner in Newport, and commission a giant house on Fifth Avenue at 65th Street. Although Alva had now outgrown her New York City social role, the choice of the architect and the French château style for a new double house must have made Alva laugh—she had had won the battle of 1883.

Caroline was aging, but she still enjoyed her position as society queen. The new house would enlarge her ballroom space three-fold, allowing her to host 1,200 guests. The new house on a 100 by 100-foot square lot would be a double dwelling for herself, her son and his family and meant that she would not need to spend her final years alone, except for her servants, in her old house. She would launch her son as successor to Astor family status and gave the prime position of importance in the new house to her son who, with his family, had the southern corner with windows all along the side street facing south. Mrs. Astor's nephew replaced his house with a large Edwardian hotel as he moved to England. The Waldorf Hotel loomed over the garden and the house of his aunt.

The Astor double house was completed quickly, bringing Mrs. Astor 30 blocks above her old neighborhood, now swarming with stores and guests in her nephew's hotel, the Waldorf, which cast a long shadow. Caroline Astor demolished her almost 40-year-old house to build the Astoria Hotel. The combined Waldorf-Astoria Hotel would set the tone for the grand Edwardian hotel in New York City, with its Peacock Alley, exotic reception rooms, a hotel restaurant that featured dishes created by a series of notable chefs. The restaurant, and indeed the hotel, bore the Astor imprint, making the dining room among the first acceptable places for society women to eat in a public place unaccompanied by a man.

There is something almost sad about the double house at 840 and 841 Fifth Avenue. It feels rather as if Caroline Astor had been vanquished by the new money and even her attempt at a new house was only keeping up. She was too old-fashioned a Knickerbocker to throw away money, and made a double house with principal rooms that were less grand than the rooms of the Vanderbilts, but could nevertheless be opened up for major parties. The French style Hunt used required less carving than that of Alva's house and Astor did not call in the grand French decorators as had become common. She brought her old furniture, now in need of renewal. Mrs. Astor's pictures, never well selected, formed the wallpaper on the gallery/ball room, but there was an air of defeat in the echoing big house. There were no rumors of gold bathroom fittings, and, in the end, no major balls. Within a decade in her new house, Caroline sank into dementia and likely suffered a series of small strokes. Attended by two loyal servants, Caroline retreated into holding evening parties but without any guests. Her imaginary dinners seemed to bring her era to an end.

Her husband had not been generous to Caroline, but, as we know, the family Schermerhorn properties had become surprisingly valuable. Still, when she died in 1908, and an inventory was made, her furnishings were rather dismissed as in bad condition, her tapestries were tattered and many of the pearls on her famous long chain were fake. The world of Mrs Astor was over. In the next decade her son, John Jacob Astor IV, would have a short stay in the house, redoing the house as his own with the work now done by Carrere & Hastings.[10] John Jacob Astor IV would die, gallantly, on the Titanic and just a few years later, the house disappeared faster than his mother's old house had, going down after 30 years to be replaced by Temple Emanu-el. The world of exclusion practiced by Knickerbocker society was well and truly over.

The first phase of houses built across from Central Park proved a location for many Knickerbocker figures who now were forced by commerce to leave their brownstone world. When Mrs. Astor, Catherine Lorillard Kernochan, the Watts Shermans and the like bought and built their earlier mid-Fifth Avenue homes, it would

THE CAROLINE
SCHERMERHORN ASTOR
HOUSE, WITH HER SON,
VIEW FROM THE SOUTH

*Dementia took Mrs.
Astor within a decade.
In her mind, the world
of the 1870s carried on
as she hosted imaginary
dinner parties. Here
we see her now-worn
out furnishings and
her famous portrait by
Carolus-Durand draped
in mourning black.*

never have occurred to them that they would need to build again some
thirty blocks higher, now directly facing Central Park. The pressures
of many new families who aspired to an address on Fifth Avenue, and
the commercial push in what would now be the streets of the 20s, 30s
and 40s forced most to abandon their houses for the new section of
the city. Did these people realize how short a life their new abodes
were destined to have? Again, the pressures would implode on the
houses in the 1920s as the apartment houses became accepted and
sought-after addresses on Fifth Avenue. The life of the first phase of
brownstone New York would prove a generation to a generation and
a half and the same affliction would condemn the new wave of houses
facing Central Park in the 1920s.

CHAPTER 15

FASHION ARRIVES ON THE UPPER AVENUE

Senator Copper of Tonapah Ditch
Made a clean billion in minin' and sich
Hiked from Noo York, where his money he blew
Buildin' a palace of Fift' Avenoo.

Wallace Irwin

THE YEARS AROUND 1890 saw these upper avenue blocks become the most prestigious portion of the city as commerce in the streets of the 20s and 30s as well as the growth of retail pushed social figures some 30 streets north. Mrs. Kernochan moved from 384 Fifth Avenue, the Watts Shermans from 102 East 25th Street. Leaping uptown, the second wave of house owners now faced existing row houses and the new arrivals would totally tear down and rebuild or to re-front and rearrange within the exterior side walls. Often, the rear wall would be removed, light wells created, and the house extended into the back lot, making a larger house with more light within the interior. The choice was to stay in the familiar home and endure the crowds and, now, commercial neighbors, or to pull up stumps and join the northward parade.[1]

The Sugar King
At the north corner of 66th Street, with the entry on the side street, was the unusual and artistic house built for the industrialist, entrepreneur, and sugar refiner Henry Osborne Havemeyer by Charles Coolidge Haight, an architect with family connections to Trinity Church Corporation but little house design presence. Haight rarely designed private homes, but for the "sugar king," Havemeyer, Haight designed a fine house in the manner of H. H. Richardson, whose heavy, blocky stone style was just coming to an end. Haight's composition is very restrained, making the house wildly unlike any other on Fifth Avenue, but not an outrage to its neighbors. Havemeyer settled down in the

H. O. Havemeyer House, on the northeast corner of Fifth Avenue and 66th Street

The sugar magnates in 19th-century New York were German families. The Havemeyers achieved a baronial level of success with one brother in a fine house on Madison Avenue and H. O. here on Fifth Avenue. The H. O. Havemeyer House was designed by an architect, Charles Coolidge Haight, who was not a player in grand house building, and the design was unusual in its day with thick turrets and fine brickwork.

now most fashionable part of the Avenue. He was certainly wealthy enough to be on Fifth Avenue, but his art-infused, restrained house did not fit into the prevailing picture of statement houses that were built by aspirants seeking admission to society.

Havemeyer and his brother, Theodore, took on the family sugar refining business with great success, making respectable fortunes. Theodore Havemeyer lived the gilded age lifestyle, building a tall, mansard-roofed house on Madison Avenue and filling it with the contemporary vision of European grandeur. Henry O. Havemeyer's house did not fit in with the rather pretentious taste of the time and his collections did not blend in either. Old masters and less safe, but great, modern French painting distinguished Havemeyer walls. Havemeyer and his wife, Louisine, with their close friendship with the American artist, Mary Cassatt, had amassed one of the greatest collections of pictures in New York, which was set within a Tiffany-suffused artistic interior (as the house itself, the Havemeyer interior was at the tail end of the style of the 1880s, but one of the best examples of what could be done). The Havemeyer's remarkable Tiffany fittings were in direct contrast to the pomp of their neighbors – they rose above the taste of the time.[2]

An odd aspect of the commission was the building of a self-contained house under the northern wide turret. Entered from Fifth Avenue, unlike the main house, which had a side street door, the purpose of the small house is a mystery. Was it perhaps for the children and their tutors? Or for the young when they grew up? In the end, it was rented to the bachelor Standard Oil partner, Oliver Payne, who had Stanford

H. O. HAVEMEYER
HOUSE, INTERIOR,
TIFFANY FLYING
STAIRCASE

*The Havemeyers broke
the conventions of their
day. Unlike most Fifth
Avenue house owners,
they created an artistic
house and collected
paintings of importance.*

White decorate it. He was doing the same for W. C. Whitney's house a block away so these mortal enemies were neighbors, sharing the same designer to make their homes important.

The loss of the Havemeyer house, while enriching The Metropolitan Museum with some of their best pictures, was unfortunate for New York. The gift of the paintings was a triumph, but this was a special house, and its survival would have enhanced the city. Indeed, the *petit château*, the W. C. Whitney house, and the Havemeyer home are large losses to the formation of a sophisticated gilded age taste in America. All are gone without any protest at demolition.

Speculative Buildings

The speculative builders remained active through the early 1880s, starting the development of the 66th Street block in 1871 with a Jardine brownstone, easily recognizable as the Jardines usually had a projecting porch entry at the top of the stoop. Another speculative team, Lamb and Wheeler, arrived in the 1880s around Fifth and Madison Avenues at 67th Street. Lamb and Wheeler became Lamb and Rich, and they did rather fanciful late Victorian houses on these blocks, as well as Amsterdam Avenue, West End Avenue, and Henderson Place in Manhattan. It seems possible that Lamb and Wheeler, then Lamb and Rich, were the first developers to create some small sets of row houses in varied styles, a miniature version of the variety of new houses on Fifth Avenue. Lamb and Rich composed artful arrangements of independent stylistic features often reflecting on exuberant version of English Queen Anne and Pont Street Dutch.

P. D. Armour House,
on the corner of
Fifth Avenue and
67th Street

_____

*Speculative developers
and designers Lamb
and Rich designed the
most varied rows of
the city. Working on
Madison Avenue, the
Upper West Side, and,
here, Fifth Avenue, the
brick-fronted houses
were composed of
artful arrangements of
independent features
often reflecting an
exuberant version of the
United Kingdom Queen
Anne and Pont Street
Dutch.*

The Chicago meat packer, Philip Danforth Armour, bought the corner house on 67th Street, which was likely the Armour house, whose interiors were shown in *Artistic Houses* of 1883–84. Lamb and Rich's vigorous designs impressed Theodore Roosevelt, who hired the firm to do his Sagamore Hill house in Oyster Bay—they did a number of houses in summer resorts, including Bellport, Long Island. Would that these men had left records: where did they get the capital? How did they mingle in the small-scale developer world of the 1880s? The patrician critic of American architecture, Montgomery Schuyler, really disliked the work of Wheeler, Lamb and Rich. The variety and range of materials and shapes were interesting to many, but not to Schuyler.[3]

Across 67th Street a speculative corner house at 857 Fifth Avenue built in 1882–85 for William H. Fogg—on the south corner with a witch's turret—was torn down by George Gould in 1907 for a much grander house, which brought the architect Horace Trumbauer to New York City (when the widow of Cornelius Vanderbilt sold her big house to become Bergdorf Goodman's department store, she bought the Gould house where she would expire in 1934). Just to its north at 858 Fifth Avenue, on a mid-block location, Isaac Stern asked William Schickel to design a house for him in 1893. Schickel, with Henry Fernbach, had built Stern's great department store on 23rd Street. The house was large with 55 feet on Fifth Avenue and went 115 feet deep into the lot. Thomas Fortune Ryan, who bounded all over on Fifth Avenue, would later own the large stone house.[4]

*857 Fifth Avenue was
an extremely awkward
house of the mid-19th
century. Poorly designed,
the house had features
clipped on, including
the witch hat turret at
the corner of the block.
The house was known
as home to George
Gould, son of Jay
Gould. Gould would
replace his own house
c. 1907 by demolishing
it for one designed by
Horace Trumbauer. The
Trumbauer House, one
of his first in New York
City, blended well with
the house next door of
Thomas Fortune Ryan.*

The northeast corner of 68th Street was the location of Schickel's
huge house of 1881, with its brick and stone front of 54 feet on Fifth
Avenue.

871 Fifth Avenue

Steam engines transformed life in the 19th century. Steam would
supply power to the first elevators, to presses printing the daily
newspaper, and would power the manufacture of cheap sugar, making
it available to all. Strict Presbyterians, Robert L. Stuart and his brother
Alexander emigrated from Scotland in the early 19th century and
harnessed the power of steam in the processing of sugar cane, which
made candy far less expensive. Ruinous to teeth, the inexpensive
process made the Stuart brothers very rich.

Robert L. Stuart collected paintings in the years after the Civil War,
which were proudly hung in his brownstone at 20th Street and Fifth
Avenue (the house was later broken up into studio spaces used by
Stanford White, among others). The beginnings of commerce in the
area pushed the Stuarts northward. They purchased a plot 55 feet
wide on Fifth Avenue itself, going eastward 200 feet on 67th Street,
and a huge, if ungainly, house by William Schickel was built on the
site, perfect for displaying the paintings. The Stuart interior was
designed by William Bigelow, working for the Herter firm (former
partner of McKim and Mead and briefly a brother-in-law to McKim).
It is possible that he was also McKim's real life partner, rather than
his sister, Annie Bigelow, whom McKim married. Annie Bigelow

*The Stuart brothers
made a great fortune in
sugar processing. Robert
Stuart and his wife leapt
to 67th Street from their
home on 20th Street. The
house was overwhelmed
with architectural details
and a great mansard
roof.*

HOME OF MRS. ROBERT L. STUART, NO. 871 5TH AVENUE

would accuse her husband of "acts of indecency," perhaps witnessing something between her brother and McKim, and divorce him in 1878, withholding their new-born infant, yet William Bigelow remained with the firm for another year and a half.

Robert Stuart promptly greeted his new construction by departing from life in 1883, leaving his widow to finish the house. New York art lovers salivated for the collection at the death of Mrs. Mary Stuart in 1891, as there were no heirs. She left behind a big building, already out of date, for a grand purchaser and bequeathed the art to the Lenox Library, then three blocks away.[5] The house went to Amzi Lorenzo Barber, the asphalt king (the house may have been rented as Amzi Barber and his brother were building his life-time home in Ardsley, New York). Levi P. Morton may have also rented the house (Morton lived in numerous houses on Fifth Avenue—indeed Edith Jones made her debut in a house of Morton's on 42nd Street). In 1897, just a few years later, Barber sold the house to the capitalist with political connections, W. C. Whitney, and moved to his home in Irvington, Ardsley Tower. W. C. Whitney was living at 57th Street at the time but needed to escape the ghost of his late wife, Flora, and Oliver Payne. Whitney bought the Stuart house, declared it horribly out of date, and for his new wife, Edith May Randolph, Whitney started to

redo the house. Stanford White gutted the Stuart home, pulling out the interiors of his predecessor at the firm of McKim, Mead & White, William Bigelow (the firm was McKim, Mead & Bigelow for its first years).

Edith May was one of the beautiful May sisters from Baltimore, belles of the 1870s involved with notorious figures like James Gordon Bennett, newspaper man, and Thomas Garner, yachtsman. Edith May was a widow of breathtaking beauty (the former paramour of J. P. Morgan whom she had hoped to wed—how small was the social world of the day). Whitney may well have taken up with Edith before his wife Flora died, and after Flora's death, Whitney waited the expected three years, then married Edith. Flora's brother, Oliver Payne, likely knew of the long affair and his rage towards Whitney was not containable. He turned to the four children of Flora and offered them his estate if they would leave their father. Two children took up with Payne and two stayed with their father.

The Robber Baron

Whitney had lived extremely well with Flora's fortune. Clearly, Whitney began to baulk at being funded by the Paynes; after all, he had lived off his wife for twenty years, which may explain his need

871 FIFTH AVENUE

The Stuart House was sold to William Collins Whitney, who hired McKim, Mead & White to tame the detail. The house was less special than its interiors. Stanford White, now more of a dealer and decorator than an architect, made these rooms truly spectacular. Would that this house had survived.

to make his own fortune. Whitney became so intensely desirous for Medici-esque wealth to validate him that he made increasingly corrupt deals. He used his political contacts in New York's Democratic party to get a street railroad set up in New York and, using insider trading tips and other forms of buying political favor, as well as stock watering efforts, he made himself very rich. But he also ruined his reputation. Even his own cronies in the Democratic party, such as Abram Hewitt, felt he had become hopelessly sinister and untrustworthy. Whitney was now isolated from real relationships but society still attended his parties. Whitney's stepdaughter was hostess for the opening of his house, which was attended by virtually everyone in the city, including Edith and Teddy Wharton (clearly Whitney is a model for some characters in Wharton's novels). A second party, hosting the social debut of Charles T. Barney and his sister's young daughter, would also take place at the house.

Whitney wanted his house to be in the same New York category as the Astor house just to the south and the mansions of Vanderbilt Alley. The most patrician of the great men of wealth, his goal was to achieve the status of the great Rothschild homes in England and France and Sir Richard Wallace's Hertford House in London. Both the Rothschilds and Wallace assembled vast arrays of treasure from aristocratic residences to imprint their houses with infusions of grandeur.

In the second half of the 19th century, many decorative ornaments and fittings from old buildings were available on the art market. Haussmann ripped out the medieval core of Paris, causing household features to appear on the art sale market—fireplaces, fabrics, ceilings, furniture, and the like—while in the French countryside, railroads plowed through manor houses, and decorative items went on sale. Florence, like Paris, had been trashing its medieval core. A painter, Stefano Bardini, rose from the role of demolition picker to become a wealthy dealer, searching the sites after work each day and amassing a great inventory of old goods. Furthermore, death duties forced many old families to sell parts of their homes. In Florence, paintings appeared in good number as well, which the new wealthy of America, Prussia, St. Petersburg, and Luxembourg, as well as the Victoria & Albert Museum, found important. Tapestries – woven arts were not popular in the second half of the 19th-century in Europe – also came on the market, often in poor condition, but large and cheap. To Americans, a tapestry was a great asset to cover a big wall and not break the bank, and tapestry purchases came to adorn all the houses of importance in this period. So treasured in America were tapestries that benefactions of individual wills often specify the gifts of individual tapestries to close friends. These treasures would soon fill American homes, especially Whitney's new palace.

Whitney took a personal interest in the house and the fittings. His commissions were on a scale with the Vanderbilts and, as he was a major client of Stanford White, he enriched his antique purchasing career magnificently. Whitney wanted the very best with provenances that could be traced back to aristocrats of France, Italy, and England. Stefano Bardini supplied the major pieces, although Whitney turned to Emile Gavet as well as Vital and his brother Benjamin Benghiat, who came to New York offering rugs and textiles for Whitney and other wealthy men of the day. In the album of large-scale photos of the house under construction, in the MM&W archive, there a photo is on a wall showing J. F. Millet's *The Sower*—clearly considered, but not purchased. Whitney was looking for pictures of aristocratic stature, not homely pictures (W. H. Vanderbilt would have loved the picture).

The entrance to the five-story house was set on 68th Street. Security was maintained by a large protective gate brought from the Palazzo Doria in Genoa. The vestibule, perhaps part of a house from the destruction of Florence's old quarter (a special forte of Bardini) was lined with green onyx.[6] The reception hall featured a complex Venetian-style mosaic floor patterned with constellation circles, provided by Antonio Salviati, a theme Joe Wells and Stanford White would use in many places. The magnificence of the interior fittings was clearly dazzling. Whitney had it all: ceilings from Italian palazzi, fireplaces of the Henri II era, furniture, velvets, paintings, and tapestries, but nothing from home-grown, dour New England ancestors. It was truly splendid—outdoing all the other palaces of the robber barons. Whitney interspersed his paintings throughout the house, unlike in the houses of the Astors and Vanderbilts, where the pictures were concentrated in galleries.

Sadly, while riding in a Whitney property in Aiken, South Carolina, Edith, his second wife galloped into a low branch, causing severe brain damage. She was brought back to New York City, where she could watch riders prancing in Central Park. She died soon thereafter in 1899, leaving Whitney with two of his children, circled by a band of enemies who did not approve of his business and political moves at this time.

Nevertheless, Whitney remained interested in society and grand dances (A. T. Stewart and W. H. Vanderbilt had ignored the ballroom in their houses). The most unusual addition to the house was in the hallway to the ballroom. Whitney had installed intarsia panels of 1547 from a chapel at the Château de la Bastie d'Urfe in France. A *trompe l'oeil* of *The Last Supper* of micro pieces of exotic woods done at the height of the Urbino Studiola graced the walkway. This great work was a rather inappropriate backdrop to the bejeweled ladies bedecked in Worth splendor, and formally dressed men, who passed it on the way to the ball. In 1947, the family of Gertrude Vanderbilt Whitney would donate the work to The Metropolitan Museum.[7]

Whitney's house is largely forgotten, and his race to top the Astors and Vanderbilts lost its place in the legends of Fifth Avenue. His house should have been fully preserved, but during World War II, it was broken up and sold off. The explanation lies with the changed character of Whitney himself. From a well-born and well-educated gentleman to a fraudster, Whitney had garnered many enemies. Several years after his niece's debutante ball in 1901 (Charles T Barney had married Whitney's sister), Whitney returned home late at night going through the Palazzo Doria gate and fell. Physicians were called (Dr. Bull, McKim's old friend), but Whitney soon expired. The official word was appendicitis, but Rita DaCosta Lydig, the rather remarkable, glamorous figure of the day, who told stories of her peers in her book *Tragic Mansions*, writes that Whitney was stabbed and died of his wounds in 1904. Given the forgotten tale of the house, and the list of enemies led by former brother-in-law Payne, one suspects Lydig is correct. The likely quiet scandal may have caused attention to the house to disappear.

The house, fully intact, was sold to the strange man of great wealth known as "Silent" Smith, who died soon afterwards. Then Whitney's loyal son, Harry Whitney, and his wife, Gertrude Vanderbilt Whitney, from across the intersection on 57th Street, bought the house back and restored it to the family. If only this house and W. K. Vanderbilt's mansion had been left as monuments to the attempt to create an aristocracy for America among the newly rich. Perhaps as astonishing as the *richesse* of the treasures in the houses of the robber barons is the speed with which it would melt away, all forgotten, by the public.[8] We will see Whitney's children in three other houses on Fifth Avenue; indeed, Dorothy, a young child at the time of his death, and her first husband built the final house of the story.

Statement Houses
Across 68th Street on the southeast corner was another very large

CHARLES YERKES
HOUSE, ON THE
SOUTHEAST CORNER
OF FIFTH AVENUE AND
68TH STREET

*The upper Fifth Avenue
blocks abandoned the
"stamped out repetition"
on the lower blocks.
Each house had its own
character and style.
Walking up the Avenue
was a chance to study
architectural periods
and details all done by
splendid artisans in fine
materials.*

stone house with 60 feet on the Avenue, built in 1893 for Charles
Yerkes. The society architect, Robert Henderson Robertson, designed
the home for the transportation king. Yerkes, who rose to importance
with some skill in political bribery and blackmail, developed the
Chicago mass transit system before moving on fully to New York
in 1899. In 1900, Yerkes set his sights on the London tube system,
developing the Bakerloo line before his financial collapse and death in
1905. Yerkes assembled a fine art collection while in Chicago which
was this house in New York at the time of his death.[9]

Brought up in Millbrae, California, with a love of thoroughbred
horses, the financier Ogden Mills settled in New York and married
Ruth Livingston in 1882. The Livingstons were the patrician family
of the Hudson Valley, placing Mills instantly in the midst of society.
Ogden Mills commissioned Richard Morris Hunt to do a restrained,
but substantial, Venetian Gothic house on the southeast corner of
69th Street. Next door at 6 East 69th Street, Hunt designed a matching
house for Mills's father-in-law, Maturin Livingston, a fixture in Mrs.
Astor's set. Across the street at 880, a different set of Herter Brothers,
recently arrived from Germany, built a house for businessman
David Dows. These Herter Brothers, who would build many of
the tenements on the Lower East Side, are often confused with the
decorative firm, which was then working with W. H. Vanderbilt on
his big house. The Dows house, built in 1879, was then above the
fashionable part of the city and was rather modestly built, costing a
mere $25,000 for a double house. The David Dows were relatively
uninterested in the social scene, but did buy American paintings—

indeed, the great Frederick Church painting, *Heart of the Andes*, a prize in its day, was in their collection and, still beloved, now is in the Metropolitan Museum. In 1909, the financier E. H. Harriman bought the large carcass of the Dow house and totally redid it with the services of Grosvenor Atterbury, making it a Harriman family home.

The neighbor to the north was Heber Reginald Bishop, who commissioned the Astor real estate architect, Charles W. Clinton (67th Street Armory) for another double house in 1880. The Bishop house, built just as the depression was ending, came in at over three times the cost of David Dows's home next door. Bishop, a member of Mrs. Astor's social set, was a city businessman who also had business interests in mid 19th-century San Francisco. His wife's sister was married to Darius Ogden Mills (the father of Ogden), making Bishop close to the neighbor who was shortly to start building a few doors to the south. Adolph Lewisohn, a merchant banker and metals investor, would later buy the house with its own stable. Lewisohn was very generous to New York City, endowing Lewisohn Hall at Columbia College and Lewisohn Stadium.

The next house, 883 Fifth Avenue, was built for John Sloane in a Queen Anne mode by R. H. Robertson. On the corner was a very early house of 1870, built when this block was well above the fashionable zone and briefly considered by "Big" Jim Fisk, a Wall Street schemer, stock manipulator, and investor. Despised by the business community for his extravagant behavior, Fisk came into a big win in 1871 and dreamed of building a French château on Fifth Avenue. Unfortunately for this 36-year-old man, his rival for the affections of a belle of the day, killed him in January of 1872. Fisk's flamboyant behavior and subsequent death allowed the property to pass to Josiah M. Fiske, a New York City businessman who was successful in the flour business (no relation to Jim Fisk). The house, built in the depression of the 1870s, was one of the first big houses above 59th Street. There were Griffith Thomas brownstones in the 80s, but the Fiske house was the first of the major statement buildings in this region. The house, begun in 1871 and built by Stephen Decatur Hatch, was expensive and the Buildings Department permit filed for a house costing $120,000. Although perhaps not Hatch's best work, one wonders if the client was a problem for the architect. The turret on the corner perhaps suggests that Hatch might have known Hunt's design for the unbuilt Fisk château.

Titans of Collecting

The Scottish businessman, Robert Lenox, arrived in New York in the late 18th century. His only surviving son, James Lenox, educated at Columbia College, was a scholar and a collector. As we know, when his father died, James Lenox left his business pursuits and devoted himself to collecting rare books and objects. Lenox never married and, as the years passed, became a recluse, seeing only his old friends and immediate family. Lenox bought, but did not catalogue, his purchases and his books and pictures rested in the house we have already discussed at 53 Fifth Avenue. As Lenox aged his thoughts turned to the collection, which now included a Gutenberg Bible and 30,000 volumes. Robert Lenox had advised his son not to sell the uptown farm that he had bought in the early century, and James Lenox owned some 38 acres of property between 68th and 73rd Streets, Madison to Fifth Avenue with a hill at its center. James Lenox kept the property, but by the later 1860s was getting ready to donate the hill in the middle of the land, the block between 70th and 71st Streets along Fifth Avenue, to create the Lenox Library. Surely his books and paintings would now receive the attention they deserved? Lenox donated the land, set up trustees (men from the world of "old" establishment New York), and brought R. M. Hunt in to do the library. Hunt's wonderful building took six years to finish, opening in 1877, endowing New York with a second great gentleman's library (the Astor Library was earlier). Hunt's building, indebted to the great Parisian Bibliothèque, was a superb Néo-Grec addition to the city but, as is the cannibalistic theme of this city, the solidly built, rather perfect library did not last 30 years. The library site was sold

Lenox Library at Fifth Avenue and 70th Street

The Lenox Library, a gift to the city to house the library and treasures of James Lenox. Designed in the style of Parisian libraries, two wings flanked an internal courtyard. The exquisite detail of the building inspired friends to create a monument honoring its architect across the Avenue. Two generations later, the library would be gone—the monument to Richard Morris Hunt remains.

The Lenox father and son owned this land, which we see as empty, east of the Lenox Library.

NEW YORK CITY.—OPENING OF THE ART GALLERY OF THE NEW LENOX LIBRARY, FIFTH AVENUE AND SEVENTIETH STREET, JANUARY 15TH.

to H. C. Frick, as a New York City Public Research Library was to be created and, the Lenox Library holdings were absorbed into the new holdings, The Frick house, then Frick Collection, replaced the building. Poignantly, the memorial to R. M. Hunt was built into the Central Park Wall across from his Lenox Library—at the time of its erection it was never contemplated that Hunt would face the holdings of a later titan.[10]

Henry Clay Frick had created a successful business converting coal to coke for the Pittsburgh steel mills. Frick went on to combine forces with Andrew Carnegie, although the two men did not personally like each other, so it was a relief when J. P. Morgan bought them out and created U.S. Steel, and the two men decamped to New York City. In 1905, Frick signed a ten-year lease on the W. H. Vanderbilt house, then inherited by George Vanderbilt, who did not want to reside in his parents' house. Frick moved into the house while searching for a property appropriate to his remarkable fortune. Carnegie, while living around the corner from Frick on West 51st Street, had bought a full block far to the north and completed his roomy house along with his own private "park." How could Frick upstage his former business associate? In 1907, when the Lenox Library site was put up for sale Frick bought the entire lot. In 1912, Frick commissioned Carrere & Hastings to build an important, but not "gauche" house at the heart of fashionable New York, standing behind a huge front grassy lawn. Surely Frick, as he filled his new house with art treasures, could feel superior to Carnegie. Yet Frick would only be able to live

*W. Pickhardt, an
impoverished German
immigrant made a
fortune in the dye and
chemical business—and
commissioned the house,
which he reconfigured,
rebuilt, and seemingly
never inhabited. Rather
unexpectedly, an old
New York gentry couple
bought the house for
their immense china and
silver collections, with
some idea of turning the
collection into a museum.
As was now happening,
a developer bought the
house in 1916 and tore
it down for a 12-story
apartment house by
Warren & Wetmore.*

in his splendid statement for four years —he died in 1918 and his widow died in 1931. Under Frick's will, the house and collection were to become a museum at his wife's death. In 1935, John Russell Pope effected this change and visitors can now enjoy the house and collection.

Acquisition and Development

As we know, some plots along Fifth Avenue at 72nd Street had been purchased in anticipation of a northward movement and would remain empty until the turn of the century. Moving above the Frick house, James A. Burden would leave his old house at 139 Fifth Avenue to build a relatively wide brick house on the southeast corner in 1891. Society architect R. H. Robertson, who did a number of houses in the area, designed this house. We will see Burden again on 91st Street.[11]

Curiously, the Edison Electric Company, now that houses were beginning to use their system, planted the company branches right on Fifth Avenue. Arabella Worsham Huntington once considered the northeast corner of Fifth Avenue at 72nd Street as a possible house site; she owned the property but did not carry through with the project. John D. Rockefeller had been interested in the site as well. The corner had a wooden shack where passengers for the Fifth Avenue Bus Company might await the coach and Arabella left standing the shanty, which sold soda water and cigars—as did several other such wooden buildings on the Avenue. These humble wooden shack-like structures that stood on Fifth Avenue amid the grandeur served the useful function of covering the property taxes until an auspicious development opportunity arose. In the fall of 1893, Arabella leased the property to the Edison Electrical Workshop and hired commercial architects, Buchman & Dreiser, to build the offices on the site.[12] A number of vacant lots, many grand houses, saloons and a few old shacks still co-mingled.

The two corner plots between 73rd and 74th Streets were built early in the 1880s. The rest of the block filled in much later. The southern corner was built by the aging Arthur Gilman of Boston, who had been working in New York City for a decade. Gilman was a fine builder, spending a good $80,000 sum in 1881 for the house for Mrs. Francis E. Quintard (possibly a Norwalk cabinet maker?). A traditional brownstone, it appears to have had a new stoop facing south away from the neighbor to the north.

Just to the north in 1898, Randolph Guggenheimer built a bow-fronted English basement house, with a central doorway and no

stoop. There was a loggia at the top of the house guarded by two pairs of caryatids. The architect was Robert Maynicke, best known for many loft buildings on the lower Avenue.[13] Guggenheimer was a politician, but he was also an attorney with Samuel Untermeyer, which enhanced his income greatly, elevating him to the exclusive class of Fifth Avenue builders. Just beyond Guggenheimer's house was George Warren's house designed by his brother, Whitney Warren, friend of the beautiful Lily Price.[14]

On the north corner another house was built in 1881 for W. Pickhardt, who had made money in chemicals and dye products, designed by the English-born Henry G. Harrison, who was prominent amongst "old" New Yorkers in the 1860s. The design for the brownstone front was super wide at 52 feet on Fifth Avenue and went 125 feet deep into the plot. A very costly house at almost $300,000, it cried out, somewhat awkwardly, for attention, as can be seen in several instances. Pickhardt made unreasonable demands—he was haunted by the dream of a grand house on Fifth Avenue, purchased the plot and set Harrison to work on the design, but was fated never to occupy his dream house. He demanded unusually deep foundations and changed his mind repeatedly as the building progressed. The shell was built, but the family never moved in, and at some point, the architect also abandoned the house. Some fifteen years later, the unfinished house was sold to Alfred Duane Pell, who bought the enormous building for his china collection. Pell's idea of leaving the house and his vast collection to the city as a museum of china faltered, and the house was demolished in 1916, replaced by an apartment house.[15]

Jacob Schiff commissioned a house in 1884, 50 feet north of 74th Street, when the block was still under-developed. The designer for Schiff's house is not recorded. Some years later, Schiff bought a wide plot a block and a half to the north, deeding over this house to his son, Mortimer, as a wedding gift. The house at 932 featured a relief by Augustus Saint-Gaudens of the two Schiff children, Mortimer and Frieda, with a borrowed great dog, which was executed as the house opened. The relief is now at The Metropolitan Museum.

Mid-block in 1883 came Alfred M. Hoyt, who sat on many boards of banks and new corporations.[16] He asked the young McKim, Mead & White to create a double house in brick with a central entry. The wide house with a bow front to one side of the entry was an early venture in breaking away from brownstone fronts. The architects were starting to work with the Perth Amboy terracotta company, and this house used the new speckle brick and their terracotta molded

SCHIFF HOUSE, 932 FIFTH AVENUE

Jacob H. Schiff bought two houses on Fifth Avenue only blocks apart. Schiff first lived here at 74th Street before buying a huge speculatively-built house near 78th Street. The house here was the original location for the great Augustus Saint-Gaudens's relief of Schiff's son and daughter. Schiff gave his son this house as a wedding gift and moved to his second house up the street.

No. 934 Fifth Avenue.
New York City.
View looking S.E.

ornament. The Hoyts owned old boweries and engaged in some land speculation on the emerging West Side, which proved to be less successful than the Astor estate's own speculations. The Hoyts built the full block with an inner court yard, named Belnord, on 86th Street between Broadway and Amsterdam Avenues, which remains today.

The two houses north of Hoyt's were re-fronted in the early 20th century, as had become the custom when new owners bought an existing brownstone and gave them an up-to-date facelift. The corner house was for one of Jay Gould's sons, Edwin Gould, done "in good taste" by Carrere & Hastings.

The Northward Parade

Extensive revision took place on these blocks in the early 20th century. Many of the first owners of 1880s brownstones had sold their houses and a wealthier set of buyers were now willing to leave the lower part of the Avenue, seeking to flee to the mid 70s blocks in the north as the commercial invasion started to transform their residential blocks. On the north corner of 75th Street, Edward S. Harkness gave his son a gift, a fine new row house. The Buildings Department permit in 1907 was for the architects to be Hoppin & Koen, although other sources state it was an early work by Mr. Harkness's Yale room-mate, James Gambrel Rodgers.[17] The superbly finished house faces the side street, which allowed for more light. E. S. Harkness was a significant philanthropist and the Harknesses did not aspire to a place at the top of New York society. Indeed, this house, which was gifted to the Commonwealth Society, is a rare survival of houses of this period. Harkness, Oliver Payne, Charles Pratt, and Henry Morrison Flagler were early partners of John D. Rockefeller and all would achieve fortunes from the success of Standard Oil.

The Harkness house left a nice space between its northern side and the then new huge Temple Beth-El, its neighbor. Temple Beth-El was built in 1890 as the blocks of the 70s were beginning to attract once downtown families. The building with its lavish "high hat" dome was by Arnold Brunner who then started his brief partnership with Thomas Tryon. To the north, the block between 76th and 77th Streets would not be built on until the early 20th century.

As the century turned, former Senator William A. Clark built the grandest house of all, the symbol of all that was excessive in this house building competition. Clark, a copper and silver mining owner from the west, as well as a corrupt politician, was identified by Mark Twain as the most disgusting creature that the Republic has produced since

ALFRED M. HOYT HOUSE, 934 FIFTH AVENUE, MID-BLOCK FROM 75TH TO 76TH STREETS

Alfred Miller Hoyt, a successful banker, retired in 1881 and purchased the land for this house in the same year. Far above the fashionable portion of the Avenue, Hoyt hired a new firm, McKim, Mead & White, to do this splendid brick and terracotta-trimmed house. The unusual placement of the door made the house plan have two sets of rooms on either side of the entry hall. This house sat alone on the Avenue for years.

the days of Tweed. He bought a parcel of land purchased earlier by Samuel Untermeyer and held in reserve. Clark also had the dream of living on Fifth Avenue, but perhaps only to show off his wealth, not because he wanted join the clubs or high society. Clark's wife had died, and the mature man took up with an actress, with whom he had a daughter, Huguette. The family of three lived in the palace for just over a dozen years.

Far left:
WILLIAM A. CLARK
HOUSE NORTH EAST
CORNER OF 77TH STREET

*The most extravagant
and flamboyant of all the
Fifth Avenue palaces. An
amazing ego effort for a
corrupt man who would
never be invited into the
houses of his neighbors.
The copper king helped
poison the Gilded Age.
His daughter lived to
great old age and is the
subject of a book,* Empty
Mansions.

*Left:
William A. Clark House
in demolition.*

Clark hired architects who were not from the main house building
world, Lord, Hewett & Hull, for a nine-story, 120-room mansion.
The house, incredibly costly, was filled with treasure, but its sheer
excess caused amazement and much criticism. The house, with
its Alice in Wonderland growth elixir, took its lead from Parisian
buildings, but was described as too big, too heavy, too large for its
plot and far out of character to the Avenue.

One can only wonder what Clark intended. His family consisted
of just three people and we can speculate whether he knew of the
politically tainted A. T. Stewart and his huge house for just two
people, which was then in the process of being demolished. The Clark
house was described as we know as having 120 rooms, 31 baths, and
a swimming pool. Clark bought paintings which he offered to the
Metropolitan Museum, but with the condition that the pictures be in
a special, named gallery. In the first move of its kind, the Metropolitan
Museum turned the gift down and the pictures went to the Corcoran continued on page 232

Senator Clark

Senator Copper of Tonapah Ditch
Made a clean billion in minin' and sich
Hiked for Noo York, where his money he blew
Buildin' a palace of Fift' Avenoo.

"How" sez the Senator, "can I look proudest?
Build me a house that'll holler the loudest."
None of your slab-sided, plain mossyleums!
Gimme the treasures of art 'an museums!

Build it new-fangled,
Scalloped and angled,
Fine, like a weddin' cake garnished with pills:
Gents, do your dooty,
Trot out your beauty.
Gimme my money's worth. I'll pay the bills."

Forty-eight architects came to consult,
Drawin' up plans for a splendid result;
If the old Senator wanted to pay,
They'd give 'im Art with a capital A.
Every style from the Greeks to the Hindoos,
Dago front porches and Siamese windows,
Japanese cupolas fightin' with Russian,
Walls Sengambian, Turkish and Prussian;

Pillars Ionic,
Eaves Babylonic,
Doors cut in scallops resemblin' a shell.
Roof was Egyptian,
Gables caniption.
Whole grand effect when completed was — hell.

When them there architects finished in style,
Forty-nine sculptors waltzed into the pile,
Swinging their chisels in circles and lines,
Carvin' the stone work in fancy designs.
Some favored animals – tigers and snakes;
Some favored cookery – doughnuts and cakes –
Till the whole mansion was crusted with ornaments,
Cellar to garret with garden adornments,

Lettuce and onions,
Cupids and bunions,
Fowls o' the air and fish o' the deep,
Mermaids and dragons,
Horses and wagons —
Isn't no wonder the neighbors can't sleep.

Senator Copper, with pard'nable pride,
Showed the grand house where he planned to abide;
Full of emotion, he scarcely could speak;
"Can't find its like in New York – it's uneek.

See the variety, size and alignment,
Showin' the owner has wealth and refinement,
Showin' he's one o' the tonier classes —
Who can't help seein' my house when he passes?
Windows that stare at you,
Statoos that swear at you,
Steeples and weather vanes pointin' aloof;
Nothin' can beat it —
Just to complete it,
Guess I'll stick gold leaf all over the roof!

The American writer and humorist Wallace Irwin wrote many
such ditties.

Gallery. The house was sold for three million, as the cost of demolition would be prohibitive.[18]

Was Clark trying to counter his diminished reputation with a house that proclaimed that having a great fortune was all that mattered? He did reside in this house, where he died in 1925, but the house came crashing down the following year (his daughter, Huguette Clark, lived a very long and strange life, dying after thirteen years in Beth Israel hospital, where she inhabited a room even though she was not sick. There is a recent book, *Empty Mansions*, about Huguette's strange existence, surrounded by dolls.

Millionaires' Row

Just to the north of the construction for Clark, a speculative builder working with a high-end construction team built a house for a millionaire. Wide, dignified, and available for purchase, Jacob Schiff bought the house in 1900 and moved there, giving his son the older house a block away. He called in William Baumgarten and Company to make the interiors in a fine and historically sublime manner. Jacob Schiff, while he was a respectable banker, was Jewish and therefore was not included in the society events of the day. He avoided the neighbors' potential displeasure by buying an already-built house and was cautious about the appearance of his home, matching the best taste of the day. No one could object to the purchase, at least openly. Schiff, a remarkably scholarly and philanthropic man, was

*A big, awkward
pile built above the
fashionable blocks.
Henry H. Cook bought
the entire 78th to 79th
Streets block in 1879.
Two years later, he
commissioned William
Wheeler Smith to create
a home. The Cook house
was begun as the Hoyt
house was, in an empty
section of upper Fifth
Avenue. A late nod
to the colors of High
Victorian Gothic, with
three colors of granite
making a polychromatic
statement. Cook added
grand interior detail to
the solid house.*

generous to numerous organizations (we will encounter his house for his daughter soon at the end of the tale).[19]

In 1888, the corner house on the block, with its wonderful wide corner tower, was built for William Lawrence, a real estate and pharmaceutical mogul, in the now-prevailing French Renaissance mode of R. M. Hunt who, in his recollections, credits the design of the house as his elder son's work. Lawrence's large house extends down the block of 78th Street, but takes the address, 969 Fifth Avenue. Lawrence is little known today, but he was a sturdy member of New York society and he and his wife, Sarah Bates Lawrence, swam rather quietly in the society stream. Lawrence purchased a large tract of land in Bronxville and soon hired a firm, Bates & Howe (Bates was not related to Mrs. Lawrence) to lay out a rather lovely English-styled suburb, Lawrence Park, where there was also big house for Lawrence and his family (rather as had A. T. Stewart in Garden City, Long Island,). In the 1920s following the death of his wife, William Lawrence created, Sarah Lawrence College next to their property in Lawrence Park.[20]

On the north corner of 78th Street sat the mansion of railroad magnate, Henry H. Cook. Heavy and solid, the large home faced down 78th Street with the address at 1 East 78th Street. Cook was a successful investor, who engaged in an unusual property scheme around his house. Seeing the success Astor and the Mason heirs had with their once too-far-uptown investments, Cook bought, literally, the entire block for a reported $300,000. The price for the land, so high in 1873, declined until 1879 when Cook got this very good price. The Cook block from 78th Street to 79th Streets, Fifth to Madison Avenue was to await the great days when mansions would join his single house. Cook had to wait two decades, but his investment with its strict residential covenant specifying only high-grade private houses, did fulfil his vision, and several fine houses were built there. The Cook block has remained as it was when the great builders were there. Henry Cook, as had Mary Mason Jones and the Astor grandchildren, sited his own home on the land to be developed, hiring William Wheeler Smith to build a big family home, embellished with fine paneling, fireplaces, and costly details, and completed in 1883.[21] The Cook house was big, solid and imposing with its façade detailed in three colors of granite.

By the time his lots were ready for great buildings, Cook had aged enough to decide to sell off his own home and move into the northern half of a co-joined house McKim, Mead & White were building for Payne Whitney, the son of W.C. Whitney and his wife, Flora Payne. The commission, undertaken just before the murder of their designer, Stanford White, was a particularly fine example of White's design in the early 20th century. The architectural firm made the bow and flat front houses a pair that almost appears to be a single home. Beautifully detailed, the houses were among the finest work done in the city. Stanford White's skills as an antiquities dealer can be seen in the purchases he made for the home of an American "prince," and he paid special attention to the Payne Whitney house, a truly treasure-filled home.[22]

In the early 20th century, the Duke brothers from North Carolina formed, with help, the American Tobacco Company, which produced ready-made cigarettes, and became extremely wealthy. James B. Duke did not marry until his middle age, when he made a brief and unhappy union, which ended in divorce. Duke soon after made a more successful second marriage. As a gift to his new wife, Duke danced around the purchase of the leaden Cook house for two years and, in 1909, he decided to demolish the house and create an elegant new residence. A year after Cook's death, James B. Duke started negotiations to buy the Cook house, but these property negotiations stalled until 1909. Duke paid $350,000 less than his original bid. Duke thought about rebuilding Cook's sturdy 25-year-old mansion. Duke called in Horace Trumbauer for an exquisite homage to a Hotel Labottière in Bordeaux. The gutting and demolition of Cook's house was not easy—amazingly only 25 years after construction. Duke considered

using C. P. H. Gilbert, the architect of the Fletcher house on his block, but switched instead to a Philadelphia architect, Horace Trumbauer, helping to launch Trumbauer's career in New York. The Duke house, which set a new standard for a fine house in Manhattan, was inspired by a patrician residence in Bordeaux translated into "American" by Julien Abele in the Trumbauer office, who is often noted to be one of the first architects of African American ancestry. The house was not even Duke's primary address, as he considered Duke Farms in New Jersey to be his main residence. The New York house was inhabited by just three people: Duke, his wife Nanaline, and new baby, Doris. Somehow, Duke must have thought it was a "requirement" to have such a house as a sign of his success, but the irony of this fine house is that Nanaline did not choose to join the social whirl of fashionable New York, and the impressive house was not used at first to shoehorn the Dukes into elite circles. In fact, many of the last of the big house builders did not mingle in the increasingly moribund social whirl. Neither Clark, Carnegie, nor this Duke brother made an effort to join the social world.[23]

DUKE HOUSE, FIFTH AVENUE AND EAST 78TH STREET

On the southern corner of 79th Street, on Cook land, the businessman, art collector and museum benefactor Isaac D. Fletcher had the

The Cook's large block property remained empty for sixteen years. Isaac Fletcher bought a northeast corner for a house in the style after Vanderbilt. C. P. H. Gilbert erected a signature form of a grand medieval mansion. The limestone house would be home to three important owners.

Isaac Fletcher gave the house and his collection of paintings to the Metropolitan Museum across the street. The museum sold the house to oil company founder Harry F. Sinclair. The teapot dome scandal ruined Sinclair. Augustus Van Horne Stuyvesant and his sister moved in. The last descendants of Peter Stuyvesant lived in the house until their deaths.

ISAAC BROKAW HOUSE

*Isaac Vail Brokaw, a
successful retail clothing
store owner, hired a
commercial architecture
firm, Rose & Stone,
to make a great solid
house on the corner of
79th Street. The French
château-style house of
1887 was heavier and
awkward in contrast
to the Fletcher House,
soon to appear across the
street.*

architect, C. P. H. Gilbert, build him a fine limestone château 1898—a generation after the success of the Vanderbilt house known as the Petit Château, New York residents noticed this fresh wave of the Gothic house. A neighbor two blocks below, the young Frieda Schiff, daughter of Jacob, admired Gilbert's work, and a decade after she married Felix Warburg, the couple chose to emulate this Fletcher house.

The Fletcher house was given to the Metropolitan Museum who sold it to Harry F. Sinclair, an oil man involved with the teapot dome scandal, which was the major political scandal of the first half of the 20th century, involving bribery and the Warren G. Harding presidency. Sinclair would sell it to the last of the Stuyvesants, the bachelor, Augustus Van Horne Stuyvesant, who had been living at

3 East 57th Street just east of the Mary Mason Jones home. Commerce was attacking this block, it was surely time for a move. With the retained ownership of a large part of the old Bowery Estate (62 acres), Stuyvesant was spared from working; he took a walk every day and remained within the house. As the office buildings arrived in 1930, this seventh-generation Stuyvesant, unmarried and with his two spinster sisters, paid $450,000 for the Sinclair house and died within it in the 1950s.

On the north corner of 79th Street, a wide crosstown street, Isaac Vail Brokaw, a merchant with a very successful store selling boys' attire, commissioned a very large granite house in the style of Hunt. Brokaw used a commercial firm, Rose & Stone, to design the house in an imitative château style and some years later, he had houses for his children built around his home by the same firm. Brokaw left a complex will, which meant the Brokaw houses on Fifth Avenue survived until the 1960s, long after the private homes had been replaced by apartment houses. The Brokaw houses and their demolition was a key part of New York City's new landmark law battle, losing to a banal replacement apartment building.[24]

Just above the Brokaw houses, Simon H. Stern, the father of the well-known political figure, Henry Root Stern, built a stone house at 986 Fifth Avenue in 1899. That very year, speculative builders Welch and Smith designed and built 987 next door, which became the home of William B. Leeds, the tin plate king. Leeds's widow remained in the house and expanded her social ambitions to the courts of Prussia and Paris, then seen as a wealthy appendage to the declining New York social scene (Leeds bought Rough Point in Newport as well, selling it to the industrialist James B. Duke when Mrs. Leeds settled for a Parisian social life). Just beyond the Leeds house were two houses by R. H. Robertson, one for John Sloane.

The corners had a C. P. H. Gilbert house built in that same year for Frank Woolworth of 5&10-cent store fame.[25] Across the street was a house of 1880 by Henry Hardenbergh for William A. Doaley, resembling work Hardenbergh would soon do for the Clark family on Central Park West.[26]

Up in the 80s

The Fifth Avenue frontage in the 80s was controlled by strong deed restrictions in the manner of the Henry Cook block. The only free building site was one August Belmont Jr. bought on the northern corner of 81st Street. Belmont saw how overrun his parents' block

*McKim, Mead &
White's limestone
luxury apartment house
changed the direction
of the Avenue. The
firm did some early
apartment houses, but
this 150-foot-tall block
opens the future of
the Avenue. 998 Fifth
Avenue, the apartment
house that made the
large multiple dwelling
acceptable.*

on 18th Street had become as factories and loft buildings dug into the streets, so he bought far above the fashionable area intending, one day, to build his home there.

He would sell the parcel to a syndicate, including James T. Lee, grandfather of Jaqueline Kennedy Onassis. As this property did not have the deed restriction for first-class dwellings, it would become the great apartment building at 998 Fifth Avenue, designed in the office of the second iteration of McKim, Mead & White in the early 20th century. This well thought-through venture here was built around an internal court, and the high-grade rental building paid off. The real estate man Douglas I. Elliman wrote on August 2, 1915 that the rents for such buildings on Fifth Avenue were about $12,000–$20,000 annually. The early tenants included the constantly moving man of Fifth Avenue, Levi P. Morton, as well as Elihu Root, a daughter of W. H. Vanderbilt, Mrs. Elliott Sheppard, and several Jewish tenants from the top layer of Goldman Sachs. The success of that apartment block opened the dam and in the next decade, first-class apartment

APARTMENT HOUSE
AT FIFTH AVENUE AND
85TH STREET

*As Fifth Avenue reached
Midtown, the blocks
of the mid 80s were
quite empty. A low-end
apartment developer
built a big block
building at 85th Street.
The market for tenants
was Yorkville to the
East, not a Fifth Avenue
group.*

buildings would run onto the Avenue like rushing water. The 1920s
would see a huge number of houses give way to apartment buildings;
the same would happen again in the 1950s.

Today, almost no residences survive on the Avenue. Those that do
were often speculative ventures designed by Welch, Smith & Provost
for successful developers like W. W. Hall, who built a number of
very high-end private dwellings that they would lease, at 997, 1007,
1009, 1014, 1015, and 1046. The house on the southern corner of
82nd Street was briefly home to tobacco millionaire James B. Duke's
brother, Benjamin Duke, and his family. The press noted in 1901
and 1902 that those who desired a house were seeking one that was
already created, which a person might lease and just open the front
door—the era of commissioning of new houses was coming to an
end. Indeed, the pattern was now reverting to the speculatively built

row house of the earlier decades on the lower part of the Avenue. Once in contract, these speculative houses would have different lease times, so, ironically, it is speculative houses built by Welch, Smith & Provost that survive to this day, while those in family hands were sold to apartment builders in the 1920s or 1950s. The narrow brownstone house, with its front and back parlor with inter-connecting doors, was seen by many in the late 19th century as rather like the cars of a railroad train. In 1909, Lloyd Warren, an architect and brother of the more famous architect, Whitney Warren, would take two of these houses which were narrow at 22 feet across and combine them into a new configuration, opening them up to a more elegant layout of rooms and avoiding the "usual, ill-proportioned drawing- rooms, shaped like Pullman cars."[27].

Uptown Brownstones

The first sets of brownstones on and near upper Fifth Avenue were those by Griffith Thomas for the heirs of the early department store magnates, Arnold and Constable, whose department store was a fixture in New York for a century. The daughter of Aaron Arnold would marry James Mansell Constable, combining the two partners names into the store name. Richard Arnold built several speculative houses in 83rd Street at the end of the 1870s depression in 1877 and 1878. Although these houses were in an empty section of the city, Constable correctly assumed that the relentless push northward would reward his wisdom while the economic recession had made the costs of building tempting to a man with some capital. The resulting brownstone row extended down 83rd Street east of Fifth Avenue. Many of these brownstones were re-fronted around 1900 to bring the 25-year-old houses into the fashion of the day. Prescient in real estate trends, he had Griffith Thomas build brownstones for them far above the inhabited part of the boulevard. But when the houses on the Avenue had reached 83rd Street, Mr. Arnold and his mother Henrietta both passed away and it would seem the death of important members of the family put this bit of early speculation on hold.

Arnold's house, so far above the developing city, remained empty for some 15 years when William Salomon, Senior bought the long empty brownstone at 1020 Fifth Avenue. Trowbridge & Livingston built a house for Salomon who, after considering extensive renovation on the existing brownstone, bought two plots next to it and commissioned a brand new and large house. Salomon had been the head of the Baltimore and Ohio Railroad but was now ready to start his own banking firm. He celebrated in 1901–06 with the new house and a lengthy sojourn in Europe, buying the requisite tapestries, paintings, fireplaces, ceilings, and furniture for the new home, which he memorialized in 1912, with a lavish, large format volume with images of the rooms in the house. The curious volume has no title nor text and must have been a gift the proud homeowner shared with friends. The house, with its interiors of European items, seemed to be virtually worthless sixteen years later when Salomon died. The auctioneer received no bid for the property and the house was demolished for an apartment house.[28]

From 84th to 85th Streets the corner and four more houses (possibly speculative units) were built by S. D. Hatch for H. N. Spencer Trask, a banker and broker who is mainly known for his home in Brooklyn, in 1870, very early for the upper avenue. Trask had a fine house named Yaddo in Saratoga, New York, now a summer retreat for authors. The "Countess" Annie Leary, who had been awarded the title by Pope Leo XIII, which she frequently used, in 1903 in gratitude for her generosity to the Church, lived at 1032, one of the Trask houses, until she moved back to lower Fifth Avenue.. Annie Leary and her brother Arthur, deeply Catholic, were allowed into Ward McAllister's 400, which usually forbade all but Protestants (Papal Countess, the first in America).[29]

The Upper Avenue

Beyond an empty lot, the first true apartment house was built on Fifth Avenue in 1889. The Fifth Avenue Apartments was a six- or seven-story (there were differing accounts in the papers) block by Philip Braender for Frank Wennemer (Wennemer had a practice in building apartment buildings in the German area to the east in Yorkville). Really more of an upper-end tenement than a grand apartment block, the building drew its residents from the new German community in Yorkville. The apartment tenants were middle class families. This mundane apartment house directly on Fifth Avenue reinforces the ordinary sense of the location, which was to change very rapidly. New York had a height restriction on apartment houses under the 1885 Daly Law, when the Fifth Avenue Apartment building was finished, so the land cost must have been modest. If it had been costly, the six-story limitation would not have made the building a viable option.

Across 85th Street a house was built early in 1868 as 1040 Fifth by W. W. Gardner for G. Hoffman, with a then-fashionable mansard roof. In 1908, Horace Trumbauer replaced the earlier house, turning it inward as 1 East 85th Street for the railroad executive James B. Clews.[30] To his north were three brownstones turned into English basement entries by removing the stoops and smoothing away existing old-

WILLIAM STARR MILLER
HOUSE, 1048 FIFTH
AVENUE, ON THE
SOUTHEAST CORNER
OF FIFTH AVENUE AND
86TH STREET

*William Starr Miller
Jr. lived at 39 Fifth
Avenue in "old" Fifth
Avenue. In 1912 he
commissioned Carrere
& Hastings, major
figures of their day, to
build a large town house
on the corner of 86th
Street among many
ordinary brownstones.
The red brick and
limestone house was
indeed distinctive with
its high-pitched Mansard
roof. Miller, an attorney,
married very well: Edith
Caroline Warren, an
heir to the Warren and
Phoenix Estates. Mrs.
Miller's brother was
the architect Whitney
Warren, who built
the couple's Newport
house. Curiously, the
Millers selected a rival
firm for the 86th Street
house. The Millers'
daughter, Edith Starr
Miller, married Almeric
Paget, first Baron
Queensborough, in 1921.
The grandchildren lived
in England. Almeric
Paget was previously
married to Pauline
Payne Whitney.*

*The house contrasts with
the earlier brownstones
on the left.*

fashioned ornament. This may also be the work of Lloyd Warren. To the southern corner was the small flats building we already saw, which was built for eleven families. The tenants at the Fifth Avenue apartments changed over several decades. 1048 Fifth Avenue became William Starr Miller's new home as he moved north from 39 Fifth Avenue, where he lived with his wife, a Warren of New York and Albany (the Millers had a house in Newport by Whitney Warren, a relative of Mrs. Miller). Their daughter married Sir Almeric Hugh Paget in 1921. The tall townhouse of brick and limestone stands out among the brownstones. Several American women married Pagets, including the green-eyed Minnie Stevens, whose adventures with her mother are discussed in the section devoted to Marietta Stevens. The building was bought by a developer in about 1924 who would demolish the Fifth Avenue apartment and an empty lot to its south for an apartment building by J.E.R. Carpenter, still standing. Later the house became the last residence of Grace Wilson Vanderbilt, the rather notorious wife of Cornelius Vanderbilt III who was unwelcome by the family. She would die there in 1953. The house is the Ronald Lauder Museum of Austrian and German Art, today the Neue Galerie.

James Speyer, whose family banking business was most successful, married Ellin Prince Lowery. Speyer, who was Jewish, and his bride, a Christian, were accepted in society by none other than Mrs. Astor. The couple lived at 207 Madison Avenue in an area where bankers, such as George F. Baker, also lived. Commerce pushed the bankers

to the north. Speyer followed J. B. Duke to the Philadelphia architect Horace Trumbauer. The Speyer house was very wide at 75 feet (3 lots) on Fifth Avenue, and deep down the side street. Precious interiors were designed by Ogden Codman. The Speyers had a fine art collection. Speyer left the house to the Museum of the City of New York, who sold it for an apartment house in 1951.

A Steel Magnate's Mansion

As we know, the hoped-for model of land being bought well above the inhabited part of the city yet being developed in a lucrative way a lifetime later, led some, with capital, to buy parcels on "the upper Avenue" in the 1880s. The upper avenue referred to land in the blocks of the 80s and 90s, then sparsely inhabited with the home of an unusual millionaire and some middle-class brownstones. We have seen that August Belmont's sons bought plots for future homes they would never build, while a few new-monied men purchased these plots and built large homes with an ample amount of open space for gardens, driveways, and extra buildings. In 1901, a humbly born man from Pittsburgh with a fortune made along with Frick and Carnegie in the steel factories joined the other two and moved to New York City. Henry Phipps, like Carnegie, came from an impoverished neighborhood where the elder Phipps was a shoemaker. After U.S. Steel was created, Phipps likely settled into a fortune of about a hundred million dollars. Phipps and Carnegie did not fully forget their beginnings. Each man conceived and executed a series of philanthropies which would assist newcomers to America get started on a decent life.

Phipps and Carnegie built large homes three blocks distant in about the same years—Phipps purchased lots from Perry Belmont and E. H. Van Ingen on the north corner of Fifth Avenue. Phipps wanted a house in a grand setting with a carriage turn-around, garden spaces, and an orangery. He hired Trowbridge & Livingston, a young firm starting out in the mansion business to design an exquisite home facing the city to the south. The house took four years to build and decorate with help from a young English architect whom he had met in Pittsburgh, Alfred Charles Bossom. Bossom arrived in New York in 1903 from England and remained and worked in the American south until he returned to England in 1926. The fine marble mansion was completed as Phipps took on other properties such as a big house in Great Neck, Long Island.

Phipps was able to move in the highest levels of American society by the early 20th century, renting a Scottish castle for the shooting season in August and hosting grand parties. The shooting parties took place near the estates of the royal family in Balmoral, and were much frequented by British bankers, giving Americans an opportunity to establish relationships with businessmen, as well as aristocrats, in the United Kingdom. Phipps invited C. F. McKim, Edith Wharton, Beatrix Ferrand, and others to be his guests at the "shooting parties." Inspired by his success in meeting people in the United Kingdom, Phipps's son, John Shaffer Phipps, would import materials, such as slates from Wales and other fine materials, from British makers for his Westbury house. Some of the treasures from the 87th Street house reside today in Phipps's son's great house Westbury Gardens (the house and garden are open to the public).[31]

Phipps thought he would protect himself by buying two lots just east of his orangery on 89th Street, but it did not prove enough

*Henry Phipps Jr. was
closely associated with
neighbor Andrew
Carnegie. Phipps
managed to enter
high society despite
his humble roots. His
philanthropic work was
extensive. Two years
after Carnegie purchased
his "hill," Phipps bought
a plot belonging to
Perry Belmont. The
architects, Trowbridge
& Livingston, built
an elegant palace
approached via a
semi-circular drive. An
"orangerie," a rarity in
New York City, sat on
the east side of the white
limestone house.*

forethought. In 1915, as fashionable apartment houses began claiming former homeowners, the land to Phipps's east was sold for a twelve-story block of apartments. Horrified to be in the shadow of the new building, Phipps sold his house for a future apartment house within twelve years of moving in; it was built just after World War I by J. E. R. Carpenter, who would build many of the first generation of fine apartment blocks in the 1920s. His grand and gracious apartment building, such as 1060 Fifth Avenue, would make Fifth Avenue apartment buildings acceptable when they began to replace the houses.[32] Perhaps the superb Phipps house may have had one of the briefest lives on Fifth Avenue, although ironically, Phipps Tenements, built as part of his generosity on West 42nd Street, are still standing today.

To the north of Phipps's house and begun the same year were two speculative houses for H. M. Weed designed by Janes & Leo. In keeping with the new addition to the neighborhood, the two houses were built at the very highest end, costing $150,000 for the southern abode and $200,000 for the corner house. Leo Stein, of the Baltimore/San Francisco eccentric and artistic family, leased the southern house at 1068. His sister, was Gertrude Stein, and he would eventually move to Paris into a house by Le Corbusier.

The second of the two speculative houses developed by Hamilton Weed at 1069 Fifth Avenue was bought from foreclosure by Mrs. James B. Reynolds, the heir to the Spingler/Van Buren farm at 21 West 14th Street, the last of the farms near the fashionable growth of Fifth Avenue in the mid 19th century. Weed went bankrupt in the banking crisis of 1907. Mrs. Reynolds only lived uptown for six years, dying in 1914. The two houses would be demolished in 1929.

Proceeding across 88th Street were more high-end speculative houses and a house for George H. Penniman of 1897. The architects, Babb, Cook & Welch, then a rather out-of-date practice, would notably be chosen by Andrew Carnegie for his new house two years later.

The Huntington House

At the southern corner, Benjamin Duke, of tobacco and textile fortune, who had moved frequently, finally built his own house. In 1908 Duke joined the fan club of the architect C. P. H. Gilbert and requested a house to cost $190,00 on the site. The block would soon attract Moses Taylor and Archer M. Huntington. Archer Milton Huntington was born in 1870 and lived with his mother, Arabella, on 54th Street, then 57th Street in the big house his likely true father Collis P. Huntington built for them. We have seen both these houses in the chapter on the streets of the '50's. Collis Huntington died in 1900 leaving a third of his estate to Archer. Two years later Archer bought two of the high-end speculative houses at 1082 and 1083 Fifth Avenue, part of a three-house row by Turner & Killian. Archer had a life interest in the family house on 57th Street house, which was to go to Yale if he had no children (actually, Huntington tried to sell the house in his lifetime and the case was taken on by John Lambert Cadwalader, a high-profile attorney of the day much involved with causes like the New York Public Library).

Huntington rented 1083 Fifth Avenue, hiring in 1913 the equisite socialite and sometime architect Ogden Codman Jr. to re-front and transform it into an elegant townhouse with an L-shaped wing around the corner. This was home to Archer and his second wife, Anna Hyatt Huntington, the sculptor. At her death in 1940 the house became the National Academy of Design and Art School.

Archer Huntington's likely father was a coarse, ill-mannered man. Arabella, Collis Huntington's second wife, while self-trained, was a far more sophisticated person, learning to speak French well and devoting herself to the collection of first-class works of art. If Arabella had any idea of joining the New York social scene, it

ARCHER M.
HUNTINGTON
PROPERTY, 89TH–91ST
STREETS, INCLUDING THE
HUNTINGTON HOUSE AT
1083 FIFTH AVENUE

*The block with
the Archer Milton
Huntington House was
part of a group of bow-
fronted houses of good
size and uses a variety of
materials. The group was
built by George Edgar.
Huntington bought
several of the houses
and asked the socialite
and sometime architect
Ogden Codman Jr.,
to redo his property at
1083 Fifth Avenue, in
1913. In 1940, the house
was bequethed to The
National Academy of
Design.*

failed with a possibly true tale of Ward McAllister. We do know
McAllister both worked for the newspapers and accepted fat fees
for bringing a person into society. The story has it that McAllister
hosted a party for Collis Huntington and Arabella and had them
present at a society event, making these arrangements in exchange
for a $9,000 gift to McAllister, although it is impossible to know if
this occurred. It is reported that Huntington did not pay McAllister
after the deed was done and McAllister had the press write negatively
about Huntington's manners—probably condemning them as too
crude for social acceptance. But Collis's son Archer Huntington was
a gentleman and a scholar, who devoted his life to learned societies,
creating Audubon Terrace on upper Broadway and funding many
cultural institutions. Archer Huntington's deepest devotion was to
Spanish culture, then little studied in Protestant America, and he
created the Hispanic Society with a magnificent library of books on
Spanish subjects in upper Manhattan.

Archer Milton Huntingdon had no children. The will of Collis
Huntington promised the valuable family home site to Yale after
Archer's death. As Arabella aged and died, Archer tired of the property
taxes and went to court with Cadwalader to fight the restriction
promising Yale the money from any sale, which he eventually won.
Huntington had all the money he needed and no heirs and only
wanted to remove taxes and upkeep on the house. He did not live
there and was willing to give the sale funds to Yale University.

Archer gave the great art collection in the 57th Street house to the Metropolitan Museum. Of the big, sturdy house, Archer remarked that his father liked to build things well, which proved a problem in the widening of Fifth Avenue. To make the roadbed wider, the bay window and Fifth Avenue detail needed to be removed. Given the intricate stonework in the gray granite castle, the removal of projecting portions of the house spoiled its rather dim aesthetic appeal and caused unwelcome disruption in the house.

The Houses of the 90s

Andrew Carnegie, born in 1835 in Scotland, arrived in Pittsburgh as a poor laborer. By the later part of the century, he had invested well in many growth parts of the economy, as well as creating the Carnegie Steel Company. When J. P. Morgan united his company as U.S. Steel, Carnegie became, arguably, the richest man in America.

Carnegie had a house just west of Fifth Avenue for many years. Carnegie married rather late in life in 1887, giving his bride, ten years his junior, a Second Empire house on 51st Street just west of Fifth Avenue, the most fashionable part of the city. The Carnegies lived in New York, but when he sold the steel works, he came to New York City as a full resident (he did have a castle in Scotland). Carnegie and Henry Clay Frick went from associates to rivals for New York City properties, as each was determined to acquire a full block on Fifth Avenue. Frick achieved this by demolishing the Lenox Library in the second decade of the 20th century, as we know. When the Carnegies had a daughter, Margaret, after a decade of marriage, Mrs. Carnegie insisted upon a new house to raise their daughter. Carnegie himself was content to rebuild the 51st Street house, but his wife insisted on a large place for the child. Using an attorney, Carnegie bought a number of plots on a rather empty part of the Avenue twenty blocks above his house, purchasing several plots as he wanted control of the future of the neighborhood. A lemonade stand and shacks stood nearby, while the Fifth Avenue Riding Academy was on the block he bought, which he quickly demolished. Carnegie's site needed modern engineering to level the hill for the comfortable and modest house Carnegie claimed he envisioned. He wanted all the latest tech for the house, but in a building of unostentatious appearance.

The Carnegies had traveled to Europe on their honeymoon in 1889 and became friendly with the conductor, Walter Damroche, whom they met on the boat. Carnegie had been involved with the creation of Madison Square Garden, but pulled out as he came to dislike the McKim, Mead & White's partner in charge of Madison Square

*Andrew Carnegie lived
in fashionable New York
when he and his wife
had their first and only
child. His wife insisted
their new daughter
needed light and air.
Carnegie, who wanted
to rival his soon-to-be
former partner, Frick,
demanded a full block
on Fifth Avenue as
Frick would also obtain.
Carnegie asked Babb,
Cook & Willard to
design a "modest, plain,
and roomy house."
Carnegie's house was a
replica English Georgian
manor, and is heavy
and rather oppressive.
Brick and limestone, it
was indeed roomy. The
large, landscaped garden
is an important portion
of Carnegie's vision for
his new house. Carnegie
had married late in life,
and his daughter was
born in 1897, just before
the house was completed.
Seems a mighty large
home for three people.*

Garden, Stanford White, and built his own music venue, Carnegie
Hall, which has survived to the present day. When it came time to
select a firm to design his new 91st Street house, Carnegie rejected
McKim, Mead & White and their former protegés then doing the
fancy houses on the Avenue.

He narrowed it down to three firms, choosing Walter Cook of Babb,
Cook & Welch, then not at their prime. Babb, a great Victorian
architect, had aged and was out of style. Cook, of Scottish descent,
ran the firm. Cook's mother's family were old-time New York City
landowners, who had just finished the Penniman house a block away.
Carnegie claimed he selected Cook as he was the only architect in New
York who did not beg for the commission. The house of brick and
limestone is rather heavy and oppressive; with a most sophisticated
plan.

To Mrs. Carnegie, a large garden for the child was vital, and she did
get her wish fulfilled. Carnegie's huge brick and stone house/mansion
sat with a carriage entry at 1 East 91st Street on the north. A large
garden, the largest plot of nature on the Avenue, faced, or protected,
Carnegie to the south. New York noticed the wealth of Carnegie
and his ability to buy a number of developable sites, leaving them
unbuilt. While Carnegie wanted control of his house and immediate
surroundings, his extra plots were now to be sold to people who he
might want to have as neighbors.

Carnegie was a complex person who tried to keep his "generous man of the people" image by making remarkable benefactions, including the system of Carnegie Libraries in the United States and United Kingdom, as well as numerous other philanthropies, yet assume a baronial lifestyle. The requirement that the house be unassuming while taking up a full block, along with his insistence on vetting future neighbors, displayed the contradiction of his thinking.[33]

Carnegie's entry faced 91st Street. A few side streets in Manhattan would garner an especially brilliant tone and 91st Street would become one of the finest blocks in the city. Henry Hope Reed, the dean of classical architectural appreciation in the mid-20th century, led walks of the block and featured it as a cover story in the magazine section of the *New York Herald Tribune* on October 21, 1962. The north corner remained empty for quite a while until Otto Kahn built his new house, one of the best and last mansions on the Avenue. But just east at 7 East 91st Street, James A. Burden Jr. would have Warren & Wetmore build a house in 1902. Burden had at least three houses on Fifth Avenue. We have seen his 1893 house on 72nd Street (907 Fifth Avenue). Two years later he married a very wealthy woman (907 Fifth Avenue was the first building on the upper Avenue to be demolished for a 12-story apartment house in 1916 well before the boom in apartment houses after World War I). At this time, several of the great families of New York were presenting their children with houses at their marriage, so when Burden married a Vanderbilt great granddaughter he received a house on 91st Street from his father-in-law. Next door, a Vanderbilt sister married John Henry Hammond and also had a new house by Carrere & Hastings. Carrere & Hastings completed the house at 9 East 91st Street. The limestone house had an internal court with a fountain. Music was important to the Hammonds. They hosted Benny Goodman, who would marry their daughter, Alice. No. 7 East 91st Street was a wedding gift for James A. Burden and his Vanderbilt/Sloane bride. The elaborately detailed Beaux Arts stone house was designed by Warren & Wetmore. The house, as was the optimal arrangement in the early 1900s, had a low set of steps rather than the older stoop entry. The wedding house at 11 East 91st Street for groom John B. Trevor and his bride, Caroline Wilmerding, was a fine limestone house, with perfect proportions and subtle detail, built by Trowbridge & Livingstone in 1909-11. Although only 26 feet wide, the Trevor house held its own against its more florid neighbor at 9 East 91st Street. The three houses would represent the ideal for urban houses of the first decade of the 20th century. Ironically, of course, these smaller, but fine, houses would

Right:
Trevor House, 11 East
91st Street

*91st Street was a special
group of houses on
what was now being
called "Carnegie
Hill." In 1909 the
architects, Trowbridge
& Livingston, created
a fine limestone with
perfect proportions
and remarkably subtle
detail for John Bond
Trevor and his bride,
Caroline Wilmerding.
Only 26 feet wide, the
Trevor House held its
own against the more
florid neighbors on the
Avenue.*

live on while the Fifth Avenue mansions of a generation earlier would
die. New York City retains these early 20th-century individualized
and fine row houses when all the Fifth Avenue mansions were
replaced by apartment blocks in the 1920s and 1950s. How quickly
that world would end.

Later, in 1913, Otto Kahn, a man known for both his business and
social skills, was allowed to buy the empty corner plot from Andrew
Carnegie and built the last and superb New York version of the
Palazzo della Cancelleria in 1917. How amazing that a newcomer to
America could liken himself to a Cardinal, the builder of the original
Palazzo della Cancelleria, who was said to have built his palace on

Otto Kahn House

1 East 91st Street was built on land purchased by Otto Kahn from Andrew Carnegie. Carnegie did not sell plots to just anyone. The house was commissioned rather late in 1917 to C. P. H. Gilbert and J. Armstrong Stenhouse, who brought the Italian Renaissance palace to a German born American banker. The stone courtyard was a private drive. Kahn brought European grandeur even to an Adam-style ceiling in the music room. He built a house with a most sophisticated plan.

the winnings of gaming. The model was especially interesting for a German of Jewish heritage (the house would eventually become part of the Sacred Heart Roman Catholic School). J. Armstrong Stenhouse and C. P. H. Gilbert created this huge family home. If Alva Vanderbilt claimed Caen stone was the stone of her "*petit château*," Otto Kahn actually used it for his 1917, 80-room house. Kahn liked his houses and built fine homes in New Jersey, then Huntington, Long Island for weekend houses.

In the opposite spirit of wedding gift houses, Felix Warburg of a German banking family married Frieda Schiff whose father was a partner in Kuhn, Loeb in 1895. The couple initially lived at 18 East 72nd Street before buying the 100-by-100-foot plot on 92nd Street from Perry Belmont for $400,000 in 1907. As we remember, Frieda Schiff Warburg requested a version of the Isaac Fletcher house on 79th Street near her parent's home. The couple commissioned the Fletcher architect, C. P. H. Gilbert, to do another version of his château style for which he had become famous. In 1907, Gilbert began the Warburg house for Frieda's husband, Felix Warburg. Jacob Schiff at first was

FELIX WARBURG HOUSE

The range of design practiced by C. P. H. Gilbert can be seen in these two houses located so close to each other. As unlikely people to join the old ways of the wealthy, both Otto Kahn and Felix Warburg used cultural generosity to garner respect. Frieda Schiff Warburg wanted the château-styled houses that were a specialty of C. P. H. Gilbert. The Warburg house is now the Jewish Museum. The Schiffs continued to work with Gilbert on their large country house in Oyster Bay.

unhappy about the house but relented once it was finished.[34] He may have resented the couple starting the house without consulting him or may have been concerned that the very lavish brief given to Gilbert might cause jealousy and inappropriate notoriety for the couple, perhaps causing an anti-Semitic reaction locally. These two C. P. H. Gilbert houses were built for men who did not play the social game. Frieda and Felix finished their house with a generous, post-completion gift from Jacob Schiff. The house today is the Jewish Museum.

On the corner of 93rd Street was a very early house for the brewery magnate Jacob Ruppert. The turreted, rather coarse house of 1881, built by William Schickel, was far above the developed part of the

JACOB RUPPERT HOUSE, SEEN FROM PARK AVENUE

We see how very empty Upper Fifth Avenue was when the family built a long-lost castle on East 93rd Street. William Schickel was the architect in 1880 for a fellow German New Yorker.

Avenue. Sitting in splendid isolation, but only a few blocks west from the Ruppert brewery on 91st Street and Third Avenue, the Ruppert interiors were done by the Herter Brothers, who were working for W. H. Vanderbilt 40 blocks to the south. Ruppert's father, William Schickel, and the Herter Brothers were all German speakers, which may explain the selection of the contractors.

Willard Straight skipped a block and at 94th Street commissioned Delano & Aldrich to design a sophisticated English-styled house in 1915. Straight worked for J. P. Morgan with a specialty in Asia and especially China. The house signaled a departure from castles, châteaux, and palazzi in favor of British good taste, and Straight returned to the old deed restriction program found on the East side. The deed mandated that the house was to be used for small scale residential purposes only, which explains its survival. The Willard Straight house signaled the end of the aspirations of new money to seek European pedigree, reflecting instead the absorption of a high-minded, principled approach to an American gentleman. Straight began such a life as the husband of Dorothy Whitney, whose money supplied the funds for his life. Sadly, this was cut short by the 1918 Spanish flu and his early death deprived the diplomatic community of

Delano and Aldrich.
Willard Straight House,
1915. View from the
west.

the nation. Dorothy Whitney Straight moved to England and became a subject of the United Kingdom.[35]

Rather like music which starts out in a familiar and low tone, then progresses towards a crashing crescendo, Fifth Avenue began in an atmosphere of quiet civility and ended with a blazing triumphal chorus. Was Fifth Avenue always destined to be the vehicle that would pull the city to the north? Would the old Knickerbockers of Brevoort's era imagine the spectacular future of the Avenue in seventy some years? Slowly and steadily, more money and bigger ambitions created a street which left behind convention for what was a boxing match of architectural styles. As the new group of men popularly known as robber barons emerged, they seemed to require strident and huge houses to extend their identity. The big houses made the builders famous for spending so very much money with only an elusive goal.

Did these builders realize that polo and yachts in Long Island, major social events in Newport and grandchildren in other locations would end the need for a signature house? By the time these huge houses were being built, social recognition had faded as corporate identity became the motivational factor in social mobility. While Mrs. Astor had become irrelevant, J.P. Morgan had consolidated family businesses into corporations. The message of the houses was now about corporate projection: did anyone imagine the life of the house on the Upper Avenue would be less than a single generation?

CHAPTER 16

THE FIFTH AVENUE ADDRESS STARTS TO FADE

"The avenue would be greatly improved in appearance when deluxe apartments would replace the old-style mansions."

J. E. R. Carpenter, Architect. Height restriction court case, 1923.

BY THE EARLY 20TH CENTURY, the New York City house was no longer a central need in the lives of many Fifth Avenue families. The upkeep of a house in Manhattan was costly and tedious and living in the Marais or Mayfair seemed more enticing many families with Fifth Avenue addresses were now living abroad. Other families now had country estates in Westchester or Long Island, summer "cottages" in Newport or watering holes in the northeast, sport-shooting plantations in the south, as well as Adirondack camps.

The issue of servants was an increasing vein of contention for those managing the houses. Reliable house staff retired, and new household mechanical appliances started to change household work patterns. The automobile was beginning to appear, soon to replace the horse-drawn coach, which would limit the need for coachmen. Searches for new staff were burdensome, and anxieties were compounded by sinister stories from friends, as well as accounts in the newspapers, of crimes involving household staff—these were especially alarming for absentee house owners.

J.P. Morgan and other investment bankers were enlarging and combining the older companies into large new corporations. As corporations began to replace individual and family businesses, the company founders became rather irrelevant and the need to project one's business or brains via a great house had evaporated. The 75-year saga of the house as image creator and sustainer faded quickly.

The Tide Turns

The Record & Guide on July 13, 1912, reflected upon the development of first-class houses. The editor noted that the customary northward advance of a block a year had been maintained between 1890 to 1900, but by 1905 the center of fashion had moved three blocks northward. By 1905 the center was at 58th Street, two years later at 62nd Street, then by 1910 the center was branching to the east on streets emanating from Fifth Avenue.

By the early years of the 20th century, it was obvious that only really costly houses could now be built. House construction on Fifth Avenue went from 779 houses in 1889 to just 56 in 1903[1] as restrictive covenants inhibited non-residential development in many parts of Manhattan. The Cook properties might be the best known example, but there were many other deed restrictions. A big blow to real estate development came in the early years of the 20th century when Columbia College, with its 11-acre property, once the nursery of Dr. Hosack, stopped enforcing their deed restriction of 1859, which had barred buildings housing multiple dwellings, commercial buildings, and (heavens!) industrial use on their residential rowhouse property. With the covenants removed, the 60-year-old brownstones descended into a wild array of uses; brothels and speakeasies sprang up among the rooming houses and other illicit businesses. Columbia's action must have angered Benjamin Altman, who had just built his art gallery behind his rental house at the same time, while the Vanderbilts, who had bought a property across the street from their house to curtail commercial development, also had to give in to development of the property. Columbia, with their brownstone rental houses, had helped establish the neighborhood three generations earlier. Now, Columbia needed to build their third campus at Morningside Heights and showed no concern for their neighbors in the region, throwing the 11 acres and surrounding properties under the proverbial bus.

The Triumph of Commerce

By 1909, the battle with taller commercial buildings on the Avenue had ended. On the Langham Hotel site (once the Osborne), the Vanderbilts gave up the long and expensive battle and sold the property for the 12-story Dutton building. Three more commercial buildings were quickly constructed. Commercial developers of hotels and office buildings were prepared to pay far more for property and very quickly, over the course of about five years, the prime residential area of the blocks in the 50s had transformed into the new reality. By 1912, residential life had ended below 59th Street. A tall building loomed over Arabella and Archer Huntington on 57th Street, which had become virtually a business street by World War I. All signs seemed to point to great change rushing onto the Avenue. One can only wonder why William Kissam Vanderbilt Jr. hired McKim, Mead & White to double the house of his parents at 666 Fifth Avenue; his new house would survive only 21 years.

By 1913, even the young John D. Rockefeller Jr. saw the potential for commercial buildings on the west side of Fifth Avenue in his very own neighborhood. Rockefeller had lived in these streets for some 35 years yet, when the local Episcopal Church, St. Thomas, suffered a massive fire in 1907, even he thought of buying the site for commercial development. St. Thomas disappointed Rockefeller by deciding to rebuild and would have Ralph Adams Cram and his partner Goodhue design the church, which is still on the site today. Rockefeller interests would overtake Vanderbilt purchases on these blocks. The aging daughters of William Henry Vanderbilt, Mmes Twombly and Webb, who had commissioned Snook to build them houses as part of "Vanderbilt Alley" in the early 1880s, were ready to abandon their 53rd Street homes next to St. Thomas and move northwards, and Rockefeller bought them out. By the 1920s, all the Vanderbilt women had moved uptown, across from Central Park. Even Alice Claypoole Vanderbilt moved into the George Gould house at 857 Fifth Avenue when her mansion was sold for Bergdorf Goodman's future store.[2] In about 1927 Rockefeller demolished the Vanderbilt homes, and built a six-story commercial building, putting the swanky Revillion Furrier in the ground floor in 1929 (*Record & Guide* asserts Rockefeller owned Revillion at this time, but I could not find any confirmation). The Da Pinna store, which opened on erstwhile Vanderbilt and now the Rockefeller site at 642–650 Fifth Avenue at 52nd Street, sold merchandise that stressed fine tailoring, but it closed in 1959.

Height Restrictions

A new group had formed in 1907—The Fifth Avenue Association—with a mandate to protect the Avenue from encroaching factories in the loft areas around 30th Street. The role of the Association grew with the concept of holding down the height of new buildings on the Avenue. Moving northward, the Fifth Avenue Association required buildings to be up to 125 feet high, depending on the width of the street. The Association would be a key factor in the 1916 New York City Zoning Resolution, which tried to work with issues of light, air, and the bulk of the building. The Fifth Avenue Association's professed height for apartment buildings on Fifth Avenue met a severe test on the Upper Avenue in the years after World War I. In 1919 a big apartment building was constructed at 1067 Fifth Avenue, just above the Phipps house, by C. P. H. Gilbert, who had turned his collar around from architect of fine private houses to designing the new, large apartment house. In 1921 the height rule was challenged, and in 1924 the Court of Appeals of New York State overthrew the Association's height concept. The apartment building boom would quickly follow.

The final factor which ended the private home on the Avenue was a version of the phenomenon that drove the builders to the street across from the park—looming neighbors. The tall commercial buildings pushed the private homes to the blocks above 60th Street. Many of these plots were deeper (115 rather than 100 feet), allowing the builders to create light-wells in the middle of the houses. By moving to the north, house owners had misguidedly assumed that the park would protect their investment on Upper Fifth Avenue. They thought they would have protection from commercial buildings, but even though the office buildings would not proceed to the areas across from Central Park, they did not figure on the 1920s apartment boom.

Some of the Fifth Avenue house owners who no longer needed a city residence conferred with developers wishing to build ten-story deluxe apartment houses on the Avenue, realizing that the height restriction of 150 feet allowed for such buildings. In 1922 New York City reduced the height to 75 feet, which only allowed a five-story building. Some developers and the well-born architect, J. E. R. Carpenter, fought and overturned the mandated height the next year, opening the flood gates to the arrival of the high-grade apartment house. The Jabez Bostwick house, was the subject of a major legal case in the early 1900s, when the house had been demolished and architects were seeking to construct a tall building on the site, an inevitable result of the rise in land values. In a decision of April 1, 1924 in the Court of Appeals, the height restriction on the Fifth Avenue frontage was raised to 150 feet, a height that would make an apartment building a viable investment.[3] This would quickly doom the remaining houses as the sums being offered for them were now fantastic.[4]

As the apartment houses took over the Upper Avenue, commerce took over the midtown locations. The Fifth Avenue address from 34th to 59th Streets was morphing from house owners to commercial office buildings and department stores. Fifth Avenue would retain its magic for a while, but now for a different world. And, today, even that is gone as department stores reach the end of their lifespan.

CHAPTER 17

TRADING A HOUSE FOR AN APARTMENT

"She [the nanny] wanted us to have the party in Robert's father's house on 70th Street in the first place. I'm serious. She doesn't <u>like</u> this apartment. It embarrasses her! ... Do you know who runs the East side of New York? The nanny mafia."

Tom Wolfe, *The Kandy-Kolored Tangerine-Flake Streamline Baby*, 1965

TRADE AND BUSINESS pushed residences out as tall buildings brought numerous employees to the blocks near Fifth Avenue and the new skyscrapers cast great shadows, killing the back gardens of the houses. Larger numbers of people flooded the once-quiet streets. This happened very quickly in the area we call midtown today, especially in the streets of the upper 40s and 50s. Astors and Rockefellers tried to stop the commercial invasions of a rapidly-growing midtown business district, which was tied to close-by Grand Central station, bringing commuters from northern suburbs. The rich and seemingly powerful did not succeed in stopping the commercial building boom. Even the Vanderbilts, whose west side of Fifth Avenue was known as Vanderbilt Alley, found their property facing commerce across the Avenue.

Stemming the Tide
On the east side of Fifth Avenue between 55th and 56th Streets, William Waldorf Astor hired Clinton & Russell (by now Astor architects building on Astor properties on the Upper West Side) to build four first-class dwelling houses in 1895. The elaborate houses were to be up for rent as 721–25 Fifth Avenue. These houses were built as an early attempt to preclude commercial development in this premium area.[1]

When the east side of the Avenue between 51st and 52nd Streets came on to the market, the city's most important club, the Union Club, grabbed the southern corner, moving up from their old club house.

Surely private homes would join the club on the block? Sure enough, in 1901, plans were revealed for an 18-story apartment house on the rest of the block. The Vanderbilts still intended to remain in their houses and in order to prevent the huge shadow-producing building, they unhappily had to buy out the developing syndicate. It cost the family a million dollars for the land and another million to have Hunt & Hunt build the "marble twins," two houses, as a place saver. The two identical houses were rented out, one to Robert Goelet, who had tired of his house twelve blocks below. Soon though, the Vanderbilts sold the corner plot to Morton F. Plant for his beautiful house by R. W. Gibson (now Cartier). Within one of the "twins" the Vanderbilt family would later have their last residence on Fifth Avenue.

No sooner had the east side frontage been saved, the Hotel Langham on the corner of the next block, the former home of Mme. Restell, was pulled down for redevelopment, and the Vanderbilts had to buy that corner as well. What to do with it? At first, in 1902, the family thought of building a house there, then "Silent" Smith offered to buy the land and build a house. A few years later, after William C. Whitney died and his house came on the market, "Silent" Smith bought the Whitney house, and the Restell site went to Frederick G. Bourne of the Singer Sewing Machine Company. Bourne showed an interest in the corner for a while, but did not build. With the New York City decision of 1908 to widen the street part of Fifth Avenue for the new automobiles, the sidewalks were pushed to the edge of the actual buildings, forcing the house owners to chop off green spaces, stoops, ornamental projections, and the like. Suddenly, it felt as if change was unstoppable and Fifth Avenue was losing its charm. The Vanderbilts gave in and sold the corner, once the notorious home of Mme. Restell, to a commercial developer for a boring new office building—even the grandest of families could not stem the tide. Some of the family moved farther up and just off Fifth Avenue, others gave up on New York and lived elsewhere and abroad, while some went to those new apartment and hotel buildings. The apartment house loomed as a way to remain in the area and downsize while selling your now very valuable property. By 1914, the *New York Evening Mail* reported that it was virtually impossible to sell a property for private residential use south of 59th Street.[2]

Multiple Dwelling Units

We have always considered New York to have been a city of houses in the manner of London and the concept of unrelated people living separately under a single roof is thought to be a post–World War I phenomenon. Yet the fluidity of movement in New York, with neighborhoods changing every generation, created intensive land speculation and often wildly high prices. To remain in the city in a convenient or respectable location challenged the person searching for a home. Those already in possession of a property which was costly to support, were faced with an obvious solution: a house could become a boarding house, or a place where roomers could rent a space, or even a building built purposely to make living together as comfortable as possible. The stealthy conversion of the solid house in a good neighborhood into a home for more than one family was well established by the middle of the 19th century. The English-born architect, Calvert Vaux, who built the High Victorian Gothic house for A. C. Gray on lower Fifth Avenue, suggested apartment houses in 1857 at a meeting of the new American Institute of Architects. He spoke of Scottish multiple dwellings and his talk as published in the December 19, 1857 *Harper's Weekly* as "Parisian Buildings for City Residents."[3] As houses were built on the lower Avenue some became, and others were created to be, stealth multiple dwelling addresses. Did anyone notice that more people than one might think entered a house on a regular basis?

The older boarding house concept continued, but the idea of a dignified and distinct interior arrangement for several unconnected families flourished. Different arrangements and different levels of features made for consumer choices. A family wishing to live in the city in the winter only might take such a place, while a widow or mature couple might find this arrangement comfortable. What about single respectable women? Or a newly married couple? The bachelor flat was an entirely separate and now forgotten subspecies—a clever way to use flexible space in the upper part of a building, creating small units with two rooms, some closets, and a bath for unmarried men, who could dispense with household systems—no kitchen nor laundry. There were numerous such apartments in later 19th-century New York. Edith Wharton's character Undine Sprague in *The Custom of the Country* has been brought to New York to rise in the fashionable world. Her parents had purchased a fine house on a new boulevard in the city but were forced to move into a hotel to keep Undine fashionable. "Undine had early decided that they could not hope to get on while they 'kept house'—all the fashionable people she knew either boarded or lived in hotels."[4]

The narrow plot of the New York row house, traditionally 25 feet across and 100 feet deep, creates a building which is dark in its midst, not an ideal formula for conversion to a multiple dwelling. Perhaps the best way of exploiting the space was to rent rooms out or adopt the boarding house principle of offering meals for those living in individual rooms, and this was a widely used residential choice, especially in the older sections of the city. As we know, the fashionable area fairly leapt northward, making the first blocks above Washington Square vulnerable to reorientation as multiple dwellings. Number 3 Fifth Avenue would become a boarding house by the end of the Civil War. The owner, N. L. Beers, added an addition on the house shortly thereafter.

By 1870, the Richard K. Haight house at the southeast corner of 15th Street, one of the early houses of 1848 by Trench & Snook and briefly the New York Club in the 1860s, was reworked by S. D. Hatch, who added two stories and a mansard atop the once private house. The new Haight House was to be occupied by suites of apartments on each of the five floors, while the mansard housed more rentable units. The reworked house had a central kitchen. The top area under the mansard was a set of bachelor flats—small spaces without housekeeping facilities. The Haight house worked well as it carried the status of an old family residence, even if it was now home to many.

In 1872, the Albany society gentleman and first student from America to study at the Ecole in Paris, A. H. Thorp, altered the upper floors of a house on the west side of the Avenue just north of 26th Street that probably belonged to his father. The following year, the widow of Paran Stevens took over the completion of her husband's massive apartment building a block above, the Victoria. As we know that idea was premature, or perhaps a combination of the overwhelming size of the building, combined with an element of social rejection of Mrs. Stevens, kept the Victoria with its lavish fittings unoccupied. The neighborhood surrounding the Fifth Avenue Hotel had become a social center, and another block of flats by the great early apartment house designer of Boston, Arthur Gilman, came to 25th Street.

In that year, 1873, Henry Van Schaick converted August Belmont's first house at 82 Fifth Avenue into flats, hiring D. J. Jardine to create a five-story apartment house. In 1874, as the nation slid into depression, Peter Townsend converted his house at 129 Fifth Avenue into a boarding house. The same year, at 388 Fifth Avenue, William H. Barmor created a private hotel and boarding house from his personal house, adding an extension to the building. In 1876, Griffith Thomas attempted to convert his new house on 42nd Street, now owned by William H. Webb, into flats with the addition of more floors. The expensive renovation cost some $200,000 and opened not as apartments but as the Hotel Bristol.

In 1876, a further three multiple dwelling buildings were created. At 72 Fifth Avenue a hotel for long term stays was opened, while at 170 Fifth Avenue, John Hoey had his house at 22nd Street enlarged to accommodate a store on the ground floor, perhaps the first such alteration on Fifth Avenue. Tenement rooms were set on the upper floors (there is a slim line between a high-end tenement and lower end French Flats). In August of that year, Detlef Lienau altered J. H. Gautier's house to become part of the Grosvenor, 35 and 37 Fifth Avenue, a building of French flats started by Cottenet. The following year, as we know, John H. Sherwood, a property owner and architect, would build in the mid 40s, starting with a building of French Flats on the northeast corner of 44th Street.

The March of the French Flats

As the nation emerged from the economic collapse towards the end of the 1870s, two more buildings of French flats rose on Fifth Avenue. Now, the estate of Mme. Restell rehired Robert Mook to alter her corner home, 657 Fifth, into flats at a cost of $60,000 and Levi P. Morton, a man who played Fifth Avenue property games, turned a row house at 503 Fifth Avenue (where Edith Jones made her debut) into a family hotel, adding a fifth floor where the mansard had been (J. E. Terhune, $30,000), enlarging it again as flats. Often, it is the identity of the owner of the property that would ensure its success. While Levi P. Morton was a well-known figure, who succeeded in renting out all his flats, the Restell/Lohman property, as we have already seen, was tarnished with Mme Restell's notoriety as a well-known abortion provider, and people avoided the Lohman building.

One of the first major fashionable apartment buildings was the Knickerbocker at 245 Fifth Avenue. As the name of the building asserts, this multiple dwelling was for Knickerbocker society in New York—a big building of 1882–83 by Charles W. Clinton with some development assistance from the young Ernest Flagg, who was not yet an architect. The developers were Hubert, Pirson & Co. The notable and socially connected contractor and builder David H. King built the million-dollar stone and terracotta building and leased apartments to Mrs. Astor's crowd.[5] While a number of apartment houses would be built on the west side, only the 1885 Fifth Avenue Apartment building would join the Knickerbocker as a large apartment house. The seminal building would be the apartment house at the northern corner of 81st and Fifth Avenue 35 years later, which ushered in the fashionably acceptable apartment house.

The professional architectural press recognized the future would be

apartment houses and wrote a sensible front-page article in 1870 called
"European Homes," extolling the financial wisdom of the multiple-
occupation dwellings on pricey land.[6] In 1874, James Richardson
wrote an important article, "The New Homes of New York, a study
of Flats," in *Scribner's Monthly*,[7] in which he lauds the importance of
building apartments for the future.

The first apartment/flat builders wanted to be certain to differentiate
the flats from the multiple dwellings which rose above the working-
class tenement house. The renting out of rooms on a floor in a row
house was known as a "flat," using the earlier term of European
origin—Flats—One floor. To distinguish the building from a then-
loathsome tenement, a "flats" building had a bathroom within each
unit. The fine points were kitchens and laundries: some of the higher-
end flats had central kitchens and laundries in the basement which all
could use; others had a staff to send the cooked meal and clean laundry
to the units; others had the kitchen and laundry in the back of the
unit for self-catering. A dumb waiter helped bring the heavier items
to the individual homes and became an important enticement to gain
tenants. The essential feature by 1880 for the higher-end buildings was
an internal elevator, usually with a person operating the lift.[8]

The buildings which acknowledged the purpose of multiple family
homes needed a proper name rich in association with European urban
grandeur. For the lower-end apartments, women's names, such as
"the Louise," were adopted over the entry marking the building with
an appellation. The building names may still be found atop the entry
doors. Higher-end apartment buildings stayed with the street number
or associated the building with European royalty.

Some of these buildings had no stoop as the tenants could be elderly
and found it difficult to manage the steps. Some had very fancy lobby
spaces with marble or mural finishes, employing young men, who sat
on a chair in the hall on each floor to aid the residents. The owners of
the building worked hard to attract renters as the units were costly,
at $1,000 to $2,000 per year. The location was an important factor to
many, the glamor to others, while the discreet sense of the building
being a private home still counted as well. The developers understood
that the multiple dwelling building would only be the answer to the
city's housing needs if New Yorkers did not still cling to the old
idea of the sanctity of a private house. Whatever the subtleties of the
buildings might have been, it was paramount that they were perceived
as being far from a tenement, ensuring that no one might mistake a
multiple dwelling unit for a home to the working class.

8908. HOTELS NETHERLAND AND SAVOY, NEW YORK.   COPYRIGHT, 1905, BY DETROIT PHOTOGRAPHIC CO.

Providing a Service

A final factor in the multiple dwelling story was service. Everyone needed some household help, and obtaining ideal service people was a common topic for discussion amongst society women. The huge immigration numbers provided a constant pool of African Americans, Irish and German speakers, but actually finding help, ensuring staff were honest and retaining staff were problems that beset many households. By the 1890s, another multiple dwelling specialty appeared, the Apartment Hotel. This new concept rose in fashionable areas such as the Plaza and offered hotel-like service in a semi-permanent apartment to older, now childless couples or an affluent, older person (London had serviced flats at this time, which were quite similar). The family hotel allowed for the sale of the old row house, enabling the new tenants to benefit from services that they did not need to engage, and for which they were not responsible. The goal was to provide all the comforts of a house, including service, while still ensuring that each unit was completely isolated from any other.[9] Indeed, instead of looking at the giant new apartment houses, a renter could now live within the big building and look down on the older neighbourhoods.

On a smaller scale, the residential hotel became a home to many who tired of running a house and wanted hotel service. In 1890, Judge P. Henry Dugro with an investor named Stagman, had R. S. Townsend create the twelve-story Hotel Savoy on Fifth Avenue across the street from Grand Army Plaza and the new Plaza Hotel. The location

HOTEL SAVOY, EAST 58TH TO EAST 59TH STREETS

Hotel Savoy, home to many as they downsized. On the east side of Fifth Avenue at Grand Army Plaza and the opening of Central Park, the apartments gave the residents the chance to live within one of the buildings then casting a shadow on their row houses. Ralph Townsend architect, 1892.

was pleasing, near Central Park and a fashionable part of the city and the staff of the hotel catered to their residential population. The apartment hotel was marketed to older couples happy to be served as in a transient hotel. Apartments were advertised in the *New York Times* as furnished or unfurnished, and for weeks or a season.[10]

William W. Astor carried on his great-grandfather's role as the hotel builder—the first Astor had built a hotel near St Paul's Chapel. W.W. Astor purchased the property just above the Savoy in 1891 and built the 17-story New Netherland Hotel, which was a rival to the Savoy. This side of the Astor family would build numerous hotels in New York, then in London.

By the middle of the 19th century, the answer to living quarters for many modestly-wealthy and middle-class families was a multiple dwelling unit. From immense land-holding developers like the patrician Stuyvesant Rutherfurd to speculative builders on the edges of the city, the apartment house was the answer—the bigger the building the better to amortize the high land and building costs, making living in the city more comfortable. The other choice was the new suburbs. But at this stage, some American families were not yet ready to live under a roof with other families they did not know, and the acceptability of the apartment for many in higher societal ranges was truly slow. Although, the elderly, widowed, or newly-married might live briefly in an apartment, the leaders of fashion did not accept an apartment abode until the 1920s.

The terms "flats," "French flats," "family hotel" would combine into the designation "apartments" by the end of the century—the sensible way to live in a city without the responsibilities of a private house. By the end of World War I, well-born architects like Cross & Cross built apartment buildings on the east side for those in their class.[11] The 1920s would see an enormous acceptance and building of apartment houses on the Upper East Side and Upper West Side, replacing row houses within a generation of the row house construction. Today, most residents in Manhattan live in apartment houses.

CHAPTER 18

UPDATING HOMES AS SIDEWALKS SHRINK

"The fun of being a New York painter is that landmarks are torn down so rapidly that your canvases become historical records almost as soon as the paint is dry."

John Sloan, Painter (1871-1951)

As we know, Fifth Avenue across from Central Park developed in spurts with an occasional house, a few brownstone rows, and a few odd large houses such as the Rupert mansion and the Cook house. The remaining blocks were empty until late in the 19th century, when escapees from the lower Avenue built on empty blocks. *The Record and Guide* reported on the Upper Avenue in 1890 that there were over 80 buildable lots between 72nd Street and 86th Street and over 70 above 86th Street. As the new homes appeared, usually those of individuals rather than speculative rows, the block assumed a higher architectural tone. The existing brownstones were in a now-emerging neighborhood, but were out of date—indeed, the row house was expiring as the acceptable home for the middle- and upper-classes and the cost of the row house was slowing their creation. We know there were a few high-end speculatively built town houses in the blocks above 79th Street. The porous nature of New York's social world was drawing wealthy people to the city and these newcomers were often in a hurry to arrive and not eager to undertake all the work needed to build a house. A quick solution was to buy one of those high-end, just-finished speculative houses, which provided an instant address on Fifth Avenue.

An Architectural Art Gallery
As Edith Wharton and Henry James had railed against the uniformity of the, to them, dreary brown-colored stone and cookie-cutter facades of the multiple house rows, the next generation opted to

The brownstone had a rather brief time in the sun. Here we see a house removing the stoop and changing to a street level entry. Temple Emanu-El behind on the left.

buy an individual rowhouse and then set to work updating it. Probably the first example of a "re-fronting" took place at 39 West 57th Street, on a most fashionable block. The woollen manufacturer and merchant, David L. Einstein had originally commissioned the Jardines to build a Queen Anne-style house in 1880 and was most proud of it; the tasteful interior appeared in the four-volume luxury publication *Artistic Houses* of 1883–84 (Einstein seems to be the only Jewish patron whose home appears in that vanity publication, which required a cash contribution for inclusion). Einstein was part of an upper end of Temple Emanu-El society and descended from several important early settlers in America in the optical instrument and banking businesses. He came to appreciate England and was in London for his daughter's wedding—perhaps this was when he fell in love with the Queen Anne style? In 1894 he commissioned an architect named Manly N. Cutter to remodel the house, removing the Queen Anne window detail and flourishes—the style had faded out of fashion and Einstein wanted his house to look more up-to-date.[2]

The speculative row was out, and individual design was in. Even the once-homogenous rows constructed by speculative builders had some stylistic variety in the group of houses. The old appearance of Fifth Avenue and its neighboring houses just to the east became, as the wags of the day would remark, an art gallery of architectural styles. In these renovations, the stoop was taken away and replaced with a central ground floor entrance, and every trace of brownstone was carted away. Often, an extra story would be put atop the house and private house elevator(s) would now be installed to justify a taller house. The house would, usually, receive a full interior renovation. There was now an entry hall, sometimes with light wells to bring in more daylight in the center portion of the house and skylights might be added over staircase. The house could be enlarged back into the once deep garden and might now stretch 70, even 90 feet into the back garden.

Many of these houses then received a rather showy façade done by a leading architect of the day. The blocks just off Fifth Avenue now rivaled the Avenue in the high design of each house. The dull brownstone rows were totally recast as houses on a par with their brothers and sisters on the Avenue itself. These re-fronted houses survive today and give the Upper East Side its substantial tone of elegance.[3]

The Widening of Fifth Avenue

The recognition of beautiful cities was dawning on Americans in the later 19th century. A growing awareness of the glories of European capitals led to a movement to create beautiful boulevards in the cities of the United States. The early phase of the movement focused upon Fifth Avenue for political reasons (the loft buildings of lower Fifth Avenue made many civic minded people think that Fifth Avenue should be the center of the city planning story), but it was also the most architecturally rich concourse in the nation. Streets that had been crowded with horse drawn vehicles now also had to accommodate the first automobiles. This first stab at creating a wider Avenue was to take away the broad 15-foot sidewalk that had been accepted as part of the private properties to the street line for over 60 years, embellished by early residents with plantings and enrichments of design. The wider street forced a new sidewalk, and this was now to move closer to the actual house, demanding that the owners cut off projecting bay windows, stoops, gardens, lawns, porticos, and eliminate the old area ways. The celebrated entry at the W. K. Vanderbilt house had to be taken off and the same amputations were needed at Arabella and Archer Huntington's house. The issue of the widening of the streets percolated through the first decade of the 20th century, and was ultimately carried out between 1909 and 1912. The urban balance did shift, and the aspect of a building did change;

The New York Times,
June 27th, 1909

"Probably no local
Improvement made to
the city at nominal cost
to the municipal treasury
was ever received by
the people most directly
affected with so much
regret as the widening
of Fifth Avenue now in
progress."

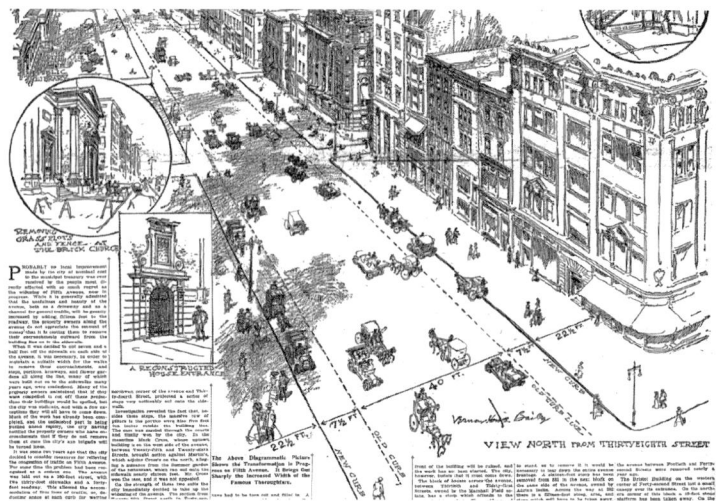

the pushing of the sidewalk to the building edge undoubtedly spoilt the appearance of many buildings, and the University Club looked less imposing after the loss of its sidewalk space.[4]

The 'shaving' of the houses, gardens and entries and the like, took a valuable part of the city away from viewers and pedestrians. The car was winning and the busy streets of Manhattan were losing their charm. The character of houses and blocks was diminishing and now shadows from tall buildings were changing the light on rear gardens and on the streets. The century had indeed changed the city, ushering in an era of deep canyons, towering skyscrapers and seething traffic. Working men and women now walked the streets once reserved for promenades by the elite.

CHAPTER 19

CONCLUSION

… And on the pedestal these words appear:
"My name is Ozymandias, king of kings:
Look on my works, ye mighty, and despair!"
Nothing beside remains. Round the decay
Of that colossal wreck, boundless and bare
The lone and level sands stretch far away.

Percy Bysshe Shelley, Ozymandias, 1818

MULTIPLE FORCES brought the street of fashion to a close. The new apartment house, world war, children living abroad, country estates, corporate buy-outs, and now a change in high society, which increasingly came to value celebrity over pedigree…all of these factors brought the statement house to a close. By the beginning of the 20th century, the determined and brash aspirants, such as the Mariettas, Alvas, and Mrs. Leeds, widow of the king of tin plate, had court dress gowns as well as invitations to all the social functions. Charles Dana Gibson, the American illustrator whose images characterized aspects of the nation for 30 years in *Life* magazine, depicted newly-wealthy women attempting to storm society. By the early 20th century "Mamie" Fish, otherwise known as Marion Graves Anthon Fish, the wife of Stuyvesant Fish, was perhaps THE hostess who killed old society. The famous party for a prince who turned out to be a fully-attired monkey known as Prince del Drago was a rebuke to a newly-rich Fifth Avenue resident. Mamie Fish's events were a celebration of amusement and glamor where once forbidden actors and celebrities mingled with society members. Edith Wharton's world was lost—perhaps this is a reason she remained in Europe.

No longer was a grand house essential to conquer New York City. Commercial pressure, retail establishments, value of land, and the ability to build buildings that seemed to scrape the sky reduced New York Society to a few cliques that no longer needed a Fifth Avenue address. Miss Wendel, one of the unmarried grandchildren of the original Astor, was one of the last house owners in the midtown streets of the 40s, who stayed on walking her dog Toby as people went to the office, shopped, ate ice cream in parlors, and bought hats where she had once had neighbors. She did not mind. Rather like a line of dominoes, the houses of the rest fell with loud crashes in the 1920s and 1950s. The "old school" congregated on Long Island's North Shore, in Southampton, Greenwich, Rumson, and in Palm Beach, returning only to Manhattan hotels, especially the Plaza, for the occasional debutante party. The private schools had to admit those that were willing to pay for an education that was not in the public realm. The clubs lost core members and began to scramble in order to have enough "appropriate" members. Tom Wolfe writes amusingly of the end of the era in his book of 1965, *The Kandy-Kolored Tangeringe-Flake Streamline Baby*. He has nannies complain to each other of their embarrassment that the parents of their charges live in apartments and long for birthday parties to be held in the grandparents' houses in Carnegie Hill.[1]

Did the development of Fifth Avenue have any significant impact on architectural styles? Were the house plans the same until the very end? In the early 19th century, a derivative style was necessary as similarity was stressed; innovation was not required, although fine materials and workmanship excelled. Fifth Avenue houses, as they were filled with furnishings and paintings which seemed to resemble the appearance of households in Europe, played an important role in the transfer of European aristocratic values to America.

At first an established social position, and subsequently social advance, were announced through the possession of a Fifth Avenue address. The houses in this famous avenue primarily made a social point, acting as an ever more extravagant statement of arrival. The profligacy of the Gilded Age, and the vaunting ambitions of New York's wealthiest class, were played out in the lavish overstatement of the houses of Fifth Avenue. Staff dressed for the costume ball given by the Bradley Martins. The new Waldorf Astoria was the setting for this amazingly extravagant ball. The publicity for this event drove the Bradley Martins out of New York to the United Kingdom. On February 18, 1897, the guests dressed as kings and queens of history. The expensive event poisoned the well of the grand costume ball in the United States as many people, including the clergy on their pulpits, chided the lavishness of the ball and such Gilded Age extravagances came to an end. However, the Europeans were inspired by the American example and began to hold balls and events that were every bit as lavish as the Bradley Martins' ball; six months

after the Bradley Martin ball, at their Devonshire House in London, the Duke and Duchess of Devonshire held their own version of this extravagant party.

And then it did not matter. Few were expressing regret at the demolition of the houses. The extraordinary remnants that were left after these grand houses were demolished went largely unnoticed. John Ringling, the great circus king, did pay attention, and Mrs. Astor's fireplace is in the Ringling Museum in Florida. Hearst also did so, and filled his extraordinary house at San Simeon in California with objects purchased from an earlier Gilded Age house; San Simeon survives to this day. But few others noticed the exquisite carnage in the demolition wagon and many objects, which no longer had any market value, were given to loyal household staff.

What Fifth Avenue did do was to pull the city up the island in the 19th century, in much the same way as Regent Street had in London a century earlier. Fifth Avenue also established New York as a place for *pied-à-terre* for the very wealthy—a well-located apartment might be retained as a place to dress for events, the opera, and the like. Perhaps it was even a great eyrie at the top of a building—colossal sums were paid for a nest in the sky. A penthouse with a view replaced the row house and did not require full-time presence in the city.

In a mere century, the houses of Fifth Avenue evolved from a respectable residence to a house where the family conducted business, to a brownstone, then an aspirational palace and, poof, it was all gone. A Fifth Avenue address brought many a place in the new American aristocracy, that emulated, and mixed with, European high society. Just as the Americans reached a semi-acceptance, the First World War broke out, and a new café society began to emerge. The celebrated and amusing people who were promoted by society hostesses, such as Mamie Fish, crowded out the old names at parties. Now, it was entertainers and celebrities who were receiving invitations, and the days when wealthy women tried to get invited to Yankee and Knickerbocker Society were long gone.

The social figures of importance were now far less wealthy than the industrialist class, and while they needed to assert their status Fifth Avenue was no longer the center of their identity. America's self-created aristocrats retreated to Palm Beach, Greenwich, Long Island's North Shore, and locations other than New York City. How quickly this world was built, but, like the houses, how rapidly it fell. Consuelo Vanderbilt Balsan seems not to have shed a tear as her petit château was demolished for a commercial building. She lived in France, Palm Beach, and Oyster Bay. She never returned to Fifth Avenue.

Well-built houses lined Fifth Avenue for only a short time before society moved on and social climbers and newly-wealthy arrivistes found a fresh canvas on which to exhibit their wealth and ostentation. Commerce overwhelmed the domestic life of the Avenue. How quickly the street was created and how rapidly it vanished.

CHAPTER NOTES

James Boorman developed nos. 1–7. Seen here are 5 and 7 Fifth Avenue, built c. 1830s.

CHAPTER 1

[1] Edith Wharton, *The Custom of the Country*, New York: Charles Scribner's Sons, 1913.

CHAPTER 2

[1] Luther S. Harris, *Around Washington Square: An Illustrated History of Greenwich Village* (Baltimore: Johns Hopkins University Press, 2003), chapter 1.. The Harris book is superb coverage of the early history of this part of the city. The volume was of immense help sorting out the complex time of the late 18th and early 19th centuries.

[2] Harris, *Around Washington Square*, 6–9.

[3] Emily Johnston de Forest, *John Johnston of New York*, Merchant (private printing, 1909).

[4] The country house of John Taylor, later to John Taylor Johnston. A wooden version of the Greek Revival with square piers instead of columns, it stood on a hill on the empty land of Fifth Avenue at 40th Street. A picture of it in 1840 can be found in Henry Collins Brown's *Fifth Avenue, Old and New*, (New York: Fifth Avenue Association, 1924), 85.

[5] Samuel Thomson was also the builder of the new Main Building for what would later be known as New York University and the U.S. Customs House, now called Federal Hall.

[6] Henry James, *Washington Square* (New York: Harper & Brothers Publishers, 1901).

[7] For a good account of 1834–35, see William Ross, Esq., Architect, "ART IV Street Houses of the City of New York," *The Architectural Record* 9 (1899–1900): 53–56.

[8] For a good account of New York City c. 1850, see Charles Mackay, *Life and Liberty in America* (London: Smith, Elder and Co., 1859).

[9] Mariana's younger brother, Frank Gray Griswold, wrote about the old Knickerbocker Society of his youth as 50 families made up exclusively of their fellow merchants of the port. *Stolen Kisses*, for example, was privately printed in 1914 and dedicated to his sister. *Afterthoughts* was also privately printed in 1936.

[10] Mariana's grandfather, Saul Alley, was a rare example of a man who moved up from being a working class "mechanic" to the top of the business world. Backed by the second wealthiest man in Charleston, Mordecai Cohen, who sent him from Charleston with a large consignment of cotton, Alley was able to ship it and establish himself in the cotton and shipping trade. His business on Pine Street was next to another in "The Row," Shepard Knapp, who was in the leather business, as was Peter Lorillard, the snuff king who also came to "The Row." Saul Alley and Stephen Allen of Number 1, The Row, were principals in an attempt to bring clean water to NYC. Alley is a curious figure. He was born in Providence, possibly to Jewish/Irish parents. How he ended up in a trusted circle of Cohen's in Charleston is unknown to us today. Frank Gray Griswold wrote about Cohen's plantation in a story demonstrating two generations of connection. Alley is buried in Green-Wood Cemetery in Brooklyn.

[11] The 19th century, with its amazing spurts of financial growth, also endured market collapses. Some of the merchants of the day, not those in The Row, invested in the cotton plantations in the South and brokered cotton from the Port of New York to the textile mills of Manchester via the port at Liverpool. Many of the New York merchants married South Carolinian belles with plantation properties. As the Civil War began, New York's merchants split between those with heavy investment in the South and Charleston and Savannah wives and those wishing freedom for the slaves of the South. Many Members of the Union Club, New York's first important social club, founded in 1836, maintained connections to the South, and endured a split when some of their members who wanted a Union and opposed slavery in turn formed their own Union League Club in 1861.

[12] See "Growth and Prosperity," *Evening Post*, April 17, 1845; and "Second Avenue," *Evening Post*, January 14, 1846.

[13] Mariana Van Rensselaer, *The Century* (November 1893): 5–18.

CHAPTER 3

[1] Annette Blaugrund, *The Tenth Street Studio Building*, Ph.D. Dissertation, (New York: Columbia University, 1987).

[2] A room in the house appears in *Opulent Interiors of the Gilded Age*. Arnold Lewis, James Turner, and Steven McQuillin, *Opulent Interiors of the Gilded Age* [Dover Reprint of *Artistic Houses*] (New York: Dover Publications, 1987), Figure 198.

[3] Obituary for William Tilden Blodgett, *New York Times*, November 18, 1875.

[4] See: Harris, *Around Washington Square*, 114. New York City, Directory of Streets, c. 1850; Photocopy of some unsourced pages in the Office for Fifth Avenue, Office for Metropolitan History. The William M. Halsted house in the northwest corner of 14th Street is strikingly similar in appearance to the Brevoort house. The house was at the top of the city when it was completed in 1835. These would have been the first houses on an empty avenue. See Brown, *Fifth Avenue, Old and New*, page 39 for an image of the house.

[5] The surviving brownstone with some Gothic detail at the northwest corner of 8th Street was likely

finished just as the younger Brevoort died. Number 10 Fifth Avenue has an extra story, but it is still in use as a restaurant with apartments on the upper floors.

6 Unsourced Street Directory page, Office for Metropolitan History.

7 Ellen Weill Kramer, *The Domestic Architecture of Detlef Lienau* (Conshohocken, PA: Infinity Publishing, 2006). Michael Lienau, a brother of the architect, was very successful in Jersey City. Detlef Lienau designed a number of buildings in Jersey City. The connection to Savannah in mid-19th-century New York was deep and Lienau built in Savannah after the Civil War.

8 Christopher Gray, "Streetscapes: The Architecture of Jacob Wrey Mould, A Study in Contrasts," *New York Times*, May 13, 2010. Another book on Mould, *Hell on Color, Sweet on Song*, by Francis Kowsky was published by Fordham University Press in May 2023.

9 Brown, *Fifth Avenue, Old and New*, 39.

BREAKOUT
1 William Ross, "History from a Garret," vol. 9, 1899–1900.

2 A very negative assessment of the ubiquitous brownstone at the end of the era, but by the important critic of the day, can be found in: Montgomery Schuyler, "The Small House in New York," *Architectural Record* 8 (April–June, 1899): 368–73.

3 Charles Lockwood, *Manhattan Moves Uptown: An illustrated History* (Boston: Houghton Miffler Company, 1976), 185–95.

CHAPTER 4
1 David Black, *The King of Fifth Avenue: The Fortunes of August Belmont* (New York: Dial Press, 1981). Black's text is the classic account of Belmont.

2 Most of the houses on Fifth Avenue continued to be architect-designed, even at this time when architects were coming to the United States for the first time. From England came several who were rather more advanced than the builders or craftsmen of the decade earlier. Frederick Diaper was the only man with credentials from an architect's office in his home country. Joining the "English" architects were German speaking polytechnic-trained men who gained work from successful German-born clients. Strikingly, the Danish architect who trained in Paris, Detlef Lienau, earned a reputation close to that of Diaper. Lienau completed a few commissions on the Avenue. He had observed and worked in Paris before coming to America in 1848, the year of revolutions. Lienau had an easy settlement as his brother, Michael, was well established across the Hudson River in New Jersey. Kramer, *The Domestic Architecture of Detlef Lienau.*

3 Unsourced New York City Directory page, Office of Metropolitan History.

CHAPTER 5
1 Jonathan D. Sarna, "Anti-Semitism and American History," *Commentary* 71, no. 3 (March 1981): 42–47. A good account of the development can be found in Henry Collins Brown, *Fifth Avenue, Old and New*, 52–55.

CHAPTER 6
1 "Obituary for Griffith Thomas," *The American Architect and Building News*, January 25, 1879, 29.

2 The Bristol Hotel property was owned by the Livingston estate—Thomas had originally leased the land and Webb had taken over the lease. The Livingstons were the most aristocratic of property owning families and property had descended on the Livingston side to the wife of Elbridge T. Gerry, who was also of a venerable lineage, tracing ties to the creators of the Constitution.

3 Robert Mook was trained by Griffith Thomas.

CHAPTER 7
1 There is an oft noted quotation from an 1861 book by Anthony Trollope after a visit to America about the growth in American's admiration for things French. "…in his tat, the American imitates the Frenchman…. I do not merely allude to the actual household furniture…the taste of America is becoming French in its conversation, French in its comforts, French in its discomforts, French in its eating and French in its manners…" Donald Smalley and Booth, Bradford Allen, 9th ed., *North America* (New York: Knopf, 1951), 204. The Jeromes, Ward McAllister, Southern Plantation families with eligible daughters, those interested in medical, geological study, and the École des Beaux Arts, and THE Mrs. Astor all headed for the court created by Louis Napoleon and his Empress, Eugenie. Even the "fixture" of the ballroom from the 1840s forward, the dance known as "The German," came to America from the court of the Second Empire.

2 Astor had bought the Thomson Farm. In 1799, John Thomson bought 20 acres of common land. He would sell the northwest corner to Thomas Lawrence and W. B. Astor. In 1840, Astor sold the corner share back to Lawrence, who sold to Daniel Parish the property going from 34th to 35th Streets and 200 feet going west. Several transactions followed, including a brief ownership by August Belmont, before Dr. Samuel "Sasparilla" Townsend bought the lot and built his house in 1852. Across the street, a farmer was cutting hay in this day.

Unidentified newspaper clipping at The New-York
Historical Society.

[3] See "Obituary for Fanny Reed," *New York Times*,
January 24, 1915, 8; and Fanny Reed, *Reminiscences,
Musical and Other* (London: 1903).

[4] Another interesting figure in the mid-19th century
Anglo-American story is that of Cornelia Adair
(1837–1921). Adair was born in Philadelphia to a
well-connected family in Hartford and Geneseo,
New York, old time settlers with large tracts of
land. She was related to many established American
landowning and gentry families including the
Wharton family, which brought her in the range of
Teddy Wharton, the husband of Edith Wharton.
Cornelia's relatives had many connections to
politics and prominent families in the mid-century
nation. Edith Wharton wrote in *The Buccaneers* of
an American woman, Miss March, who arranged
introductions for wealthy American women who
wished to launch daughters into English society.
Wharton's figure seemed to take money from these
introductions. Perhaps Wharton's Miss March was
based on Cornelia who maintained a residence on
Curzon Street in Mayfair where she entertained
grandly, including several evenings with Edward VII.

[5] "Obituary for Marietta Stevens," *New York Times*,
April 4, 1895.

CHAPTER 8

[1] The NYC Buildings Department Docket books
revealed that one section of the southern extension
was completed by Stanford White, following the
original design of the Jardines.

[2] Joseph Devorkin, *Great Merchants of Early New
York* (New York: The Society for the Architecture
of the City, 1987).

[3] *American Architect and Building News*, 1884.

CHAPTER 9

[1] In the early 19th century, some New Yorkers built
country houses. The Johnston house on Fifth
Avenue was one location, the Apthorpe family built
a similar house on 92nd Street and what would
become Amsterdam Avenue. Still more built
country houses along the East River well above the
City. Archibald Gracie, a prominent member of
Knickerbocker New York, built a country house
near Hell Gate on the East River, which has survived
as the official residence of Mayors of New York
City. Within the course of the 19th century, the city
would reach up as far as these "country" retreats and
all but the Gracie House are now gone.

[2] The stone was not true marble.

[3] Several rooms from the Stewart house appear in
Lewis and Turner's reprint of *Artistic Houses*, plates
1 8. See also: Jay E. Cantor, "A Monument of Trade:

A. T. Stewart and the Rise of the Millionaire's
Mansion in New York," *Winterthur* 8 (1975).

[4] Nathalie Dana, *Young in New York: A Memoir of a
Victorian Girlhood* (New York: Doubleday, 1963),
89

CHAPTER 10

[1] John F. Kennion, *The Architects' and Builders'
Guide* (reprinted in 2011): 20.

[2] For reference to the hill horses, see: Brown, *Fifth
Avenue, Old and New*, 18. For the Bull's Head
Tavern, see ibid., 85 88.

[3] Charles Lockwood, *Manhattan Moves Uptown:
An Illustrated History* (Boston: Houghton Mifflin,
1976), 240.

[4] Louis Sherry (1856–1926) started life in New York
as a busboy, rising to create summer restaurants
in Elberon, New Jersey and Narraganset, Rhode
Island before coming to New York City. Sherry's
restaurant was designed by McKim, Mead & White.
For an image of the building, see *American Architect
and Building News*, no. 1177 (July 16, 1898).

[5] "Obituary for Mary Mason Jones," *New York
Times*, May 30, 1891.

[6] In 1883–84, a four-volume vanity press book,
Artistic Houses, was published by D. Appleton in
New York. The subscription printing of 500 copies
seems to indicate the house owners paid to be
shown in the volumes. There is an excellent homage
to *Artistic Houses* by Dover Press in 1987, edited
and with a text by Arnold Lewis and James Turner.
Several of the houses within this volume appear in
the books, which included 92 houses within the
nation, most in New York. Conspicuously, Arabella
Worsham Huntington's residences are not included.

[7] James T. Maher has written a wonderful telling of
this story. See James T. Maher, *Twilight of Splendor*
(New York: Little Brown, 1975).

[8] John Mason and John Jacob Astor were not the
only persons to buy farms well above the edge of
Manhattan in the early 19th century. The farms were
passing to new generations, and many were sold.
Indeed, the old Murray homestead on Murray Hill,
to the east on what would be about 37th Street, had
survived two generations, and the name lingered
on as the farm acres were changing hands. Thomas
Buchanan bought a farm extending east of Fifth
Avenue (pre-Randel map, so there were no streets or
avenues then) covering what would be 45th to 48th
Streets. Buchanan had several children, including
two daughters who married into the Jones and
Goelet family, giving them Fifth Avenue property in
addition to older Goelet parcels in the lower island.

[9] Elizabeth Drexel Lehr, *"King Lehr" and the Gilded
Age* (Philadelphia: J. B. Lippincott Company, 1935),
18.

[10] See *American Architect and Building News* 9, June 11, 1881, plate 285; *American Architect and Building News*, July 8, 1881.

[11] Floating around Goelet and Vanderbilt, Rockefeller properties in the streets of the 50s, and sales of prime real estate in the neighborhood was Charles MacRae of 533 Fifth Avenue. This realtor, whom we know from the Arabella Worsham/Rockefeller transactions, conducted many of the big sales of land, including four of the lots belonging to the old St. Luke's hospital at Fifth Avenue and 54th Street when the hospital moved to Morningside Heights. The world of agents and speculators would be fascinating to explore if papers could be found.

CHAPTER 11

[1] Images of all the Vanderbilt houses can be found in an excellent book by Jerry E. Patterson. Jerry E. Patterson, *The Vanderbilts* (New York: Harry N. Abrams, 1989), 30. The house was part of a speculative row completed about 1840, rather in imitation of the houses of The Row on Washington Square North.

[2] A picture of the Staten Island house as expanded by William Henry Vanderbilt can be seen in *The Vanderbilts*. Ibid., 24.

[3] Cornelius Vanderbilt, Jr., *Farewell to Fifth Avenue* (New York: Simon and Schuster, 1935).

[4] The title of Mark Twain's *The Gilded Age* evoked the golden hue that surrounded the time period—although perhaps more like a time of dark coal than the precious metal. See Mark Twain, *The Gilded Age* (Hartford, CT: American Publishing Company, 1873).

[5] The critic of the era, Montgomery Schuyler, really disliked this house and the other Vanderbilt houses. See Jordy and Coe, eds., "The Vanderbilt Houses," in *American Architecture and other Writings: Montgomery Schuyler* (Cambridge, MA: Harvard University Press, 1961), 500.

[6] Montgomery Schuyler, the reigning critic of the day, devoted two pages to his evaluation of the house. See Montgomery Schuyler, *The American Architect and Building News*, May 21, 1881, 243–44.

[7] The vase is now at the Metropolitan Museum.

[8] There are two catalogues from the Metropolitan Museum of Art devoted to the time period, including *The Aesthetic Movement*, which features pieces from the house, and the four volumes in *Mr. Vanderbilt's House and Collection*. See *The Aesthetic Movement*; and Edward Strahan, *Mr. Vanderbilt's House and Collection* (New York: George Barrie, 1883–84). See also: Samuel P. Avery, *The Diaries 1871–1882 of Samuel P. Avery* (New York: Arno Press, 1979); Doreen Bolger Burke, *In Pursuit of Beauty: Americans and the Aesthetic Movement*

(New York: Metropolitan Museum of Art, 1986); and "Artistic Furniture of the Gilded Age," *The Metropolitan Museum of Art Bulletin* 73, no. 3 (Winter 2016): 1–48.

[9] Ibid.

[10] Vanderbilt thought the doors were bronze, but they would have been fiercely heavy, so they were ultimately only a surface version on the vestibule side.

[11] In an article published in 1881, an unidentified writer describes visiting the newly completed house for a reception given by Mrs. Vanderbilt in honor of the marriage of her youngest daughter, Eliza Osgood Vanderbilt, who married Dr. William Seward Webb on December 20, 1881. The correspondent describes the house interiors to the highly eager readers. The prose is the usual excessive fodder rejoicing that New York City has such a treasure-filled palace. The reader learns that the entry hall to the three residences was pale yellow marble with the Demidoff vase in the middle of the cube. Upon passing through a bronze door to the W. H. Vanderbilt house, the hall is the full height of the house, "square columns of a deep red marble are topped with bronze capitals with figures, wreaths and garlands of brass upon the bronze…a great wood fire burned in a bounteous fire [sic] reached to the ceiling…Mrs. Vanderbilt received in the salon, which looks out on Fifth Avenue, and the room is simply a casket of jewels… the porphyry columns are enriched with seeming amethysts, rubies, diamonds and emeralds. The gas lights shine from behind a veil of what appears to be precious stones, the woodwork is profusely carved, inlaid with mother of pearl, gilded…halls are hung with pale crimson velvet which is embroidered with flowers, butterflies (real ones in high relief) [sic], and the same cut crystals which resemble precious stones. Rich columns of onyx, inlaid with bronze outline, stained glass windows, female figures in solid silver stand holding clusters of lights before mirrors. There is perfect taste ruling over everything." See "Mr. Vanderbilt's House," *Boston Traveller* (1881): unpaginated.

[12] Amanda Mackenzie Stuart, *Consuelo and Alva Vanderbilt* (New York: Harper Collins, 2005).

[13] The full story here remains elusive. How did Alva pull off the marriage? One strange possibility is that Consuelo, their first child, may have been born two years before the family claimed. She had no birth certificate, having been born at home. Was Alva claiming a pregnancy?

[14] *The American Architect and Building News*, 1886.

[15] Specifically, W. K. Vanderbilt, Alva, and George, who would soon commission Biltmore.

[16] Curiously, Vanderbilts avoided Elberon on the

New Jersey shore, then in decline. A decade after building Idle Hour, Alva would take on Newport, Rhode Island, a destination now for high achievers.

17 *The American Architect and Building News* XXXIII (August 1891): 132.

18 Consuelo Vanderbilt Balsan, *The Glitter and the Gold* (New York: Harper & Brothers Publishers, 1952).

19 Happily, W. K. Vanderbilt donated all four of his important pictures to the Metropolitan Museum in 1920 where they hang today.

20 The long saga of the costume ball in New York has been described elsewhere in this volume.

21 The 8th Duke had sold the important pictures in Blenheim a decade earlier.

22 Richard Morris Hunt was gone by this point and W. K. Vanderbilt favored Stanford White of McKim, Mead & White from the recent Metropolitan Club construction.

23 A comparison of the two houses was made by the editors of *Architectural Record*. See *Architectural Record* 23 (May 1908): 408.

24 Surely the workmanship of the W. K. Vanderbilt house was the masterpiece of the lot.

25 "John La Farge's work in the Vanderbilt Houses," *The American Art Journal* XVI (Autumn 1984): 30–70.

26 "Obituary," *New York Times*, July 12, 1947, 13.

27 A colored lithograph of the expanded house is in *The American Architect and Building News*, August 4, 1894, 971.

28 W. H. Vanderbilt's daughters were indeed loyal to their parents' builders. Between W. K. Vanderbilt and Cornelius Vanderbilt were two houses by Snook and Charles B. Atwood, completed in 1883 at 680 and 684 Fifth Avenue for the daughters Webb and Twombley. The daughters of W. H. Vanderbilt are better known for their summer houses than their New York homes.

CHAPTER 12

1 Christopher Gray, "Streetscapes: Mme. Restell's Other Profession," *New York Times*, October 10, 2013.

2 The early brownstone on the southwest corner of 55th Street at 720 Fifth Avenue was a Charles Duggin speculative house which would later be replaced by the celebrated Duveen Gallery. The Duveen sales building was a replica of the Parisian Minstère des Marine, built in the time of Louis XV. Duveen imported the stone from France. It was demolished for an office building in 1953. See *New York Times*, January 18, 1953.

3 Isabelle Hyman, "The Huntington Mansion in New York: Economics of Architecture and Decoration in the 1890s," *Syracuse University Library Associates*

Courier xxv, no. 2 (1990).

4 See *Artistic Houses; The New York Sketch Book of Architecture* 2 (September 1875): 1, plate XXLV; and Mary Elizabeth Wilson Sherwood, "Certain New York Houses," *Harper's New Monthly* 65 (October 1882): 680–90.

5 David M. McCullough, *Mornings on Horseback* (New York: Simon & Schuster, 1982).

6 McCulloch, *Red Cloud*, 109. A description of the new house is also scattered between pages 131-40.

7 *The New-York Sketch Book of Architecture* 3 (March 1876): 1, plate X.

8 *Architecture and Building* 65 (July 22, 1899): 31, plate 1230.

CHAPTER 13

1 See *Architecture and Building*, November 2, 1895; and *New York Times*, April 5, 1895.

2 W. M. Tweed, the corrupt mayor of the mid-century, had a plan for a hotel on the site in 1870. He may have even worked a scheme with S. D. Hatch and backing by Henry Hilton, the man who destroyed the A. T. Stewart estate. Tweed would get caught for corruption and the proposal would die and be forgotten.

3 C. Howard Walker, "Joseph M. Wells," *The Architectural Record*, July 1929

CHAPTER 14

1 A June 15, 1889 article in *Record & Guide* reports on Fifth Avenue above 59th Street.

2 "Fifth Avenue Events," *Fifth Avenue Bank* (New York: 1916), 61.

3 Gerrymandering, or the manipulation of voting districts, can be traced to his ancestor.

4 Montgomery Schuyler, "Works of the Late Richard M. Hunt," *The Architectural Record* 5 (October–December 1895): 130.

5 "Residence of Mr. J. Hooker Hamersley, 1030 Fifth Avenue," *Architecture and Building*, June 3, 1899. [

6 "Fifth Avenue owners demand Right to Erect Tall Apartment houses," *New York Times*, February 19, 1922.

7 *Architecture and Building*, January 11, 1896.

8 811 Fifth Avenue, the Jardine firm designed houses, were converted into flats in about 1890. This would be the first apartment building on the Upper Avenue. The owner, Frances Loring, ran the building. The Rambusch firm, newly in New York from Denmark, did some decorative work, likely in the lobby. See the Rambusch family archives; and *Record and Guide*, June 15, 1889, 836.

9 See *Architecture and Building*, August 29, 1896; and John Tauranac, "Fifth Avenue Apartments Where the Gilded Age Never Tarnished," *New York Times*, September 23, 1999.

[10] *Architecture and Building*, March 21, 1896.

[11] *The Architectural Record* 27 (June 1910): 471.

CHAPTER 15

[1] "East Side Architecture–Fifth Avenue," *Record and Guide* 45 (May 8, 1890): 640–41.

[2] See *The Architectural Record* 1 (April–June 1892): n.p. and Thomas Farnham, "Rugs in the City: A History of the Hajji Baba Club," in Jon Thompson, *Timbuktu to Tibet: Exotic Rugs and Textiles from New York Collectors* (New York: New-York Historical Society, 2008).

[3] Montgomery Schuler, *Record and Guide*, February 3, 1883.

[4] Ryan figured in many aspects of the Gilded Age. He considered moving down to lower Fifth Avenue for a while, but then joined Levi P. Morton in moving often on the Avenue.

[5] Lewis, Turner, and McQuillin, *The Opulent Interiors of the Gilded Age*, 99–101.

[6] Perhaps a reference to W. H. Vanderbilt's vestibule?

[7] A full description of the interior detail can be found in Wayne Craven, *Gilded Mansions: Grand Architecture and High Society* (New York: W. W. Norton & Co., 2008).

[8] George Ethelbert Walsh, "City Homes of Fashion and Wealth," *Architect and Builder's Magazine* 34 (December 1901): 106.

[9] *Architecture and Building*, October 17, 1896.

[10] Sally Webster and David Schwittek, "A Digital Recreation of the Lenox Library Picture Gallery: A Contribution to the Early History of Public Art Museums in the United States," *Nineteenth-Century Art Worldwide* 17, no. 2 (October 2018).

[11] Cornelius Vanderbilt III bought the corner around 1911 to move potentially above the commercial buildings in the 50s. He would not use the property.

[12] *Record and Guide*, June 15, 1889, 836–37.

[13] *Architecture* 1, February 15, 1900.

[14] *Architecture*, May 1, 1905, plate XLL.

[15] Gertrude Rhinelander Waldo's house on Madison Avenue at 72nd Street had a similar story. It would never be inhabited, as Mrs. Waldo was an eccentric and did not have the money needed to finish the house. It is now the Ralph Lauren flagship store.

[16] The Hoyts were part of the Montauk Association's seven buildings by McKim, Mead & White—a contemporary summer colony.

[17] A roughly contemporary publication identifies and illustrates the house but does not list the owner. See *The Architectural Record* 27, May 1910, 383.

[18] See *The Architectural Record* 19 (January 1906): 27; and *Architecture* 16 (September 15, 1907): 157.

[19] See *The Architectural Record* 18 (July 1905); and *Record and Guide* 76 (July 1, 1905).

[20] *Architecture and Building* (February 29, 1896).

[21] Christopher S. Gray, "Streetscapes," *New York Times*, June 2, 2002.

[22] Christopher S. Gray, "Streetscapes," *New York Times*, July 31, 2011.

[23] For interior views, see the real estate section's cover story in the *New York Times*, January 4, 1914.

[24] See *The Architectural Record* (October–December 1891); Christopher S. Gray, "Streetscapes," *New York Times*, December 2, 2012; and Anthony Wood, *Preserving New York: Winning the Right to Protect the City's Landmarks* (New York: 2007).

[25] *Architecture* 4 (November 15, 1901): 304–6.

[26] Franz K. Winker, "Architecture in the Billionaire District of New York City," *The Architectural Record* 11 (October 1901): 679–99. Note that Winkler was an alternative pen name for the great critic of the era, Montgomery Schuyler. See also "The New Fifth Avenue," *Record & Guide* (August 3, 1907): 171; and *Record & Guide* (October 8, 1910): 565.

[27] *The New York Architect* 4 (July 1907): n.p., in a combined block of brownstones, worked inside, not on the exterior. The article has a good contemporary account of the views on brownstone interiors.

[28] *The American Architect* (July 20, 1901): no. 1334.

[29] Joy Wheeler Dow, "Lower Fifth Avenue," *Architectural Review, Old Series* 9 (February 1902): 61–64.

[30] "The Latest Fifth Avenue Mansion," *Record and Guide* 82 (November 282, 1908): 1017.

[31] *Architecture* (December 1905): Plate CII.

[32] Cornelius Vanderbilt Jr., *Farewell to Fifth Avenue* (New York: Simon and Schuster, 1935).

[33] Heather Ewing, *Life of a Mansion, The Story of Cooper-Hewitt, Smithsonian Design Museum* (New York: Cooper Hewitt, 2014).

[34] Stephen Birmingham, *Our Crowd* (Wallaby edition, New York: 1977), 313–15.

[35] *Record and Guide* (December 28, 1907).

[36] "Residence of Mrs. Willard Straight, 1130 Fifth Avenue, Delano & Aldrich," *Architecture* 41 (1920): plates 33–38.

CHAPTER 16

[1] "The Contemporary Metropolitan Residence," *Record and Guide* (June 11, 1904): 1447.

[2] *New York Times*, January 9, 1926.

[3] Christopher S. Gray, "J. E. R. Carpenter the Architect who Shaped Upper Fifth Avenue, Streetscapes," *New York Times*, August 26, 2007.

[4] "Plan to Transform 'Millionaires Row'," *Record and Guide* (April 26, 1924); and "Big Apartment Houses on 5th Avenue," *New York Times*, May 16, 1926. The *New York Times* article noted more than a score of private houses sold for development with three or four more ready to go. The report noted

there had never been such a rapid transformation on the Avenue as these last two years. The Woolworth, Burden, Ruppert, and Blair houses were already demolished. Those not selling in 1925 were Charles Lanier, Geraldine Dodge, W. Emlen Roosevelt, George L. Rives, William Woodward, Clifford Brokaw, Frederick Lewisohn, H. O. Havemeyer, E. T. Gerry, Thomas Fortune Ryan, Ogden Mills, Mrs. E. H. Harriman, Oliver G. Jennings, Mrs. Frick, Payne Whitney, James Speyer, Archer M. Huntington, Felix Warburg, and Carnegie. Fifteen new apartment buildings were planned for Fifth Avenue as replacements for demolished houses including: 1034–8 Fifth Avenue; 1136 Fifth Avenue; 1013 Fifth Avenue; 810 Fifth Avenue; 1120 Fifth Avenue; 953 Fifth Avenue; 922–4 Fifth Avenue; 817 Fifth Avenue; and 1030 Fifth Avenue. Upper Fifth Avenue became an avenue of fine apartment houses. There was little outcry as the house owners and others moved into apartments.

CHAPTER 17

[1] See Russell Sturgis, "A Review of the work of Clinton & Russell," *The Architectural Record* 7 (October–December 1897): 27; and *Brickbuilder* 9 (July 1900).

[2] Several weeks of articles in *The Record and Guide*, like "The Fashionable Residential Section: Fifth Avenue from 72nd Street to 90th Street," *The Record and Guide* 77 (December 16, 1905–January 20, 1906): 950–1102, flogged the importance of the upper Avenue, noting the variety now wished for and the magnificence of the houses. Perhaps this was a realtor's effort to keep the prices high in the resale of properties.

[3] Charles Graham, a Scottish-born builder, settled in New York in 1850. He proposed building two apartment houses on the west side on Sixth Avenue between 49th–50th Streets. Graham may have been the first to propose multiple dwellings in an area here, as we will see some built in the next generation. Museum of the City of New York Archives, vol. 1/3. Graham went on the build the eccentric Graham Apartment building on 89th Street, still extant, among other buildings.

[4] Edith Wharton, *The Custom of the Country* (New York: [1913] 1987), 12.

[5] David H. King was an important contractor. He built numerous significant buildings for men who were his peers. This was not the usual contractor of the era. King also developed properties himself on the Upper West Side and in West Harlem.

[6] *The Real Estate Record and Builder's Guide* (September 24, 1870).

[7] James Richardson, "The New Homes of New York, a study of Flats," *Scribner's Monthly* viii (May 1874),

63–76.

[8] Even Matthew Hale Smith promoted the apartment house concept. See Matthew Hale Smith, *Sunshine and Shadows in New York* (New York: 1880), 882.

[9] Ibid., 905.

[10] See "An Outbreak of Hotel Building," *Record and Guide* 48 (October 24, 1891); and Reginald Pelham Bolton, "The Apartment Hotel in New York," *Cassier Magazine* 24 (November 1903): 27–32.

[11] Peter Pennoyer and Anne Walker, *New York Transformed: The Architecture of Cross & Cross* (New York: 2014).

CHAPTER 18

[1] *Architect and Building* (April 17, 1894): 163.

[2] David L. Einstein's daughter, Florence, married Charles Waldstein, later Walston, once of New York. Walston became a prominent figure at King's College in Cambridge and in the region and remained in England.

[3] *The Architectural Record* in the early years of the 20th century reported on these changes. The observing critic of the day was Herbert Croly. For the refitting of the William Owen house at 553 Fifth Avenue, see *Record & Guide* (October 10, 1908). Mr. Owen had given 49 feet of the back lot to the Church of the Heavenly Rest next door to widen the church interior. "A Profit in Altering Old Dwellings," *Record and Guide* (December 19, 1908).

[4] See Charles Starks, "Remembering George McAneny: The Reformer, Planner and Preservationist who Shaped Modern New York City," *The Gotham Center for New York History*, August 6, 2019; and "The New Fifth Avenue," *New York Times*, June 27, 1909.

CONCLUSION

[1] J. Mordaunt Crook, *The Rise of the Nouveaux Riches in Victorian and Edwardian England* (London: 1999).

APPENDIX 1

KEY CLIENTS AND FIGURES

The Social Push, almost in. Illustration for Eighty Drawings including The Weaker Sex, The Story of a Susceptible Bachelor by Charles Dana Gibson (Charles Scribner and John Lane, 1903).

NOTE: Much of the information below has been compiled from two publications: *Moses King, Notable New Yorkers, 1896–99: A Companion Volume to King's Handbook of New York City,* New York and Boston: Bartlett & Company, The Orr Press, 1899; and Social Register, 1887, New York: Social Register Association, 1986.

Alley, Saul (?–1851): Alley was an original settler in The Row at Washington Square. Although his early story is murky we know he was connected to Mordecai Cohen from Charleston, who sent Alley to New York with a consignment of cotton. Alley established himself as a merchant of the port.

Altman, Benjamin (1840–1914): Altman was a department store creator beginning on Sixth, then Fifth Avenue. He became a collector of paintings and porcelain of high quality, which he donated to The Metropolitan Museum of Art.

Anderson, John Charles (1812–81): A tobacconist, real estate speculator and possibly responsible for a murder.

Armour, Philip Danforth (1832–1901): Armour was the founder, in 1867, of a meat-packing business, Armour & Company. He moved to New York City and had a house on Fifth Avenue.

Aspinwall, William H. (1807–75): Aspinwall was a merchant of the port who was later involved with the Panama Canal Railroad and the Pacific Mail Steamship Company.

Astor, John Jacob, III (1822–90): This Astor was a third generation of the Astor family, He was a soldier in the Civil War and a philanthropist.

Astor, John Jacob, IV (1864–1912): The son of Caroline Schermerhorn Astor, he iniated the move uptown to a double house on Fifth Avenue. He died on the *Titanic.*

Astor, William Backhouse, Jr. (1829–92): This Astor was the husband of Caroline Schermerhorn Astor, a yachtsman and a horse breeder. As the second son, he was less involved with the Astor Estate.

Astor, Caroline Schermerhorn (1830–1908): She was a major figure of Knickerbocker New York who was married to W. B. Astor Jr. Known as the "Mystic Rose" of the New York 400, she was the self-proclaimed "THE Mrs. Astor."

Astor, Charlotte Augusta (1858–1920): Charlotte Astor was the daughter of Caroline and William B.

Astor. She married J. Coleman Drayton, received a house by Mckim, Mead & White then fled to Europe with G. O. Haig, creating a scandal.

Astor, William Waldorf (1848–1919): Son of J. J. Astor, he was in the hotel business. Not as civic minded as his father, he moved the family to England, where he became 1st Viscount Astor.

Barney, Ashbel (1816–86): Barney was the president of Wells Fargo Bank. He also had railroad interests. He settled in New York in 1857 at 101 East 38th Street, later the home of his son C T. Barney.

Barney, Charles Tracy (1851–1907): Son of Ashbel Barney, the businessman, C. T. Barney married the sister of William C. Whitney. He expanded the Knickerbocker Trust Company, which failed and started the Panic of 1907. Although not financially ruined himself, he was greatly devastated at having cost others such misfortune. He shot himself in the 38th Street house.

Belmont, Alva Smith Vanderbilt (1853–1933): Alva Erskine Smith Vanderbilt, later Belmont, was a prime mover in the creation of the Gilded Age in America. Her role in a series of great houses, the petit château in New York, and Marble House in Newport sets a new level for American houses. She was married twice, to William Kissam Vanderbilt and Oliver Hazard Perry Belmont. Around 1909, Alva Belmont, now a widow, turned her life purpose to women's suffrage.

Belmont, August, Jr. (1853–1924): Son of August Belmont and Caroline Perry Belmont. A financier, he was the head of the New York Rapid Transit Company.

Belmont, (Schonberg), August, Sr. (c. 1813 or 1816–90): Arrived in New York City as a young man with connections to the Rothschild banking house in Germany. He settled in New York working with the Rothschilds and on his own with great success. The company he created would work with the Rothschilds until the 1920s.

Belmont, Caroline Slidell Perry (1829–92): Born in Charleston, she was the daughter of Commodore W. Matthew Galbraith Perry and the niece of Commodore Oliver Hazard Perry. She was a widely admired social figure in New York as the wife of August Belmont.

Berwind, Edward J. (1848–1936): A graduate of the US Naval Academy, his fortune came from coal. He was an important and early client of Horace

Trumbauer, who designed his Newport house, the Elms, and his New York City house at 2 East 64th Street. Amazingly, both of these houses survive.

Bishop, Heber Reginald (1840–1902): Businessman who started in the sugar refining business and expanded into steel and banking. He was known for his jade collection, which remained in his house at 881 Fifth Avenue until his death. The collection was given to the Metropolitan Museum.

Blodgett, William Tilden (1823–75): One of the first serious painting collectors in the United States. He was a founder of the Metropolitan Museum. He purchased a big collection of painting for the Museum in 1871. His peer collector was John Taylor Johnston.

Boorman, James (1783–1866): Born in England. He was a neighbor in The Row and partner with John Johnston in the Dundee linen business. He became a major importer of iron from Sweden and Russia.

Bostwick, Jabez Abel (1830–92): A partner with John D. Rockefeller in Standard Oil. He lived a modest life compared to other Rockefeller partners.

Brevoort, Henry (Hendrik) (1747–1841): Farming family who owned a farm from 9th to 18th Street, Fifth Avenue to the Bowery.

Brevoort, Henry, Jr. (1782–1848): Emerged from farming to join the Astor fur business. He accompanied Lewis & Clark to the West. He commissioned the first house on Fifth Avenue, which inaugurated the Avenue as a location for fine residences.

Brokaw, Isaac Vail (1835–1913) and Brokaw, William V. (1831–1907): Opened Brokaw Brothers men's and boys' outfitters.

Brown, Isaac Hull (1812–80): Sexton of the fashionable Grace Church. He was a facilitator of social events, from the visit of the Prince of Wales gala in 1860 to parties, funerals, carriages, and much more. He pronounced on those he found acceptable.

Burden, James Abercrombie, Jr. (1871–1932): Founder of the Burden iron works, Troy, New York. He married a Vanderbilt granddaughter and received a house at 7 East 91st Street.

Carnegie, Andrew (1835–1919): One of many Scottish born immigrants to make a fortune riding the industrial elevator in America. Primarily his fortune was in the steel business. He gave much of his fortune in his last decade to numerous causes in America and the United Kingdom.

Clark, William A. (1839–1925): Self-made American figure who made a fortune in mining and other businesses. He built the biggest and most elaborate house on Fifth Avenue.

Cook, Henry H. (1822–1905): Made his fortune in railroads and moved on to real estate. In 1879 he purchased a full block of empty land from 78th to 79th Streets, Fifth Avenue to Madison Avenue. He layered deed restrictions and covenants on the entire property, limiting it to first class residences. He would build a seed house on the corner and await future plot purchasers.

Cottenet, Francis (1795–1884): French born silk merchant. He was an early creator of a multiple dwelling building in Manhattan.

de Rham, Henry (1785–1873): He belonged to an old Knickerbocker family in the dry goods and banking business, and purchased and owned the Brevoort house for some 80 years.

Dodge, Geraldine Rockefeller (1882–1973): A niece of John D. Rockefeller, she married Marcellus Harley Dodge. Their house was never really occupied.

Dugro, P. Henry (1855–1920): New York Supreme Court Justice. He opted to build a great hotel, The Savoy, across from the newly completed McKim, Mead & White first Plaza Hotel.

Duke, Benjamin Newton (1855–1929): Older brother of James Biddle Duke. He was in the tobacco business as well as a textile business. He moved often in Manhattan.

Duke, James Buchanan (1856–1925): The better-known Duke brother, who was in the tobacco business. His family created Duke University in North Carolina, their home state. He commissioned one of the finest houses on Fifth Avenue for himself, his wife, and one child.

Einstein, David L. (1839–1909): American businessman in the wool business. He had a house by the Jardines on the newly fashionable 57th Street. His decorative work on the interior appears in the 1883–84 special publication, *Artistic Houses* (New York).

Eno, Amos Richards (1810–98): Made a fortune in the dry goods business, then invested it all in real estate. His major investment was the Fifth Avenue

Hotel. He continued to buy plots of land and owned a prominent block at what would become Times Square. He lived in the Hart Shiff House, and had a well-known collection of prints. He made good on a big embezzlement made by his son.

Fisk, Jim 1834–72): Wall Street investor and schemer. He was a notorious figure who was murdered over his love for Josie Mansfield in a hotel lobby in 1872.

Fiske, Josiah Mason (1823–92): Flour merchant who turned to banking. His house at 70th Street was built well above the then-fashionable streets.

Fletcher, Isaac D. (1844–1917): Banker and investor who admired the Vanderbilt Château on 51st Street. A patron of the arts, he gave the house to The Metropolitan Museum, which would promptly sell it.

Frick, Henry Clay (1849–1919): Born in rural Pennsylvania, the young Frick made coke needed for the steel industry in Pittsburgh and came to supply coke to Andrew Carnegie. Frick was involved in the famous labor action, The Homestead Strike, and was the subject of an attempt on his life by Alexander Berkman. He retired to New York, collected important works of art, and built his full block house, which is now a museum.

Gihon, John (?–?): New York City merchant who seemed to overspend to build his house on 18th Street, forcing him to sell the house to August Belmont.

Goelet, Robert (1841–99): The Goelet family were Huguenots from Amsterdam who settled in New York in the late 17th century. Robert Goelet practiced law briefly and married into another prominent family, the Warrens, making the architect Whitney Warren his brother-in-law. The Goelet land became valuable in his lifetime, allowing him to become a clubman and yachtsman.

Goelet, Ogden (1851–97): Brother of Robert and yachtsman. He also came into great wealth from long-held family property. His daughter made one of the few successful marriages to a UK aristocrat, the 8th Duke of Roxburghe.

Gould, Jay (1836–92): Speculator and warrior in the big railroad "wars" of the 1870s. Gould was unscrupulous, much disliked in his day. He personified the term "Robber Baron".

Gray, John Alexander Clinton (1815–98): Dry goods man with an interest in politics and New York City. He was a Parks Commissioner, an early supporter of the Metropolitan Museum.

Griswold, J. N. A. (1822–1909): A descendant of the 19th-century sugar and rum family business, he specialized in the China trade and lived in China for several years. He moved to Newport, although he kept a residence in New York City.

Griswold, Mariana Alley (1851–1934): See Van Rensselaer, Mariana.

Guggenheimer, Randolph (1907–99): New York City politician and lawyer.

Gurnee, Walter S. (1813–1903): Born in Haverstraw, New York, he went to Chicago where he became successful in the tannery business. He was Mayor for two terms before heading to New York City, where he became active in many businesses.

Haight, Richard Kip (1798–1862): A successful merchant, Haight made frequent trips to Europe. After Haight's death, his house on 15th Street and Fifth Avenue would be a club house and later a small apartment house called The Hanover.

Hamersley, James Hooker (1844–1901): The Hamersley family had been in New York from 1700 onward. They owned land, and a long un-mapped street even bore their name.

Hamersley, Louis Carré (1840–83): Descendant of the property-rich Hamersley family. Educated at Oxford, he was described as sickly. He married Lily Price. His widow received the income of the estate but at her death the estate went to the male heir of his cousin, J. Hooker Hamersley.

Havemeyer, Henry Osborne (1847–1907): President of The American Sugar Refining Company and third generation sugar importer. He had an important painting collection, advanced with the help of friend Mary Cassatt. Many of his notable paintings were given to The Metropolitan Museum.

Hawley, Irad (1793–1865): Merchant who made a fortune in food, then railroads, and then coal.

Hone, Philip (1780–1851): Important figure in New York City in the first half of the 19th century. He was a mayor of the City for two terms. He kept a notable diary from 1828 to his death in 1851.

Hoyt, Alfred M. (?–1903): Manhattan-born, he was an early client of McKim, Mead & White, who built far above the fashionable streets at 934 Fifth Avenue. A commission merchant, he retired early to assume the role of club man. A farm property he held on the Upper West Side was developed as a full block soon after his death. It is known as the Belnord and is still extant.

Huntington, Archer Milton (1870–1955): Son of Arabella Duval (Worsham) and adopted by her husband Collis P. Huntington, he donated a tract of land on upper Broadway to become a cultural center, Audubon Terrace, which would include his Hispanic Society, The American Academy of Arts and Letters, the Numismatic Society, and the Museum of the American Indian. His house at 1083 Fifth Avenue was given to create The National Academy Museum.

Huntington, Collis Potter (1821–1900): One of the four industrialists who united the country by rail. While overseeing the Chesapeake and Ohio Railroad he met Arabella Duval and brought her back to New York City, where a son, Archer, was born. Huntington adopted Archer when he married Arabella in 1884. A man of great wealth, he owned many properties and, with his wife, bought notable pictures.

Hutchinson, W. J. (?–?): Broker who commissioned the house at the top of the city facing the bottom of Central Park. Hutchinson lost his fortune shortly after the house was completed. A series of financial crises led him to incarceration in the Tombs prison. The house was sold to Charles Crocker, who would give it to his daughter as a wedding gift.

Ireland, John B. (?–?) and **Ireland, John L.** (?–?): Old-time landowners in lower Manhattan and Long Island. They were connected to the Lawrence and Floyd families.

Jerome, Leonard W. (1817–91): A sportsman, horse lover, gambler and speculative investor, he had to leave his mansion on 26th Street within a few years of its completion. He had three daughters who married in Europe. His daughter, Jennie, would marry Randolph Churchill and give birth to a son, Winston. Her father would create a racecourse in the Bronx, later a reservoir. An avenue in the Bronx carries Jerome's name.

Johnston, James Boorman (1822–1887): Part of the Scottish Johnston family. He and his brother, John Taylor Johnston, commissioned America's first artists's studio and gallery on 10th Street.

Johnston, John (1781–1851): Scottish born, he came to New York in 1804 to work for Robert Lenox. He married Margaret Taylor. He was part of the group of New York merchants who built and dwelled in The

Row at the north of Washington Square.

Johnston, John Taylor (1820–1893): Son of John Johnston who grew up in The Row. In the railroad business, he was one of the first real patrons of the arts in New York and built the 10th Street Studio with his brother. Johnston was the inheritor of a summer house on 40th Street and Fifth Avenue. He would become the first president of the Metropolitan Museum, where some of his paintings reside today. His daughter and her husband created the American Wing at the Museum.

Jones, Mary Mason (1801–1891): Her father, the president of Chemical Bank, bought a huge farm. Within a generation and a half, two surviving Mason daughters received the property and developed it. Mary Mason Jones built "Marble Row" between 1867 and 1869 well above the city. Mary Mason Jones positioned herself at 1 East 57th Street and waited New York to come to her doorstep. It did.

Jones, Rebecca (1801–79): Daughter of John Mason and sister of Mary Mason. Rebecca married a Jones who was a cousin to the husband of her sister. With a sister Serena, who died young, the three Mason women lived in three row houses from 732 to 736 Broadway.

Josephs, J. L. and Josephs S. (?–?): Representative of Rothschilds Frères in New York from 1833 to the banking crash in 1837. The Rothschilds represented U.S. government interest at the time and would do so until 1843.

Kahn, Otto Hermann (1867–1934): German-born investment banker. He worked in London for five years, then came to the U.S, specializing in the reorganization of railroad companies. His great love was music, especially the opera. He built the Metropolitan Opera into a serious music venue with great personal subsidies. He also built one of the largest personal properties in the U.S., Oheka Castle on Long Island.

Lawrence, William Van Duzer (1842–1927): In the pharmaceutical business, he developed Bronxville from 1889 onward as an upper-middle-class suburb. Lawrence Park was the original section. In his wife's memory, he created Sarah Lawrence College.

Lenox, James (1800–80): Son of Robert Lenox, a successful merchant who left his only surviving son a sizable fortune and a big 30-acre undeveloped property between Fifth Avenue and what would become Park Avenue. James Lenox hired Richard Morris Hunt to build a great "private" library on his father's property at 70th Street. The library would become an anchor for the development of the area, which would come to be known as Lenox Hill. The library was combined with the two other private libraries into the New York Public Library system in 1895. A bachelor, he became a recluse, living for his books.

Lewisohn, Adolph (1848–1938): German-born industrialist and music lover. He gave generous gifts to music education in New York City and the creation of Lewisohn Stadium for concerts.

Marié, Peter (1828–1903): French-born but brought up in Haiti. He worked in banking New York, and retired at the end of the Civil War with a comfortable fortune so he could devote his life to New York society. He commissioned a series of some 300 miniatures of New York debutantes, which he intended to give to the new Metropolitan Museum. The Museum refused the collection, but The New-York Historical accepted the miniatures in 1905.

Martin, Runyon W. (?–?): An attorney, he built the first house across from Central Park in 1865. The architect was Jacob W. Mould, and the house was glaringly High Victorian Gothic.

Mason, John (1773–1839): Originally a merchant, then a banker, he is credited with the maturation of Chemical Bank. He bought a farm in what we might today call Midtown (53rd Street to 64th Street. His four children included Mary, Rebecca, and Sarah/Serena. A son was disinherited for marrying an actress.

McAllister, Samuel Ward (1827–95): Savannah-born society figure who coined the Gilded Age social rules for New York City's 400. McAllister framed the playbook for determining those in and those out of the set.

Mills, Ogden (1856–1929): California-born financier. Son of the California banker and investor, Darius Ogden Mills. He came East and married into one of the oldest families in America. With money and entry to society, he could devote his life to racehorses.

Minturn, Robert Browne (1805–66): Merchant and Clipper ship owner. With his family he traveled in Europe and the Middle East on a long trip, which inspired him to think of a central park for New York. Temperance was an issue that was important to him.

Morgan, Edwin D. (1811–83): Wholesale grocer who became a banker. He was a Union general in the Civil War. A Whig, he became a Republican and supporter of Lincoln. Morgan was Governor of New York State and Senator from New York.

Morton, Levi P. (1824–1920): Merchant, cotton broker, and then banker at Morton, Bliss & Co. He was appointed U.S. Minister to France from 1881–85. He was Governor of New York State, then Vice President under President Harrison. Morton moved houses frequently in New York but kept his house in Newport and on the Hudson.

Payne, Oliver Hazard (1839¬–1917): Well-educated at Andover and Yale, he became a Brevetted Brigadier General in the Union Army in the Civil War. He invested early in oil, which he sold to Standard Oil. Angry with his former brother-in-law W.C. Whitney, who remarried after the death of Payne's sister, he offered his fortune to the four Whitney children. Two took his offer and two stuck with their father.

Penniman, George H. (1829–1909): Successful in the linseed oil business, he turned his attention to New York real estate. He built a house at 1071 Fifth Avenue 1897. The house was replaced by the Guggenheim Museum.

Phipps, Henry (1839–1930): Rose from humble origins to join Andrew Carnegie's Union Iron Mills. He joined with Carnegie in his Carnegie Steel Company. In 1901, J. P. Morgan created U.S. Steel, making Carnegie and Phipps very wealthy. His philanthropy included Phipps Houses, affordable housing in New York City.

Pickhardt, Wilhelm (1834–95): German-born, Pickhardt had a successful air heating and cooking apparatus business. He decided to build a big house on Fifth Avenue, but it seems he ran out of money and the house was sold.

Price, Lily Spencer-Churchill (1854-1909) American heiress in the Gilded Age. The beautiful Lily Price first married Louis Carré Hamersley, who died in 1883. Her second husband was George Charles Spencer-Churchill, 8th Duke of Marlborough (1844–92). She married a third time and died in England.

Randall, Robert Richard (1750–1801): From a Scottish family, Randall and his father were privateers. Randall bought the Elliot estate above the northern edges of the city. In his will he left his property to create a "snug harbor" for worn out sailors. After inheritance disputes, the Sailor's Snug Harbor was eventually created, but it would be located on Staten Island, with the Elliot Farm property used to generate support for the Staten Island complex.

Restell, Ann Lohman (1812–78): British-born Ann Trow came to New York with her infant daughter. She married a German Russian immigrant, Charles Lohman, and expanded her work as a midwife to become an abortionist. She took the name of a prominent French physician, Restell, when she began her practice in New York. Mme Restell made a solid fortune but suffered from legal actions through the last thirty years of her work. Facing legal charges against her, on April 1, 1878, she committed suicide in her bathtub.

Rhinelander, William C. (1790–1878): Son of the original creator of the Rhinelander Sugar House on Duane Street. He married a member of the Rogers family, whose land holdings were significant in lower Manhattan. The house at 14 Washington Square North would be a family home for a century. He owned additional property in the city, including the site of his once-country house on the Upper East Side.

Roberts, Marshall O. (1813–80): Roberts's family came from Wales. He was an excellent businessman and rose quickly in the burgeoning steam ship business, then moved on to railroads. His house at 107 Fifth Avenue was on the southeast corner of 18th Street across from August Belmont. Roberts was an important early painting collector. Among his pictures was the famous Emanuel Leutze work, *Washington Crossing the Delaware* (1851), now in The Metropolitan Museum.

Rockefeller, John D. (1839–1937): Rockefeller moved from upstate New York to Cleveland, where he would create Standard Oil. He lived at 2 West 54th Street until the death of his wife, Laura Spellman Rockefeller, in 1925. In a Rockefeller tradition, his houses in Cleveland and New York were demolished at his death. A devout Baptist, he was instrumental in the 18th Amendment, which banned alcohol. He created universities and medical establishments with his Rockefeller Foundation.

Rockefeller, William (1841–1922): Younger brother of John. He also started a business in kerosene and oil. He moved to New York on the northeast corner of 54th Street.

Rogers, George P. (?–?): Son of John Rogers. He built 17 Washington Square North as his country house. It was the first house at Washington Square North. After his death, the house was enlarged and turned into an apartment house by Henry Janeway Hardenbergh. It is extant.

Rogers, John (?–?): Prominent New York City landowner. He bought the Warren property at the northwest corner of Washington Square. He was the father of Mary Rhinelander (born in 1821) and George P. Rogers.

Rogers, Mary (1821–93): Daughter of John Rogers. She was the wife of William C. Rhinelander.

Roosevelt, Cornelius Van Schaack (1794–1871): He was the last true Dutch Roosevelt. Prosperous in the hardware business, he expanded into plate glass and increased his wealth. As with so many other merchants, he bought properties in the panic of 1837. He resided in Oyster Bay but had a house near Union Square in Manhattan.

Roosevelt, Theodore (1858–1919): Son of C. V. S. Roosevelt. Born at 28 East 20th Street, he would become Police Commissioner in New York, followed by Governor, Vice President, then the 26th President of the nation.

Ruppert, Jacob (1842–1915): Bavarian-born Ruppert started and ran a beer company bearing his surname. He built a big house far above the fashionable folks on Upper Fifth Avenue. The house was decorated by the Herter Brothers, who were then working for William Henry Vanderbilt. Ruppert kept a low profile and seemed to keep to the German community in New York.

Ryan, Thomas Fortune (1851–1928): Virginia-born, Ryan was a major figure in transit in the northeast. He worked with William C. Whitney, who tutored the young Ryan. He became a broker and joined James B. Duke with a joint tobacco company, The American Tobacco Company. He joined August Belmont, Jr. in the Interborough Rapid Transit Company in New York City. He lived in several places in Manhattan.

Schmid, Josephine (?–1936) née Kleiner: Her husband August, a brewery owner, died young and left his widow comfortably well-off. She went on to take over the brewery and gained property in New York. She married the fourth son of an Italian prince. The house Josephine Schmid built was closed in 1909, and she died in Italy in 1936.

Shiff, Hart Moses (1780–1851): Perhaps German-born, he came to New York via New Orleans. He became a banker and the owner of the first French mansard roof in New York. The grand house was red brick with brownstone trim.

Sloane, John (1834–1905): Born in Scotland, he ran his family furniture business with his brother

William. William was married to a daughter of William Henry Vanderbilt. John Sloane had a house at 883 Fifth Avenue and a large property in Lenox, Massachusetts. He was active in The St. Andrew's Society in New York.

Smith, Murray Forbes (1814–75): Born in Mobile, Alabama, in the 1850s he was a successful cotton commissioner. He moved to New York in 1859. He never regained his business after the Civil War. Smith was the father of Alva Smith, who married W.K Vanderbilt, and subsequently Oliver Belmont.

Speyer, James (1861–1941): American-born son of Speyer & Co. Investment bankers. He was educated in Germany and worked with railroad bonds. He was the agent for Collis P. Huntington's rail interests. He was the initiator and founder of The Museum of the City of New York. His loyalty to Germany started a slide to the end of the company in World War I.

Stern, Simon Hunt (1847–1906): Born in Richmond, Virginia, he was an attorney in New York City. He lived at 986 Fifth Avenue. His son was Henry Root Stern.

Stevens, Adele (1841–1912): Wealthy when she married Frederick W. Stevens, she built a sturdy house at 2 West 57th Street. She would later marry the Marquis de Talleyrand Perigord and move to France. When the Manhattan house was sold to Flora and William C. Whitney, the pattern would repeat, as the house was maintained by Flora Whitney's fortune.

Stevens, Marietta Reed (1827–95): Born in Lowell, Massachusetts, her father was a grocer. She was the second wife of the hotelier, Paran Stevens. In the 1860s she staged a full assault on society. She launched her daughter, Minnie, into UK society, then returned to New York to announce the engagement of her son to Edith Jones (who became Edith Wharton). The Knickerbocker Jones family did not approve, and the engagement was called off. Her last shred of wealth dissolved, Marietta died of a massive stroke in Mary Mason Jones's house at 1 East 57th Street.

Stevens, Paran (1802–72): A hotel developer. He was one of the most important figures in the hospitality world in Boston, then at the Fifth Avenue Hotel in New York. As he succeeded in his hotel world, he started to develop an apartment house near the hotel, but died as it was being finished and his widow turned it into a hotel. Stevens bought property on and near 37th Street, where he planned to move from his rental brownstone at 244 Fifth Avenue, but his death ended the plan.

Stewart, Alexander Turney (1803–76): Ulster-born schoolteacher and then merchant. He started a retail store on Broadway. He married into a New York City mercantile family and expanded into real estate. He ran successful hotels in Saratoga, New York. Stewart bought pictures and sculpture with an untrained but excellent eye.

Straight, Willard (1880–1918): Son of two missionaries to China, Straight became an expert on China and its arts. A graduate of Cornell in architecture, Straight became a diplomat specializing in Chinese issues. He married the heiress Dorothy Paine Whitney. His diplomatic career was ended when he fell victim to the Spanish Flu in Paris in 1918.

Stuart, Robert Leighton (1806–82): He and his brother, Alexander, developed a refining process for sugar, which facilitated the creation of inexpensive candy. He and his wife had a brownstone at 154 Fifth Avenue, later the office of Stanford White and soon his firm. He built a big house on Fifth Avenue just before his death. A devout Presbyterian, he forbade work on Sunday.

Stuyvesant, Augustus Van Horne, Jr. (1870–1953): The last direct descendant of Peter Stuyvesant. He and two sisters were born in their house at 20th Street and Fifth Avenue. They would never marry. They moved to 57th Street, just east of Fifth Avenue and then, when it became too commercialized, to the Cook block at 79th Street. The elderly man lived there to his death. He is in the Stuyvesant vault at St. Mark's in the Bowery, which was sealed after he was interned there.

Stuyvesant, Peter (1610–72): The director general of the Dutch West Indies Company who capitulated to the British, creating New York out of New Amsterdam. He was known for his wooden false limb as Peg Leg Pete. He assembled a vast property in the then-northeast part of the colony, in what would become Brooklyn, and a part of the area to the north. It would be known as Stuyvesant's Farm or Bowery. The land was retained for many generations.

Stuyvesant, Peter Gerard (1777–1846): A descendent of the Stuyvesant and Livingston family, he gave four acres to New York City for what would become Stuyvesant Park.

Stuyvesant, Rutherford (1843–1909): Part of the Rutherford and Stuyvesant families. To inherit his third of the Stuyvesant property, he reversed his name from Stuyvesant Rutherford to Rutherford Stuyvesant. He was celebrated for beginning the apartment house for high-born people in his social circle on his property on 18th Street. The patina of his name provided him tenants.

Thompson, Frederick Ferris (1836–99): Banker who hired McKim, Mead & White to build him a very up-to-date house at 283 Madison Avenue with an elevator and a warming area for messenger boys at the front stoop.

Townsend, Samuel P. (?–?) The creator of a popular tonic and beverage in the middle of the 19th century, Sasparilla.

Trask, Spencer (1844–1909): Venture capitalist best known for backing Thomas Edison's light bulb. His property in Saratoga became Yaddo, a retreat for writers.

Tweed, William M. "Boss" (1823–78): Political boss of Tammany Hall in New York City. He was a New York senator and U. S. congressman. Highly skilled in political kickback, he may have been one of the largest owners of property in Manhattan. Finally convicted for his crimes, he escaped to Spain, where he was recognized and returned to New York where he died in the Ludlow Street jail.

Untermeyer, Samuel (1858–1940): Corporate lawyer and prominent figure in political circles. His very successful firm included Randolph Guggenheimer, who also built on Fifth Avenue. He donated Untermeyer Park to the citizens of Yonkers, New York. His mausoleum at Woodlawn has a figure by Gertrude Vanderbilt Whitney.

Van Rensselaer, Mariana Alley Griswold (1851-1934) Often known as Mrs. Schuyler Van Rensselaer. One of the first American writers and critics of architecture. Born to a family of two merchants of the Port who met in the back gardens of The Row. Widowed early she lived a life not typical of her social position at the time. Her brother, Frank G. Griswold, was also a writer. She held a fine line between the world of the Knickerbockers and the young new architects she praised, H.H. Richardson and McKim, Mead & White.

Van Schaick, Henry (1825–1914): Son of Myndert Van Schaick, he was part of an old Dutch family that had settled when it was still under Dutch rule.

Vanderbilt, Cornelius (1794–1877): Staten Island-born, he established a ferry service that grew, earning him the nickname "Commodore". He traded ferry boats for the iron horse. He had established perhaps the largest fortune in America by the time of his

death. His family business was left to one son, William Henry Vanderbilt.

Vanderbilt, Cornelius Jr. (1843–99): Oldest son of William Henry Vanderbilt. His grandfather, the Commodore, took a strong liking to the boy and brought him into the business at a young age. He married Alice Claypoole and although prominent, he and his wife were not absorbed in the social whirl. Vanderbilt rebuilt The Breakers in Newport, after a fire.

Vanderbilt, William Henry (1821–85): A son of Commodore Vanderbilt who initially regarded William Henry poorly. William Henry finally managed to gain his father's trust and his father, who had twelve children, left him his entire inheritance. William Henry promised to keep the now large railroad empire whole. He promptly gave the company over to J. P. Morgan to organize as New York Central. His siblings brought the will to court, making a trial that became a circus full of lurid claims.

Vanderbilt, William Kissam (1849–1920): Second son of William Henry Vanderbilt. He married Alva Smith, and their New York house became a touchstone for the era. After he and Alva divorced, he devoted his later years to horse racing, yachts, and the life of a very wealthy man in America and Europe.

Waddell, William Coventry Henry (1802–84): New York City-born, he was a youth with great possibilities. He and his second wife built a "suburban" villa way above the inhabited part of the city in the late 1830s. The Waddells entertained well and were part of the Newport summer colony. The economic downturn of 1857 wiped out Waddell's fortune.

Warburg, Felix (1871–1937): German-born part of a Hamburg family banking house, he arrived in New York and joined Kuhn Loeb &. Co. He married Frieda Schiff, the daughter of banker Jacob Schiff.

Webb, William Henry (1816–99): Ship builder and creator of the Webb Institute Merchant Marine academy.

Weed, Hamilton M. (?–?): Developer. He built the Dorilton at 171 West 71st Street in New York City, an over-the-top apartment house on the newly-built upward West Side.

Wendel, Ella (?–1931): The last of the real estate Wendel family. They were amongst the biggest real estate property owners in Manhattan.

Wendel, John D. (?–1876): Son of Johann Gottlieb, he carried on the family real estate business. Clinging to a modest lifestyle, the only improvement generations of Wendels made to their 39th Street house was indoor toilets. They did not live a high life. Told not to marry for fear of a spouse claiming the properties, the sisters and brothers lived the life of their grandparents.

Wendel, Johann Gottlieb (1767–1841): German furrier who came to New York and worked with the original J. J. Astor. The two men married sisters. The Wendels bought farms and property as would Astor. Both men abandoned fur for farms above the city.

Wharton, Edith (1862–1937) née Jones: Edith Jones was the epitome of the Knickerbocker social world. Born to merchants of the port, the family were property rich but cash poor after the Civil War and spent several years in Europe, where life was cheaper. Shy, her first engagement was to Marietta Steven's son, Harry, which came to a bad end. Edith would marry a well-off Bostonian, Teddy Wharton, and dip her toe into publishing. She became the first American woman to win a Pulitzer Prize. Some of her books are heavily based on the New York she experienced when she returned from Europe in the 1870s. In the 20th century, she moved to France and would remain and write from France until her death.

Whitney, William Collins (1841–1904): Descended from John Whitney who came to New England in 1635. Eminent but not wealthy, he married Flora Payne, who died in 1893. Whitney then married one of the beautiful May sisters, which outraged Flora's brother and the two men became estranged. Oliver Payne offered the Whitney children his fortune if they would leave their father. Although Whitney lived very grandly, he was increasingly distrusted. In 1904 he died in the portico of his palatial new home. The official cause was appendicitis, but many suspected he had been stabbed.

Wilson, Richard T. (1829–1910): Southern-born Wilson made money passing off cotton blankets to soldiers in the Civil War as wool. A slightly disreputable business history did not stop him from moving into 511 Fifth Avenue, to a small house left by Boss Tweed. He and his wife moved in the top social circles, where his five children made important marriages. The family became known as the "marrying Wilsons."

Worsham, Arabella (c. 1850–1924): Arabella Duval Never Worsham Huntington. The beautiful young woman caught the eye of Collis P. Huntington. He brought her with a son and her mother to New York. Blessed with an excellent eye, she moved into the house of William Williams on 54th Street, well above the built city. Arabella created a house that was the apogee of the Aesthetic Movement in New York. She later married her husband's nephew and set up a library in Pasadena, California. A fine collector, she owned the famous painting of her era, Gainsborough's *Blue Boy* (1770). Her son, Archer Milton Huntington, was also devoted to the arts.

Yznaga, Consuelo (?–1934): Her father was a Cuban plantation owner, her mother a Natchez belle. They had a small plantation, Ravenswood, near Natchez. Her brother married Alva Smith Vanderbilt's sister. She was the godmother of Alva's daughter, named for her. She married George Montagu, Viscount Mandeville, in New York in 1876, settling into a bad thirty years during which neither she nor her husband had any money. In 1901 Consuelo's brother Fernando left her his estate, saving her financially. It seems that she became the beloved companion of William Kissam Vanderbilt and was an intimate in the court of Edward VII. She is the role model for Edith Wharton's Conchita in *The Buccaneers* (1938).

APPENDIX 2

KEY ARCHITECTS, BUILDERS,
DESIGNERS, SURVEYORS,
URBAN PLANNERS.

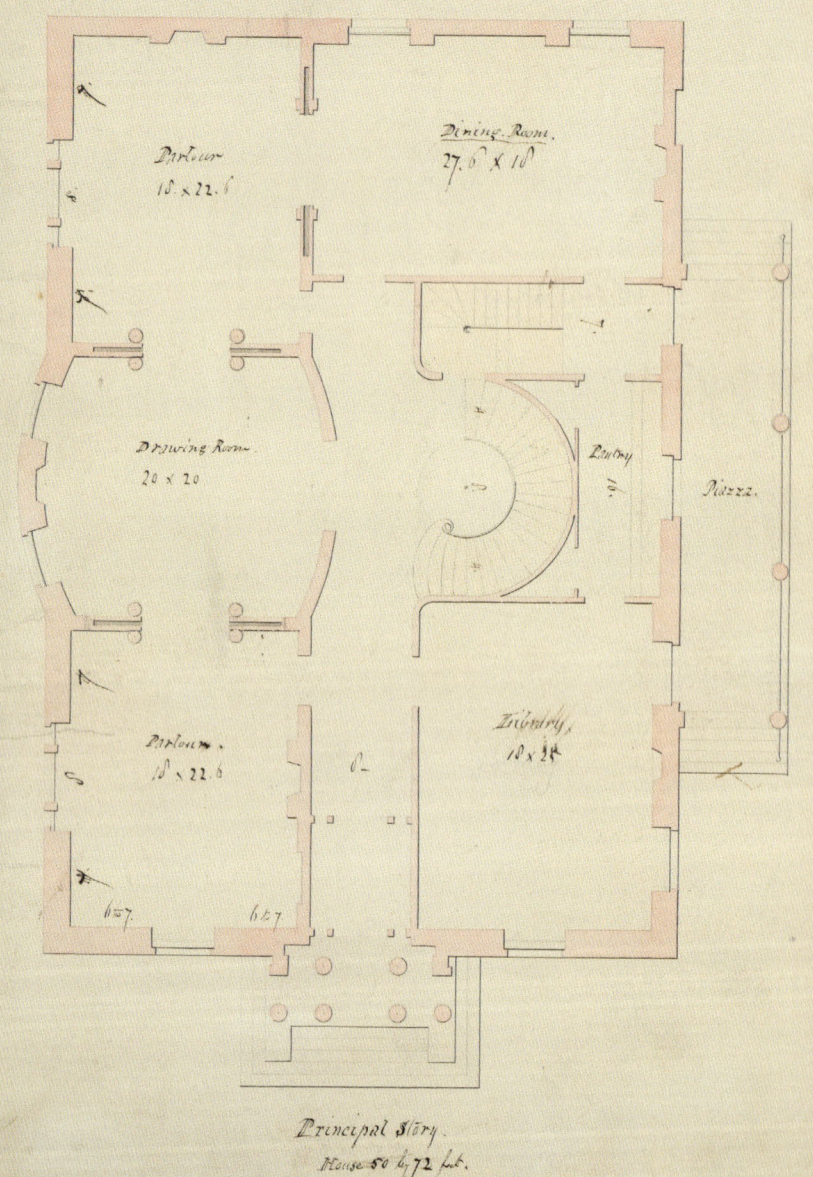

Parlour
18 x 22.6

Dining Room
27.6 x 18

Drawing Room
20 x 20

Pantry

Piazza

Parlour
18 x 22.6

Library
18 x 24

Principal Story.
House 50 by 72 feet.

24 Fifth Avenue

Brevoort/De Rham House, 24 Fifth Avenue The plan reveals an unusual central entry and hall. The house was built to be distinct from the speculative houses of its day.

Abele, Julian (1881–1950): A prominent architect with a notable career. One of the first-known-black architects, he worked as chief designer in the office of Horace Trumbauer. Abele designed buildings for Duke University.

Atwood, Charles B. (1849–95): A talented designer who may have known C. F. McKim and Schuyler Van Rensselaer at the Lawrence Scientific School at Harvard. He worked for R. M. Hunt and the Herter Brothers on Vanderbilt commissions. He went on to work with Daniel H. Burnham on the World's Columbian Exposition, where he designed the Fine Arts Building. Atwood's later career seems murky at best.

Bigelow, William A. (c. 1848–c. 1925): Well-born, Bigelow's life and career took him on a downward spiral. He was a classmate and early partner of Charles Follen McKim. He had to leave the firm after a year and a half, when his sister forced him to depart. McKim and Annie, his sister, had a short and unhappy marriage. Was the real love affair here between McKim and William Bigelow? Bigelow worked for the Herter Brothers briefly, but his later years were spent in a boarding house in Cambridge near Harvard.

Bloor, Alfred J. (1828–1917): Born in Edinburgh, (where he was possibly known to John Taylor Johnston), he settled in New York, and was likely part of the Scottish group in lower Fifth Avenue. He went to Washington D.C. with the Sanitary Commission. He was the secretary of the American Institute of Architects from 1870–88.

Bossom, Alfred Charles (1881–1965): London-born and well-educated, he arrived in New York in 1904 and worked on some large mansions on Fifth Avenue and in the region. He became a skyscraper expert with a flourishing career but chose to return to England to give his three sons a UK education. Once in England, he became a politician, abandoning his architectural career.

Brunner, Arnold William (1857–1925): Brunner was born in New York to a well-positioned Jewish family who sent him to school in Manchester, England. He then attended the new program in architecture at MIT before he returned to New York where he would remain and be active for the rest of his life. He had good social connections and served on many committees. He built notable synagogues and buildings for public service, and also undertook some city planning.

Carpenter, James Edwin Ruthven. (1867–1932): Carpenter was born in Tennessee, trained in MIT in the early day and then went to the Ecole des Beaux Arts in Paris. Carpenter worked in the South before coming to New York, where he designed the first high-class apartment building on Fifth Avenue after WW I. He was an excellent designer, fitting his buildings into their context and thinking of the residents when creating fine detailing.

Clinton, Charles William. (1838–1910): Born in New York, Clinton trained under the architect, Richard Upjohn. He was the architect of the Park Avenue Armory and numerous residences, both houses and apartment buildings. He worked for the Astor Estate on their better buildings. He also designed the John Bond Trevor house in Yonkers, now the Hudson River Museum.

Crooks, Arthur (1838–88): English-born, he arrived in New York and worked under Richard Upjohn. He was the architect of many Catholic churches in the greater New York region.

Cutter, Manly N. (1851–1931): Rather more a delineator than architect, he built in the American Shingle style.

Da Cunha, George W. (??–??): A Portuguese-born architect and developer, he was important in early multiple dwelling units, and designed row houses on the Upper West Side of Manhattan.

Dakin, James Harrison (1806–52): Dakin was apprenticed to the architect A. J. Davis. He worked in New York before settling in New Orleans, and he built through the south. His special skill was the Gothic Revival.

Davis, Alexander Jackson (1803–92): Born in New York to a working family, Davis took up painting before he was encouraged to take up architecture. He was best designer of the mid 19th century in all areas including furniture design. Davis never traveled abroad but he used the architectural library of his one-time partner, Ithiel Town, to see all the images books provided in the days before photographic illustration.

Davis, Thomas E. (c. 1785 or 1795–1878): An English-born developer who worked for the agents of the Rothschilds. He subsequently developed rows on Fifth Avenue, as well as working in Staten Island.

Diaper, Frederick (1810–1906): An experienced row house builder in New York, known for building the highest quality houses. Diaper went to San Francisco in 1869 with a German architect who also practiced in New York.

Duggin, Charles (1830–1916): One of several developer/designers in mid 19th-century Manhattan. Duggin built five houses on the northern site of the once St Luke's hospital. He built in Staten Island before coming to Fifth Avenue where he went into partnership with James Crossman.

Flagg, Jared Bradley (1820–99): A portrait painter of important figures, Flagg later became a member of the Episcopal clergy. He also dabbled in real estate. Despite his connections to notable people, his development reputation was unsavory. He was the father of the architect, Ernest Flagg.

Gilbert, Charles Pierrepont Henry (1861–1952): Gilbert descended from an old New York family. In his early career he sems to have built houses in the new American West, returning to New York where he became the master of the château town house in Manhattan. Gilbert built in other styles as well and for his clients in their weekend settings. He built many residences in Brooklyn and in his last years designed a multiple dwelling in Manhattan.

Gilman, Arthur Delevan (1821–82): Gilman's family were early settlers in New Hampshire. He attended Trinity College, then took an extended trip through Europe looking at buildings. A good designer, he worked in Boston until, perhaps, Paran Stevens lured him to New York.

Goerck, Casimir Theodor (c, 1755–1798): Possibly of Polish or German birth, Goerck came to America in the Revolutionary War. He quickly proved to be the master of turning the common land into saleable lots for the Stuyvesant estate. He began a plan for New York but died of yellow fever before he finished. The Mangin-Goerck plan was completed in 1801 with a street named for each planner.

Haight, Charles Coolidge (1841–1917): The Haight family were well-born, and his father was active in Trinity Church and the Trinity Church properties. Not a Fifth Avenue architect, Haight designed college campuses: the long-demolished midtown Columbia; buildings at Yale; and the Chelsea Episcopalian seminary.

Hardenbergh, Henry Janeway (1847–1918): A son of an old Dutch family, Hardenbergh trained under Detlef Lienau before setting up his own practice. Known for his apartment buildings in the early days

of this building type on 57th Street, he designed and built the Dakota on the Upper West Side for the Clark family. When the Daly Law stopped apartment building, Hardenberg became the master of the Edwardian hotel, building the current Plaza and hotels in Boston, Philadelphia and Washigton D.C.

Harney, George Edward (1840–1924): An elusive figure in late 19th-century New York architecture, he trained with an engineer. With no known social connections, it is mystery that he secured so many plum jobs.

Harrison, Henry G. (1813–95): An English-born architect about whom little is known. He had an active career in the mid 19th century before building records began. He had connections to the old Knickerbocker families, building in Garden City for A T Stewart's widow and the Beekmans in Oyster Bay.

Hatch, Stephen Decatur (1839–94): Seemingly untrained, he entered the office of Snook where he learned to build, mainly working on commercial buildings. He died by falling off a pier while adding on to the Equitable Life Insurance Company headquarters on Broadway.

Hunt, Richard Morris (1827–95): One of the first European-trained architects in America, he was the 'dean' of the profession, helping establish the American Institute of Architects. From a prominent family, he was educated in Europe after his father's death and was one of the first American students to work at the Ecole des Beaux Arts. He then worked for a French architect on a wing of the Louvre before returning to America. Cosmopolitan and genteel, Hunt was embraced by the wealthy of the city. His wife's inheritance (she was part of the world of the merchants of the port) allowed Hunt the freedom to choose his commissions and travel to refresh his skills. He was the architect to the Vanderbilts and even, later, Mrs. Astor. While working on the massive Biltmore estate and the Metropolitan Museum Fifth Avenue front, he died. A memorial was built on Fifth Avenue at 70th Street opposite his great Lenox Library. The library is gone but the Hunt Memorial remains.

Jackson, Thomas R. (1826–1901): English-born, Jackson arrived in America as a child with his family. He went on to work with the English-born Richard Upjohn before setting out on his own.

Jardine, David J. (1840–92): David Jardine was the first of three brothers, sons of a Scottish builder, to settle in New York. The Jardines built commercial buildings as well as numerous row houses on Fifth Avenue. The Altman store on Sixth Avenue with its cast iron front was an early Jardine work.

Jardine, John E. (1838–1920): A younger brother of David, he donated the firm's papers to the California Historical Society in San Francisco. Suffering from depression, John Jardine took his own life.

Kellum, John (1809–1871): Born on the Hempstead plain in Long Island, Kellum came to New York as a carpenter. He began working with the Brooklyn political figure, Gamaliel King, and attracted the attention of the real estate magnate and department store mogul, A. T. Stewart. Kellum lured Stewart to the Hempstead Plain to begin what would become Garden City. Working for the corrupt mayoralty in New York, Kellum designed the notorious "Tweed Courthouse".

Kendall, Edward H. (1842–1901): Boston-born, Kendall worked under Arthur Gilman on the important early tall office building for Equitable Life. Little else is known.

Kilburn, Henry Franklin (1844–1905): Born in Maine, Kimball learned of the important British architect, William Burges and went to London where he claimed he worked in Burges's office. Kilburn did theaters and tall commercial buildings on his return to New York.

King, David H. Jr. (??–1916): A contractor and developer who moved in the same social circles as his clients. He was the contractor for Madison Square Garden.

Kissam, Peter (??–??): The Kissams were an important family, probably with Dutch roots, found throughout the region of New York. Builders and bankers, the Kissams built for the Astors and many row house speculators.

Lienau, Detlef (1818–87): Born in Holstein, Lienau went to Paris and was perhaps aware of Henri Labrouste and the Ecole des Beaux Arts. Lienau followed his brother, Michael, to New Jersey. He quickly rose to the top of the house building world with many well positioned patrons.

Lord, James Brown (1859–1902): Born wealthy and well connected, the grandson of the famous attorney, Daniel Lord, he graduated from Princeton. Lord then went to Paris and the Ecole. Back in New York, he built the New York Appellate Court and in

Tuxedo Park. He died young.

Marcotte, Leon (1824–87): French-born, Marotte trained as an architect and attend the Ecole des Beaux Arts. In the atelier of Labrouste, he likely met Detlef Lienau. The two sailed for New York in 1848 where clients existed through contacts. Marcotte established a furniture business, creating elaborate furniture sets in ornate French styles.

Maynicke, Robert (1849–1913): Born in Germany, Maynicke arrived in New York as an infant. He attended night classes at Cooper Union, then worked in the office of George B. Post. He designed commercial buildings and was the master of the loft building in New York,

McKim, Charles Follen (1847–1909): Son of a central figure in the abolition cause, McKim left the Lawrence Scientific school at Harvard to go to the Ecole des Beaux Arts in Paris. He formed a partnership with William R. Mead and Stanford White, and the firm became leading figures in American architecture in the late 19th and early 20th centuries. McKim was the 'dean' of American architecture in his later years. His awareness of Fifth Avenue was intense, but he designed little upon it.

Mook, Robert (1830–1917): Son of the abattoir owner of 44th Street and Fifth Avenue, Thomas Mook, he seemingly trained with Griffith Thomas and built row houses and a cast iron store, extant in Soho today. It would seem he first created a lavish brownstone for Mme. Restell at 52nd Street in the early 1860s. He would then build the famous row of Mary Mason Jones at 57th–58th Streets and many rows on her properties in that area. He became interested in cement and reinforced concrete and created a house in Port Chester, New York, entirely of that material for the Ward family. Mook then seems to have moved from New York. He lived until 1917, but without further commissions in Manhattan.

Mould, Jacob Wrey (1825–86): English-born, Mould came to the United States in 1852 after working with Owen Jones on the 1851 Crystal Palace. His work in New York ranged from houses to the Unitarian Church, which was the first High Victorian Gothic building in the city, to the structures of Central Park. An accomplished librettist and musician, Mould wore several hats.

Pfeiffer, Carl (1834–88): German-born, Pfeiffer trained in Ohio before coming to New York where he built commercial buildings and churches.

Post, George Browne (1837–1913): New York-born, Post graduated from NYU as an engineer. He trained in the office of Richard Morris Hunt for two years before setting out on his own. He had family connections to businesses in his day, and quickly became the "king" of the skyscraper corporate form. Post built few houses.

Price, Bruce (1845–1903): An American architect with good social connections, who built houses mainly outside New York City. His American Surety Company at 100 Broadway is one of the earliest examples of a steel frame skyscraper in New York.

Randel, Jr., John (1787–1865): Albany-born and with little formal education, he became a surveyor, map maker and civil engineer. He was a force in the creation of the Commissioner's Plan of 1811 for New York, then only Manhattan.

Renwick, Jr., James (1818–95): Born in New York to a well-established family with access to education and wealth, his father was an engineering professor at Columbia College where Renwick Jr. studied the subject. He had no architectural training at all yet was commissioned to build Grace Church on land donated by his mother's family, the Brevoorts. Renwick went on to a very successful career designing St. Patrick's Cathedral in New York and the early Smithsonian building in Washington D.C. and many other notable structures.

Robertson, Robert Henderson (1849–1919): Philadelphia-born to Scottish parents, Robertson was sent to Scotland for school before entering Rutgers College. From 1875–81, he had a brilliant career at Potter & Robertson, before striking out on his own. He had very good social connections which gave him plenty of work in the styles of the era with great success.

Schastey, George A. (1839–94): German-born, Schastey trained in the workrooms of the Herter Brothers. A cabinet maker and decorator, he did splendid work in the Aesthetic Style of the 1870s in America.

Schickel, William (1850–1907): German-born with some architect's training in Germany, he crossed the Atlantic and immediately entered the office of R. M. Hunt. He worked especially for German-speaking clients and the Roman Catholic Church. His work for the Scottish Presbyterian, Robert Stuart, is unexplained.

Shapter, R. S. (?–?): A less well-known architect who, in 1922, created a house for Mrs. Marcellus Dodge, a Rockefeller heir. The house was rarely used.

Sherwood, John H. (1816–87): An American developer, instrumental in the development of Fifth Avenue after the abattoir era. A great admirer of artists, he built a famed artist's studio building on 57th Street with apartments for artists.

Smith, William Wheeler (c. 1838–1908): An American architect and businessman, who designed and developed properties he owned on Wall Street. He lived and worked from his home at 17 East 77th Street, after he designed the Cook house a block away. Successful as a businessman, he gave away his fortune to philanthropic causes. His printed book collection is now in the British Museum.

Snook, John Butler (1815–1901): English-born, he started out in his father's carpentry business. While he never trained as an architect, it would seem his business skills gave him many commissions. He worked for the Vanderbilts and numerous clients and was a master of cast iron fronts and brownstone., a far cry from carpentry.

Sturgis, Russell (1836–1909): Born to a New York family, living in Baltimore, Sturgis was educated in public schools. He went to Munich for a year and a half and joined the office of Leopold Eidlitz, a New York-based German architect. He practiced in the High Victorian Gothic mode, particularly at Yale. Sturgis gradually turned to writing, producing a number of important books.

Thomas, Griffith (1820–79): Born in London or Wales, the son of a builder, Thomas arrived in New York and set himself up as an architect. He had an important career in New York, in many modes and styles. A master of cast iron, and brownstone his may have been the most important architectural practice in New York from the 1850s to 1870s.

Thomson, Samuel (1784–1850): A Scottish-born architect, who was important in New York in the 1830s, he seems to have had disputes during his commissions. He retreated to Inwood on the Upper Island where he built houses and a small Presbyterian church.

Trumbauer, Horace (1868–1938): A Philadelphia-born man with little education, Trumbauer began working in offices before setting out on his own. Trumbauer made a career of building for recently successful men. A modest man himself, intimidated by the lack of respect shown him in the profession, Trumbauer flattered the newly-wealthy by not being superior to the clients in education and behavior. He designed many mansions in the Gilded Age and his firm were the architects of Duke University.

Tuthill, William B. (1855–1929): A graduate of the College of the City of New York, Tuthill worked in the office of R. M. Hunt. His major work was Carnegie Hall.

Upjohn, Richard (1802–78): English-born, he came to the United States as a master craftsman and cabinet maker, Upjohn recreated himself as an architect. He would design numerous ecclesiastical buildings in America.

Vaux, Calvert (1824–95): English-born and trained, Vaux was a landscape designer and architect. Downing, the American landscape designer sought out Vaux in England and brought him to America. Downing's early death launched Vaux's career and he subsequently became most famous for his work on Central Park.

Vine, William (??–??): Totally unknown other than for a sketch book left to the New York Historical Society. He must have been in New York in the early 1830s.

Washburn, William (1808–90): A Boston architect, he was brought into the Steven's project for an apartment house, which later became The Victoria Hotel.

Wells, Joseph C. (1814–60): An English architect who designed the Presbyterian Church on Fifth Avenue at 12th Street. He died on a boat returning to England.

Wells, Joseph Morill (1853–90): A little known architect, he was the creator of the best work for C. F. McKim and Stanford White. His design skills impressed his peers and McKim & White both acknowledged his importance to their firm. He died too young to become well known as a major architect.

White, Stanford (1853–1906): Born in New York to a writer, intellectual, dandy, and difficult character, White was a natural talent. He had little formal schooling in the public system and began in the office of H. H. Richardson (who built nothing on Fifth Avenue) where his ability allowed him a quick rise in the firm. He joined a partnership with C. F. McKim and the firm, McKim, Mead & White became the premier architects of the Gilded Age. White was a superb designer/decorator who would later become an important purchaser of European objects for the houses he was designing. His talents were forgotten for a time following his lurid murder. White's reputation has been fully restored.

Zucker, Alfred J. R. E. (1852–1913): A German-born architect who moved to America in the early 1870s. He initially worked in the new port city of Galveston, then moved to New York where he built row houses and loft buildings. Many of his loft buildings today form the campus of NYU.

ILLUSTRATION CREDITS

CHAPTER 1

8 Lionel Pincus and Princess Firyal Map Division, The New York Public Library, 1520730.

CHAPTER 2

14–15 *Seventh Regiment on Review, Washington Square, New York*, Otto Boetticher, 1851, oil on canvas. 24 x 36 in. (61 x 91.4 cm), The Metropolitan Museum of Art, The Edward W. C. Arnold Collection of New York Prints, Maps, and Pictures, Bequest of Edward W. C. Arnold, 1954, 54.90.295.

CHAPTER 3

24 Photograph. Sailors' Snug Harbor Image Collection, New York University Archives, Box 6, Item 4.
25 Berenice Abbott, March 20, 1936, gelatin silver print. 7 1/2 x 9 1/2 in. (19 x 24.1 cm), Museum of the City of New York, 49.282.105.
25 Brown Brothers, 1928, photograph. Milstein Division, The New York Public Library, 724012F.
28 E. Pallme, 1903, gelatin silver print. Museum of the City of New York, X2010.11.4270.
29 Samuel Landsman, c. 1915, gelatin silver print. Museum of the City of New York, X2010.11.4272.
29 Alexander Jackson Davis, c. 1834, pen-and-wash drawing. Museum of the City of New York, 49.57.2.
30 Berenice Abbott, October 24, 1935, photo negative. 8 x 10 in. (20.3 x 25.4 cm), Museum of the City of New York, 43.131.1.34.
31 Photograph, c. 1905. 75870, New-York Historical Society. Photography ©New-York Historical Society.
32 c. 1895, albumen print. Museum of the City of New York, X2010.11.4284.
33 E. M. Jenks, undated, photograph. Milstein Division, The New York Public Library, 708336F.
33 Brown Brothers, 1925, photograph. Milstein Division, The New York Public Library, 708335F.
34 Courtesy the Collection of the Public Design Commission of the City New York.
35 Robert L. Bracklow, c.

1882–94, glass negative. Robert L. Bracklow Photograph Collection, 66000_1449, New-York Historical Society. Photography ©New-York Historical Society.
35 New York University's Old Main Building, Washington Square, H. N. Tiemann & Co., 1894, glass plate negative. Photograph Collection, nyhs_PR129_b-03_110-01, New-York Historical Society. Photography ©New-York Historical Society.
36 George F. Arata, May 28, 1912, albumen print. Museum of the City of New York, X2010.11.4276.
36 Photograph. Detlef Lienau architectural drawings and papers, 1835–1886, Avery Architectural & Fine Arts Library, Columbia University.
37 George F. Arata, c. 1910, albumen print. Museum of the City of New York, X2010.11.4275.
39 Elevation and plan, Alexander Jackson Davis, 1843, ink wash drawing on paper. Alexander Jackson Davis architectural drawings and papers, 1804–1900, Avery Architectural & Fine Arts Library, Columbia University, NYDA.1940.001.00128.
39 Elevations and details of door and banister posts, 1843. Alexander Jackson Davis architectural drawings and papers, 1804–1900, Avery Architectural & Fine Arts Library, Columbia University, NYDA.1940.001.00127.

CHAPTER 4

41 c. 1855–65, glass negative. Brady-Handy photograph collection, Library of Congress, Prints and Photographs Division, LC-BH82-5228 B.
42 Mora, c. 1875, albumen print. 6 1/2 x 4 1/4 in. (16.5 x 10.8 cm), Museum of the City of New York, F2012.58.73.
43 R. B. Irmtraut, 1893, watercolor. 9.5 x 11 in. (24.1 x 27.9 cm), Museum of the City of New York, 2000.23.2.
44 George Gardner Rockwood, 1860, photoprint. RIBA Collections, RIBA13705.
45 J. Clarence Davies Street Views Scrapbook. Museum of the City of New York, X2012.61.28.42.

46 G. P. A. (George Peter Alexander) Healy, c. 1860, oil on canvas. 58 x 45 in. (147.32 x 114.3 cm), Museum of the City of New York, 51.317.

CHAPTER 4 BREAKOUT

48 The Row, built 1831–33, photograph. Sailors' Snug Harbor Image Collection, New York University Archives, Box 5, Item 6.
49 Federal row house. State Street, nos. 16–19, c. 1864, Walter M. Aikman, 1907, engraving. 8.5 x 10.9 in. (21.7 x 27.8 cm), Print Collection, The New York Public Library, 1659258.
50 Henry Collins Brown, *Fifth Avenue, Old and New*, The Fifth Avenue Association, New York, 1924, 60.

CHAPTER 5

52 William J. Roege, glass plate negative. William J. Roege Photograph Collection, nyhs_PR181_b-09_9247-01, New-York Historical Society. Photography ©New-York Historical Society.
54 Fifth Avenue Hotel, c. 1920, photographic print. Library of Congress, George Grantham Bain Collection, Library of Congress, Prints and Photographs Division, LC-USZ62-83846.
55 Fifth Avenue Hotel, view of the main dining room, October 1, 1859, print from *Harper's Weekly*. Picture Collection, The New York Public Library, 805256.
56–57 Fifth Avenue Hotel, front view, Madison Square, G. W. Thorne (George W. Thorne), print on card mount. Library of Congress, Prints and Photographs Division, LC-DIG-stereo-1s07453.
58 Leonard W. Jerome portrait, undated (possibly 1873), print. Print Collection, The New York Public Library, 1545568.
58 Leonard W. Jerome House, Madison Avenue at 23rd Street, 1875, gelatin silver print. Museum of the City of New York, X2010.11.4392a.

CHAPTER 6

62 Henry Collins Brown, *Fifth Avenue, Old and New*, Fifth Avenue Association, New York,

1924, 76.
64 1875, photograph. Milstein Division, The New York Public Library, 708751F.
65 Image courtesy the Office for Metropolitan History.
65 December 16, 1929, Irving Underhill. Milstein Division, The New York Public Library, 708765F.
66 100557d, New-York Historical Society. Photography ©New-York Historical Society.
67 Drucker & Baltes Co., 1919, black-and-white negative. Billboard photograph collection, c. 1918-1934, nyhs_PR005_b-02_59648-01, New-York Historical Society. Photography ©New-York Historical Society.

CHAPTER 7
70 Illustrated in *Judge*, November 8, 1890, Hamilton, color lithograph. Library of Congress Prints and Photographs Division, LC-USZ62-56001.
71 Samuel Ward McAllister, Prince, New York, in The Sketch 106, no. 9 (February 6, 1895): 1. ©Illustrated London News Ltd/Mary Evans.
71 Photograph. New-York Historical Society, PR020, Box 77.
72 1875, albumen print. Manuscripts and Archives Division, The New York Public Library, 1627564.
73 *Mrs. William Astor (Caroline Schermerhorn Astor)*, Carolus-Duran (Charles-Auguste-Émile Durant), 1890, oil on canvas. 83 1/2 x 42 1/4 in. (212.1 x 107.3 cm), The Metropolitan Museum of Art, 49.4.
74 John Jacob Astor III House, 338 Fifth Avenue, c. 1860, albumen print. Museum of the City of New York, X2010.11.4523.
74 August 8, 1885, scrapbook. 13 x 18 1/4 in. (33 x 46.4 cm), Museum of the City of New York, X2012.61.29.34.
75 E. & H. T. Anthony & Co., stereograph. George T. Bagoe Collection, 100556d, New-York Historical Society. Photography ©New-York Historical Society.
75 c. 1900, gelatin silver print. 9 6/8 x 7 6/8 in. (24.8 x 19.7 cm), Museum of the City of New York, 91.69.183.
77 c. 1880, albumen print.

Museum of the City of New York, X2010.11.4466.
79 Minnie F. Stevens Paget, Vanderbilt Ball, 1883, Mora, photograph. Costume Ball Photograph Collection, 83886d, New-York Historical Society. Photography ©New-York Historical Society.
81 Victoria Hotel, Byron Company, c. 1900, gelatin silver print. 14 x 11 in. (35.6 x 27.9 cm), Museum of the City of New York, 93.1.1.6740.
83 Henry Collins Brown, *Fifth Avenue, Old and New*, The Fifth Avenue Association, New York, 1924, p. 61.

CHAPTER 7 BREAKOUT
86 Mora, c. 1876, cabinet card, albumen print. 6 1/2 x 4 1/4 in. (16.5 x 10.8 cm), Museum of the City of New York, F2012.58.1310.
86 December 21, 1896, admission ticket. 2 3/4 x 4 in. (7 x 10.2 cm), Museum of the City of New York, 40.108.134.
87 *Emily Vanderbilt Sloane*, Carl A. Weidner, c. 1895, watercolor on ivory. 3 1/4 x 2 5/8 in. (8.3 x 6.7 cm). Gift of the Estate of Peter Marié, 1905.230, New-York Historical Society. Photography ©New-York Historical Society.
87 *The Daughters of Robert Minturn*, Carl A. Weidner and Fredrika Weidner, 1899, watercolor on ivory. 3 7/8 x 5 in. (9.8 x 12.7 cm), Gift of the Estate of Peter Marié, 1905.161, New-York Historical Society. Photography ©New-York Historical Society.
88 Brown Brothers, 1893, photograph. Milstein Division, The New York Public Library, 708440F.
88 March 26, 1883. Costume Ball Photograph Collection, 43334, New-York Historical Society. Photography ©New-York Historical Society.
89 Delmonico's menu for February 7, 1873. 8 3/4 x 7 in. (22.2 x 17.8 cm), Museum of the City of New York, 45.34.19.

CHAPTER 8
92 Brown Brothers, 1907, photograph. Milstein Division, The New York Public Library, 708423F.

93 Detroit Publishing Co., 1905, postcard. 3 1/2 x 5 1/2 in. (9 x 14 cm), Picture Collection, The New York Public Library, 836587.
94 Copy negative of a photograph c. 1885. H. N. Tiemann & Co. photograph collection, 1880–1916, nyhs_PR129_b-07_315-01, New-York Historical Society. Photography ©New-York Historical Society.
95 March 17, 1899, albumen print. 5 1/2 x 8 1/2 in. (14 x 21.6 cm), Museum of the City of New York, 91.69.15.
96 Museum of the City of New York, X2010.11.4721.

CHAPTER 9
98 c. 1890–1934, scrapbook photograph. 18 1/4 x 13 in. (46.4 x 33 cm), Museum of the City of New York, X2012.61.29.47.
99 Jacob A. Riis, c. 1895, gelatin silver print. Museum of the City of New York, 90.13.3.133.
99 c. 1875, gelatin silver print. Museum of the City of New York, X2010.11.4467.
100 H. N. Tiemann & Co., c. 1885, gelatin silver print. Museum of the City of New York, X2010.11.4474.
101 c. 1880, gelatin silver print. Museum of the City of New York, X2010.11.4454.
102 Mrs. A. T. Stewart's Picture Gallery, as illustrated in *Artistic Houses*, 1883. General Research Division, The New York Public Library, 1955657.
104 M. Knoedler & Co. brownstone, c. 1905, gelatin silver print. Museum of the City of New York, X2010.11.4463.
105 Wurts Bros., c. 1915. 11 x 14 in. (27.9 x 35.6 cm), Museum of the City of New York, X2010.7.1.2014.
106 Byron Company, 1897, gelatin silver print. 6 7/8 x 9 1/8 in. (17.5 x 23.2 cm), Museum of the City of New York, 93.1.1.18452.
106 View from the Latting Observatory Tower, B. F. Smith, Jr., William Wellstood, and Smith, Fern and Company, 1855, engraving. 46 x 29 in. (116.8 x 73.7 cm), Print Collection, The New York Public Library, ps_prn_cd11_166.
107 *William Coventry Henry Waddell and Family*, Mary

Pillsbury Weston, 1852, oil on canvas. 24 3/4 x 37 3/8 in. (62.9 x 96.1 cm), Gift of Alice Waddell Smith, 1956.24. New-York Historical Society. Photography ©New-York Historical Society.
108–9 Henry Collins Brown, *Fifth Avenue, Old and New*, Fifth Avenue Association, New York, 1924.
110 1889 Centennial Parade, lantern slide. The New York Public Library Archives, The New York Public Library, 465506.
111 Print. 5 1/4 x 6 1/2 in. (13 x 16 cm), Picture Collection, The New York Public Library, 805419.
111 Lantern slide. New York Public Library Archives, The New York Public Library, 465505.
112 Drawing. Murray Hill Neighborhood Association, CUNY Graduate Center Archives and Special Collections, Mina Rees Library, The Graduate Center, The City University of New York.
112 Brown Brothers, photograph.
114 Photograph. From J. F. L. Collins, Collins' *Both Sides of Fifth Avenue* (Dover Publications, 1995 [1911]), 16.

CHAPTER 10
119 Byron Company. 10 x 8 in. (25.4 x 20.3 cm), photograph. Museum of the City of New York, 93.1.1.6147.
120 Byron Company. 11 x 14 in. (27.9 x 35.6 cm), photograph. Museum of the City of New York, 93.1.1.61.61.
120 The Frank Buttolph Collection of Menus, The New York Public Library, 4037779.
122 c. 1870, scrapbook photograph. 13 x 18 1/4 in. (33 x 46.4 cm), Museum of the City of New York, X2012.61.18.39.
123 c. 1894, photographic print. Library of Congress, Prints and Photographs Division, LC-USZ62-83844.
123 1868, lithograph. 7 1/4 x 5 in. (18.4 x 12.7 cm), Picture Collection, The New York Public Library, 801631.
124 c. 1910, gelatin silver print. 10 1/2 x 13 1/2 in. (26.7 x 34.3 cm), Museum of the City of New York, 34.543.1A.

126–27 c. 1865, gelatin silver print. Museum of the City of New York, X2010.11.14182.
128 c. 1880, gelatin silver print. Museum of the City of New York, X2010.11.14188.
128 Robert L. Bracklow, c. 1890, gelatin silver print. 4 x 6 in. (10.1 x 15.2 cm), Museum of the City of New York, 93.91.92.
129 1890, printing-out paper. Museum of the City of New York, X2010.11.4778.
129 Byron Company, 1916, gelatin silver print. 9 1/2 x 13 1/4 in. (24.1 x 33.7 cm), Museum of the City of New York, 93.1.1.17215.
130 Samuel H. Gottscho, 1937, gelatin silver print. 9 1/8 x 7 1/2 in. (23.2 x 19 cm), Museum of the City of New York, 94.53.32.
131 Part of the collection of the Worsham-Rockefeller Room, built c. 1864–65; remodeled c. 1881. Mixed media. 17 1/2 x 15 1/2 ft. (5.3 x 4.7 m), Brooklyn Museum, Gift of John D. Rockefeller, Jr. and John D. Rockefeller III, 46.43.
132 Part of the collection of the Worsham-Rockefeller Room, built c. 1864–65; remodeled c. 1881. Mixed media. 17 1/2 x 15 1/2 ft. (5.3 x 4.7 m), Brooklyn Museum, Gift of John D. Rockefeller, Jr. and John D. Rockefeller III, 46.43.
133 c. 1890, printing-out paper. Museum of the City of New York, X2010.11.4876.
134 Arthur Vitols Byron Company, c. 1920, gelatin silver print. 11 x 14 in. (27.9 x 35.6 cm), Museum of the City of New York, 93.1.3.1521.
135 H. M. Tiemann & Co, 1902, glass plate negative. H. N. Tiemann & Co. Photograph Collection, nyhs_PR129_b-06_197-01, New-York Historical Society. Photography ©New-York Historical Society.
135 Frank M. Ingalls, 1906, cellulose nitrate film. Frank M. Ingalls Photograph Collection, nyhs_PR028_b-05_180, New-York Historical Society. Photography ©New-York Historical Society.
136 Wurts Bros, c. 1915, gelatin dry plate negative. Museum of the City of New York, X2010.7.1.4395.
137 Percy Loomis Sperr, 1931,

photograph. ©NYPL, 708882F.

CHAPTER 11
141 *Going to the Opera: The William H. Vanderbilt Family*, Seymour Joseph Guy, 1873, oil on canvas. 47 x 59 in. (119.4 x 149.9 cm), The Biltmore Company, BH8-00678. Used with permission from The Biltmore Company, Asheville, North Carolina.
142 c. 1895, printing-out paper. Museum of the City of New York, X2010.11.4761.
143 Henry Collins Brown, *Fifth Avenue, Old and New*, Fifth Avenue Association, New York, 1924.
143 Image courtesy the Office of Metropolitan History.
145 C. A. Brewster, 1907, photograph. Museum of the City of New York, 26908.1B.
146 Jacob A. Riis, c. 1890, lantern slide. Museum of the City of New York, 90.13.2.305.
148 In Earl Shinn [Edward Strahan], *Mr. Vanderbilt's House and Collections*, 4 vols. (Philadelphia: G. Barrie & Sons, 1883–84). The Metropolitan Museum of Art, 106.1 V28 F.
149 In Earl Shinn [Edward Strahan], *Mr. Vanderbilt's House and Collections*, 4 vols. (Philadelphia: G. Barrie & Sons, 1883–84). The Metropolitan Museum of Art, 106.1 V28 F.
151 Château de Chantilly, view taken from the terrace, c. 1910–19. Postcard printed by Curt Teich. Courtesy the Newberry Library.
153 Michel Lévy, before 1875, photogravure.
156 Mora, March 26, 1893, from a photograph album. 9 x 8 in. (22.9 x 20.3 cm), Museum of the City of New York, X2012.96.2.2.
157 Mora, 1883, albumen print. 6 1/2 x 4 1/4 in. (16.5 x 11.4 cm), Museum of the City of New York, F2012.58.1341.
157 Photograph. As published in *Architecture* V, no. 27 (March 15, 1902): 66.
158 Photographic print. Library of Congress Prints and Photographs Division, LC-USZ62-83781.
159 Byron Company, 1895, gelatin silver print. 16.3 x 19.9 in. (41.4 x

50.5 cm), Museum of the City of New York, 93.1.1.17461.
160 *Portrait of the 9th Duke of Marlborough with his Family*, including Consuelo Vanderbilt, John Singer Sargent, 1905, oil on canvas. 131 x 94 in. (332.7 x 238.8 cm), Duke of Marlborough Collection, Blenheim Palace.
161 1905–7, gelatin dry plate negative. 14 x 11 in. (35.6 x 27.9 cm), Museum of the City of New York, 90.44.1.840.
162 Byron Company, 1898, gelatin silver print. 7 1/2 x 9 1/2 in. (19 x 24.1 cm), Museum of the City of New York, 93.1.1.18035.
162 Wurts Bros., c. 1923, gelatin dry plate negative. 8 x 10 in. (20.3 x 25.4 cm), Museum of the City of New York, X2010.7.1.5613.
164 George Brown Post, Albert Lévy, c. 1883–95, photograph. Historic Architecture and Landscape Image Collection, Ryerson and Burnham Art and Architecture Archives, Art Institute of Chicago. Digital file #51210.
165 George Brown Post, Albert Lévy, c. 1883–95, photograph. Historic Architecture and Landscape Image Collection, Ryerson and Burnham Art and Architecture Archives, Art Institute of Chicago. Digital file #51211.
166 Cornelius Vanderbilt's fireplace by Augustus Saint-Gaudens, mantelpiece by David Maitland Armstrong. 1881–83. The Metropolitan Museum of Art, Gift of Mrs. Cornelius Vanderbilt II, 1925, 25.234.
167 c. 1908, gelatin silver print. Museum of the City of New York, X2010.11.4828.

CHAPTER 12
170–71 George Hayward, 1859, lithograph. Illustrated in *D. T. Valentine's Manuel*. 6 1/2 x 14 in. (16.5 x 35.6 cm), Picture Collection, The New York Public Library, 800905.
172 *Fifth Avenue, New York, From Start to Finish*, New York: Wells & Co, 1911, 50.
172 Wurts Bros., c. 1910, gelatin dry plate negative, 11 x 14 in. (27.9

x 35.6 cm). Museum of the City of New York, X2010.7.1.1620.
176 Byron Company, 1898, gelatin silver print, printing-out paper. Museum of the City of New York, 93.1.1.17410.
177 Arthur Vitols, Byron Company, c. 1920, gelatin silver print. 11 x 14 in. (27.9 x 35.6 cm), Museum of the City of New York, 93.1.3.1503.
178 Wurts Bros., 1909, gelatin silver print. 8 x 10 in. (20.3 x 25.4 cm), Museum of the City of New York, X2010.7.2.5448.
180 Byron Company, 1895, gelatin silver print and printing-out paper. Museum of the City of New York, 93.1.1.17467.
181 Byron Company, 1895, gelatin silver print and printing-out paper. Museum of the City of New York, 93.1.1.17466.
182 1872–73. Sturgis and Babb, Albert Lévy, photographer. Historic Architecture and Landscape Image Collection, Ryerson and Burnham Art and Architecture Archives, Art Institute of Chicago. Digital file #45338.
183 Courtesy of Sagamore Hill National Historic Site, National Park Service, Oyster Bay, NY.
183 Courtesy of Sagamore Hill National Historic Site, National Park Service, Oyster Bay, NY.

CHAPTER 13
186–87 H. N. Tiemann & Co., 1894, gelatin silver print. Museum of the City of New York, X2010.11.4853.

CHAPTER 14
192 c. 1870, photograph. 100558d, New-York Historical Society. Photography ©New-York Historical Society.
193 Byron Company, 1900, gelatin silver print. 7 3/4 x 6 in. (19.7 x 15.2 cm), Museum of the City of New York, 93.1.1.18056. **194** Empty blocks with wooden barricades. *Fifth Avenue, New York, From Start to Finish*, New York: Wells & Co, 1911, 78. **194** *Fifth Avenue, New York, From Start to Finish*, New York: Wells & Co, 1911, 66.

195 *Fifth Avenue, New York, From Start to Finish*, New York: Wells & Co, 1911, 51.
199 D. & J. Jardine architects. 800 Fifth Avenue, Byron Company, 1900, gelatin silver print and printing-out paper. 8 x 7 in. (20.3 x 17.8 cm), Museum of the City of New York, 93.1.1.10570.
201 Byron Company, 1900, gelatin silver print. 7 3/4 x 6 1/2 in. (19.7 x 16.5 cm), Museum of the City of New York, 93.1.1.18055.
204 Byron Company, 1893, gelatin silver print. Museum of the City of New York, 93.1.1.17178.
206 Byron Company, 1897, gelatin silver print. 7 x 9 1/4 in. (17.8 x 23.5 cm), Museum of the City of New York, 93.1.1.18060.
206 Photograph, 1890. Peter Newark Pictures/Bridgeman Images, PNP3470792.

CHAPTER 15
208 Byron Company, c. 1901, gelatin silver print. 10 x 13 1/8 in. (25.4 x 33.3 cm), Museum of the City of New York, 93.1.1.18063.
209 Image copyright ©The Metropolitan Museum of Art, MM28928. Image source: Art Resource, NY.
210 Byron Company, c. 1901, gelatin silver print. 10 x 13 1/4 in. (25.4 x 33.7 cm), Museum of the City of New York, 93.1.1.18064.
211 Byron Company, c. 1901, gelatin silver print. 10 x 12 3/4 in. (25.4 x 32.4 cm), Museum of the City of New York, 93.1.1.17185.
212 Louis Oram, 1887. 5 3/4 x 5 1/2 in. (14.6 x 14 cm), Picture Collection, The New York Public Library, 805423.
213 Byron Company, c. 1901, gelatin silver print and printing-out paper. Museum of the City of New York, 93.1.1.10548.
217 Byron Company, c. 1901, gelatin silver print and paper. 10 x 13 1/2 in. (25.4 x 34.3 cm), Museum of the City of New York, 93.1.1.17187.
218 Byron Company, c. 1900, gelatin silver print and printing-out paper. 11 x 14 in. (27.9 x 35.6 cm), Museum of the City of New York, 93.1.1.16684.
220 c. 1900, gelatin silver print.

Museum of the City of New York, X2010.11.4892.
220 January 15, 1870, illustration. The New York Public Library Archives, The New York Public Library, 57449765.
221 Wurts Bros., c. 1915, gelatin dry plate negative. 11 x 14 in. (27.9 x 35.6 cm), Museum of the City of New York, X2010.7.1.1750.
223 Byron Company, c. 1901, gelatin silver print. 13 1/2 x 10 1/4 in. (34.3 x 26 cm), Museum of the City of New York, 93.1.1.18067.
224 Wurts Bros., 1921, gelatin silver print. 8 x 10 in. (20.3 x 25.4 cm), Museum of the City of New York, X2010.7.2.363.
226 Wurts Bros., October 19, 1920, gelatin silver print. Museum of the City of New York, X2010.11.4900.
228 Wurts Bros., copy of a photograph from 1909, gelatin silver print. 10 x 8 in. (25.4 x 20.3 cm), Museum of the City of New York, X2010.7.2.5452.
229 Philip G. Bartlett, 1927, gelatin silver print. Museum of the City of New York, X2010.11.4911.
232 Byron Company, 1901, gelatin silver print. 10 x 13 1/2 in. (25.4 x 34.3 cm), Museum of the City of New York, 93.1.1.18254.
233 Wurts Bros., c. 1894–1915, gelatin silver print. 11 x 14 in. (27.9 x 35.6 cm), Museum of the City of New York, X2010.7.2.25117.
235 Wurts Bros., 1933, gelatin silver print. 8 x 10 in. (20.3 x 24.5 cm), Museum of the City of New York, X2010.7.2.5598.
236 Edmund Vincent Gillon, c. 1975, gelatin silver print. 7 x 8 in. (17.8 x 20.3 cm), Museum of the City of New York, 2013.3.1.656.
236 *The Fletcher Mansion, New York City*, Isaac Fletcher House, 2 East 79th Street, south corner of Fifth Avenue and 79th Street, Jean-François Raffaëlli, 1899, oil on canvas. 23 3/4 x 32 in. (60.3 x 81.3cm), Metropolitan Museum of Art, 17.120.228.
237 Philip G. Bartlett, c. 1927, gelatin silver print. Museum of the City of New York, X2010.11.4913.
239 1911, gelatin silver print. Museum of the City of New York, X2010.11.4924.
240 Brown Brothers, 1925, photograph. Milstein Division, The

New York Public Library, 709172F.
243 Byron Company, 1920, gelatin silver print. 8 x 10 in. (20.32 x 25.4 cm), Museum of the City of New York, 93.1.1.10084.
244 c. 1925–42, gelatin silver print. 13 3/4 x 10 in. (34.9 x 25.4 cm), Museum of the City of New York, 53.326.1.2.
246 Wurts Bros., c. 1905, gelatin silver print. 11 x 14 in. (27.9 x 35.6 cm), Museum of the City of New York, X2010.7.2.19401.
248 William J. Roege, photographic negative. William J. Roege photograph collection, 1910-1937, nyhs_PR181_b-04_9164-01, New-York Historical Society. Photography ©New-York Historical Society.
250 Robert L. Bracklow and Alexander Alland, c. 1890–1910, glass negative. 5 x 7 in. (12.7 x 17.8 cm). Robert L. Bracklow photograph collection, nyhs_pr-008_66000_1049, New York Historical Society. Photography ©New-York Historical Society.
252 Wurts Bros., c. 1905, gelatin dry plate negative. 14 x 11 in. (35.6 x 27.9 cm), Museum of the City of New York, X2010.7.1.353.
253 Wurts Bros., c. 1910, gelatin dry plate negative. 14 x 11 in. (35.6 x 27.9 cm), Museum of the City of New York, X2010.7.1.1344.
254 Wurts Bros., c. 1917, gelatin dry plate negative. 8 x 10 in. (20.32 x 25.4 cm), Museum of the City of New York, X2010.7.1.5165.
255 Photographer unknown, 1925, photograph. Milstein Division, The New York Public Library, 709192F.
256 Peter Baab, 1882–83, albumen print. 9 x 13 in. (22.9 x 33 cm), Museum of the City of New York, 2001.72.9.
257 Photograph by Jean-Louis Cohen, 2022.

CHAPTER 17
269 Detroit Publishing Co., 1905, postcard. 3 1/2 x 5 1/2 in. (8.9 x 14 cm), Museum of the City of New York, F2011.33.225.

CHAPTER 18
272 Image courtesy the Office of Metropolitan History.
274 *The New York Times*, June 27th, 1909.

CHAPTER 19
277 Byron Company, gelatin silver print, 14 x 11 in. (35.6 x 27.9 cm). Museum of the City of New York, 93.1.1.9600.
280–81 Photograph. Sailors' Snug Harbor Image Collection, New York University Archives, Box 6, Item 4.
290–91 Charles Dana Gibson. *Illustration for Eighty Drawings including The Weaker Sex, The Story of a Susceptible Bachelor,* Charles Scribner and John Lane, 1903.
302–3 Alexander Jackson Davis, c. 1834, pen-and-wash drawing. Museum of the City of New York, 49.57.2.

MAPS
332–33
1891–92
G. W. Bromley and Co., *Atlas of the City of New York, Manhattan Island, 1891–92*. Lionel Pincus and Princess Firyal Map Division, The New York Public Library, 2021204.
1897–99
G. W. Bromley and Co., *Atlas of the City of New York, Manhattan Island, 1897–99*. Lionel Pincus and Princess Firyal Map Division, The New York Public Library, 1516751.
1911
G. W. Bromley and Co., *Atlas of the City of New York, Borough of Manhattan, 1911*. Lionel Pincus and Princess Firyal Map Division, The New York Public Library, 1512200.

BIBLIOGRAPHY

ARCHIVES:

Bill books of McKim, Mead & White. 1878–1940. McKim, Mead & White Architectural Records, Series VII: Financial Records Books, Subseries V.1: Bill Books. New-York Historical Society Museum & Library, New York City, New York.

Building and alteration permits. 1866–1910. Department of Buildings, New York City, New York.

Docket Books. NYC Records & Information Services, Municipal Archives and Library, New York, New York.

Gray, Christopher S. Fifth Avenue files. The Office for Metropolitan History, New York City, New York.

The Real Estate Record (also known as *The Record & Guide* and *Real Estate Record* and *Builders' Guide*). 1868–1922. V. 1, no. 1–v. 110, no. 11. Avery Architectural Library, New York City, New York.

BOOKS:

Asher, Florence. *Women, Wealth and Power: New York City, 1860–1900*. Ph.D. Dissertation, CUNY. New York: 2006.

Auchincloss, Louis. *The Vanderbilt Era: Profiles of a Gilded Age*. New York: Scribner, 1989.

Avery, Samuel P. *The Diaries 1871–1882 of Samuel P. Avery*. New York: Arno Press, 1979.

Baker, Paul R. *Richard Morris Hunt*. Cambridge, MA: MIT Press, 1980.

Balsan, Consuelo Vanderbilt. *The Glitter and the Gold: The American Duchess—in her Own Words*. New York: St. Martin's Press, 1952.

Barrett, Walter (Joseph Alfred Scoville). *The Old Merchants of New York City*. Charleston, SC: Carleton, 1865.

Beach, Moses Yale. *Wealth and Wealthy Citizens of New York City*. New York: The Sun Office, 1842.

Beckert, Sven. *The Monied Metropolis: New York City and the Consolidation of the American Bourgeoisie, 1850–1896*. Cambridge, UK: Cambridge University Press, 2001.

Bennett, Shelley M. *The Art of Wealth: The Huntingtons in the Gilded Age*. San Marino, California: Huntington Library, 2013.

Birmingham, Stephen. *"Our Crowd": The Great Jewish Families of New York*. New York: Harper & Row, 1967.

Black, David. *The King of Fifth Avenue: The Fortunes of August Belmont*. New York: Dial Press, 1981.

Bourget, Paul. *Outre-Mer: Impressions of America*. London: T. Fisher Unwin, 1895.

Boyer, M. Christine. *Manhattan Manners: Architecture and Style, 1850–1900*. New York: Rizzoli, 1985.

Brandon, Ruth. *The Dollar Princesses: The American Invasion of the European Aristocracy, 1870–1914*. New York: Knopf, 1980.

Burke, Doreen Bolger. *In Pursuit of Beauty: Americans and the Aesthetic Movement*. New York: Metropolitan Museum of Art, 1986.

Cohen, Paul E. and Robert T. Augustyn. *Manhattan in Maps, 1527–2014*. Mineola, NY: Dover Publications, Inc., 2014.

Craven, Wayne. *Gilded Mansions: Grand Architecture and High Society*. New York: W. W. Norton & Co., 2009.

___. *Stanford White: Decorator in Opulence and Dealer in Antiquities*. New York: Columbia University Press, 2005.

Crook, J. Mordaunt. *The Rise of the Nouveaux Riches: Style and Status in Victorian and Edwardian Architecture*. London: John Murray, 1999.

Dedman, Bill and Paul Clark Newell, Jr. *Empty Mansions: The Mysterious Life of Huguette Clark and the Spending of a Great American Fortune*. New York: Ballantine Books, 2013.

Devorkin, Joseph. *Great Merchants of Early New York*. New York: The Society for the Architecture of the City, 1987.

Dodsworth, Allen. *Dancing and Its Relation to Education and Social Life*. London: Harper & Brothers, 1885.

Drexel, Elizabeth Wharton. *"King Lehr" and the Gilded Age.* Philadelphia: J. B. Lippincott Company, 1935.

Ewing, Heather. *Life of a Mansion, The Story of Cooper-Hewitt, Smithsonian Design Museum.* New York: Cooper Hewitt, 2014.

Farnham, Thomas. "Rugs in the City: A History of the Hajji Baba Club." In Jon Thompson, *Timbuktu to Tibet: Exotic Rugs and Textiles from New York Collectors.* New York: New-York Historical Society, 2008.

Field, Julian Osgood. *Uncensored Recollections.* Philadelphia: Lippincott, 1924.

"Fifth Avenue Events." In *Fifth Avenue Bank*. New York: 1916.

Fowler, Marian. *In a Gilded Cage: From Heiress to Duchess.* New York: St. Martin's Press, 1994.

Griswold, Frank Gray. Stolen Kisses. Privately printed, 1914.

___. *Afterthoughts*. Privately printed, 1936.

Hamlin, Huybertie Pruyn. *An Albany Girlhood*. Edited by Alice P. Kenny. Albany, NY: Washington Park Press Ltd., 1990.

Harrison, Mrs. Burton. *Recollections Grave and Gay.* New York: C. Scribner's Sons, 1912. *A History of Real Estate, Building and Architecture in New York City During the Last Quarter of a Century.* New York: Record and Guide, 1898.

Homberger, Eric. *Mrs. Astor's New York: Money and Social Power in a Gilded Age.* New Haven, CT: Yale University Press, 2002.

Howat, John K. and Catherine Hoover Vorsanger. *Art and the Empire City: New York, 1825–1861.* New York: The Metropolitan Museum, 2000.

Jaher, Frederick Cople. *The Rich, the Well Born, and the Powerful: Elites and Upper Classes in History.* Secaucus, NJ: Citadel, 1975.

James, Henry. *A Small Boy and Others.* New York: C. Scribner's Sons, 1913.

___. *Washington Square*. New York: Harper & Brothers Publishers, 1901.

Johnston de Forest, Emily. *John Johnston of New York, Merchant.* Private printing, 1909.

King, Moses. *King's Handbook of New York City: An Outline History and Description of the American Metropolis.* Boston: Moses King, 1893.

King, Robert B. with Charles O. McLean. *The Vanderbilt Homes.* New York: Rizzoli, 1989.

Lockwood. Charles. *Bricks and Brownstone: The New York Row House, 1783–1929.* New York: Rizzoli, 2003.

___. *Manhattan Moves Uptown: An Illustrated History.* Boston: Houghton Mifflin, 1976.

Lydig, Rita de Acosta. *Tragic Mansions.* New York: Boni & Liveright, 1927.

MacColl, Gail and Carol McD. Wallace. *To Marry an English Lord: Or How Anglomania Really Got Started.* New York: Workman Pub, 1989.

Mackay, Charles. *Life and Liberty in America.* London: Smith, Elder and Co., 1859.

Maher, James T. *The Twilight of Splendor: Chronicles of the Age of American Palaces.* Boston: Little, Brown, 1975.

Martin, Frederick Townsend. *Things I Remember.* New York: John Lane Company, 1913.

McAllister, Ward. *Society as I Have Found It.* New York: Cassell Publishing Company, 104 & 106 Fourth Avenue, 1890.

Miller, Frances. *Tanty, Encounters with the Past.* Sag Harbor, NY: Sandbox Press, 1979.

Montgomery, Maureen E. *Displaying Women: Spectacles of Leisure in Edith Wharton's New York.* New York: Routledge, 1998.

Patterson, Jerry E. *Fifth Avenue: The Best Address.* New York: Rizzoli, 1998.

___. *The First Four Hundred: Mrs. Astor's New York in the Gilded Age.* New York: Rizzoli, 2000.

Pennoyer, Peter and Anne Walker. *New York Transformed: The Architecture of Cross & Cross.* New York: 2014.

Pollen, Daphne. *I Remember, I Remember.* Private printing.

Post, John J. *Old Streets, Roads, Lanes, Piers and Wharves of New York: Showing the Former and Present Names.* New York: R. D. Cooke, 1882.

Reed, Fanny. *Reminiscences, Musical and Other.* Boston: Knight and Millet, 1903.

Shachtman, Tom. *Skyscraper Dreams: The Great Real Estate Dynasties of New York.* Boston: Little, Brown, 1991.

Simpson, Colin. *Artful Partners: Bernard Berenson and Joseph Duveen.* New York: Macmillan, 1986.

Smalley, Donald and Booth, Bradford Allen. *North America.* 9th edition. New York: Knopf, 1951.

Smith, Matthew Hale. *Sunshine and Shadows* in New York. New York: 1880.

Stern, Robert A. M., Gregory Gilmartin, and John Montague Massengale. *New York 1900: Metropolitan Architecture and Urbanism, 1890–1915.* New York: Rizzoli, 1983.
Strahan, Edward. *Mr. Vanderbilt's House and Collection.* New York: George Barrie, 1883–84.

Twain, Mark. *The Gilded Age.* Hartford, CT: American Publishing Company, 1873.

Vanderbilt Jr., Cornelius. *Farewell to Fifth Avenue.* New York: Simon and Schuster, 1935.

Van Rensselaer, May King. *The Social Ladder.* New York: Henry Holt and Co., 1924.

Wallach, Janet. *The Richest Woman in America: Hetty Green in the Gilded Age.* New York:

Nan A. Talese and Doubleday, 2012.

Wharton, Edith. *The Age of Innocence.* New York: D. Appleton, 1921.

___. *The Buccaneers: A Novel.* New York: D. Appleton-Century, 1938.

___. *The Custom of the Country,* 1913.

Wood, Anthony. *Preserving New York: Winning the Right to Protect the City's Landmarks.* New York: 2007.

Wood, George W. *The Growth of New York.* New York, 1865.

ARTICLES:

Altman, Benjamin. *"The Age of Rembrandt." The Metropolitan Museum of Art Bulletin* (Summer 2007): 30–35.

The American Architect (July 20, 1901). Architect and Building (April 17, 1894).

Architecture and Building (November 2, 1895).

Architecture and Building (February 29, 1896).

Architecture and Building (March 21, 1896).

Architecture and Building (August 29, 1896).

Architecture and Building (October 17, 1896).

Architecture and Building 65 (July 22, 1899).

Architectural Record 23 (May 1908).

The Architectural Record (October–December 1891).

The Architectural Record 1 (April–June 1892).

The Architectural Record 18 (July 1905).

The Architectural Record 19 (January 1906).

The Architectural Record 27 (May 1910). *The Architectural Record* 27 (June 1910).

Architecture 1, February 15, 1900. *Architecture* 4, November 15, 1901.

Architecture, May 1, 1905. *Architecture*, December 1905.

Architecture 16, September 15, 1907.

"Artistic Furniture of the Gilded Age." *The Metropolitan Museum of Art Bulletin* 73, no. 3 (Winter 2016): 1–48.

Artistic Houses; The New York Sketch Book of Architecture 2 (September 1875).

"Big Apartment Houses on 5th Avenue." *New York Times*, May 16, 1926.

Bolton, Reginald Pelham. "The Apartment Hotel in New York." *Cassier Magazine* 24 (November 1903): 27–32.

Brickbuilder 9 (July 1900).

Cantor, Jay E. "A Monument of Trade; A. T. Stewart and the Rise of the Millionaires Mansion in New York." *Winterthur Portfolio* 10 (1975): 165–97.

"The Contemporary Metropolitan Residence." *Record and Guide* (June 11, 1904).

Dow, Joy Wheeler. "Lower Fifth Avenue." *Architectural Review*, no. 4 (January 1902): 61–64.

"The Fashionable Residential Section: Fifth Avenue from 72nd Street to 90th Street." *The Record and Guide* 77 (December 16, 1905–January 20, 1906): 950–1102.

"Fifth Avenue owners demand Right to Erect Tall Apartment houses." *New York Times*, February 19, 1922.

"Galleries of Belmont and Blodgett." *Putnam's Magazine* 5 (May 1870): 534–40.

Gibson, Charles Dana. "Mrs. Steele Poole's Housewarming." *Life*, January 2, 1902.

Gray, Christopher S., "J. E. R. Carpenter the Architect who Shaped Upper Fifth Avenue, Streetscapes." *New York Times*, August 26, 2007.

___. "Streetscapes: The Ehrich Brothers Store; Restoration for the Final Stretch of the Ladies' Mile." *New York Times*. February 12, 1995.

___. "Streetscapes." *New York Times*, June 2, 2002.

___. Streetscapes." *New York Times*, July 31, 2011.

___. "Streetscapes." *New York Times*, December 2, 2012. "Growth and Prosperity." *Evening Post*, April 17, 1845.

Hyman, Isabelle. "The Huntington Mansion in New York: Economics of Architecture and Decoration in the 1890's." *Syracuse University Library Associates Courier* xxv, no. 2 (1990).

"John La Farge's work in the Vanderbilt Houses." *The American Art Journal* XVI (Autumn 1984): 30–70.

Kennion, John F. *The Architects' and Builders' Guide.* Reprinted in 2011.

"The Latest Fifth Avenue Mansion." *Record and Guide* 82 (November 282, 1908).

"Middle Fifth Avenue: Wholesale District." *The Record & Guide* (April 20, 1901).

"Mr. Vanderbilt's House." *Boston Traveller* (1881): unpaginated.

"The New Fifth Avenue." *New York Times*, June 27, 1909.

"The New Fifth Avenue." *The Record & Guide* (December 17, 1904).

The New York Architect 4 (July 1907).

"New York Daguerreotype." *Putnam's Magazine* 1 (March 1853).

The New-York Sketch Book of Architecture 3 (March 1876). Obituary for Fanny Reed. *New York Times*, January 24, 1915, 8.

Obituary for Griffith Thomas. *The American Architect and Building News*, January 25, 1879, 29.

Obituary for Marietta Stevens. *New York Times*, April 4, 1895.

Obituary for Mary Mason Jones. *New York Times*, May 30, 1891.

Obituary for William Tilden Blodgett. *New York Times*, November 18, 1875.

"An Outbreak of Hotel Building." *Record and Guide* 48 (October 24, 1891). "Plan to Transform 'Millionaires Row'." *Record & Guide*, April 26, 1924.

"A Profit in Altering Old Dwellings." *Record & Guide*, December 19, 1908. *The Real Estate Record and Builder's Guide*, September 24, 1870.

The Real Estate Record and Guide, October 27, 1883.

Record and Guide, June 15, 1889.

The Record & Guide, January 4, 1902.

The Record & Guide, June 21, 1902. "Residence of Mr. J. Hooker Hamersley, 1030 Fifth Avenue." *Architecture and Building*, June 3, 1899.

"Residence of Mrs. Willard Straight, 1130 Fifth Avenue, Delano & Aldrich." *Architecture* 41 (1920): plates 33–38.

Richardson, James. "The New Homes of New York, a study of Flats." *Scribner's Monthly* viii (May 1874), 63–76.

Ross, Esq., William. "ART IV Street Houses of the City of New York." *The Architectural Record* 9 (1899–1900): 53–56.

___. *"History from a Garret."* vol. 9 (1899–1900).

Sarna, Jonathan D. "Anti-Semitism and American History." *Commentary* 71, no. 3 (March 1981): 42–47.

Schuyler, Montgomery. *The American Architect and Building News*, May 21, 1881, 243–44.

___. *Record and Guide*, February 3, 1883.

___. "Works of the Late Richard M. Hunt." *The Architectural Record* 5 (October–December 1895): 130.

"Second Avenue." *Evening Post*, January 14, 1846.

Sherwood, Mary Elizabeth Wilson. "Certain New York Houses." *Harper's New Monthly* 65 (October 1882): 680–90.

"The Social Push." *Life*, January 1, 1903.

Starks, Charles. "Remembering George McAneny: The Reformer, Planner and Preservationist who Shaped Modern New York City." *The Gotham Center for New York History*, August 6, 2019.

Sturgis, Russell. "A Review of the work of Clinton & Russell." *The Architectural Record* 7 (October – December 1897).

Tauranac, John. "Fifth Avenue Apartments Where the Gilded Age Never Tarnished." *New York Times*, September 23, 1999.

"The Troubles of the Rich: At the Last Moment, Several Who Were Invited Sent Their Regrets." *Life*, February 13, 1902.

van Rensselaer, Mariana. *The Century* (November 1893): 5–18.

Walsh, George Ethelbert. "City Homes of Fashion and Wealth." *Architect and Builder's Magazine* 34 (December 1901): 106.

Webster, Sally and David Schwittek. "A Digital Recreation of the Lenox Library Picture Gallery: A Contribution to the Early History of Public Art Museums in the United States."

Nineteenth-Century Art Worldwide 17, no. 2

(October 2018).

Winker, Franz K. "Architecture in the Billionaire District of New York City." *The Architectural Record* 11 (October 1901): 679–99.

INDEX

Top: *Atlas of the City of New York, Manhattan Island, 1891–92*

Middle: *Atlas of the City of New York, Manhattan Island, 1897–99*

Bottom: *Atlas of the City of New York, Borough of Manhattan, 1911*

From the Bromley Atlas series beginning in 1891 and continuing into the mid-20th century. George Washington Bromley was an engineer. After surveying and drawing the maps to show the footprint of the buildings, they were engraved and hand colored to distinguish between brick, brownstone, and timber structures.

The New York Public Library has an extensive collection of Bromley and other maps.

Here we have three time periods for the area just north of Washington Square. Apartment buildings are replacing the older houses and the American Text Book Company has taken the place of the old Main Building of the University of the City of New York. The back gardens of houses first built are disappearing as larger buildings go up.

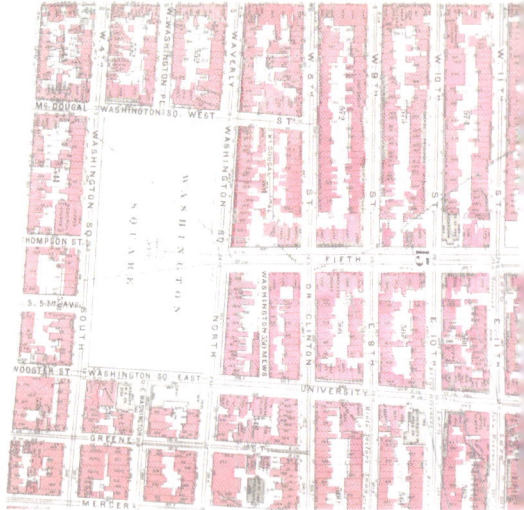

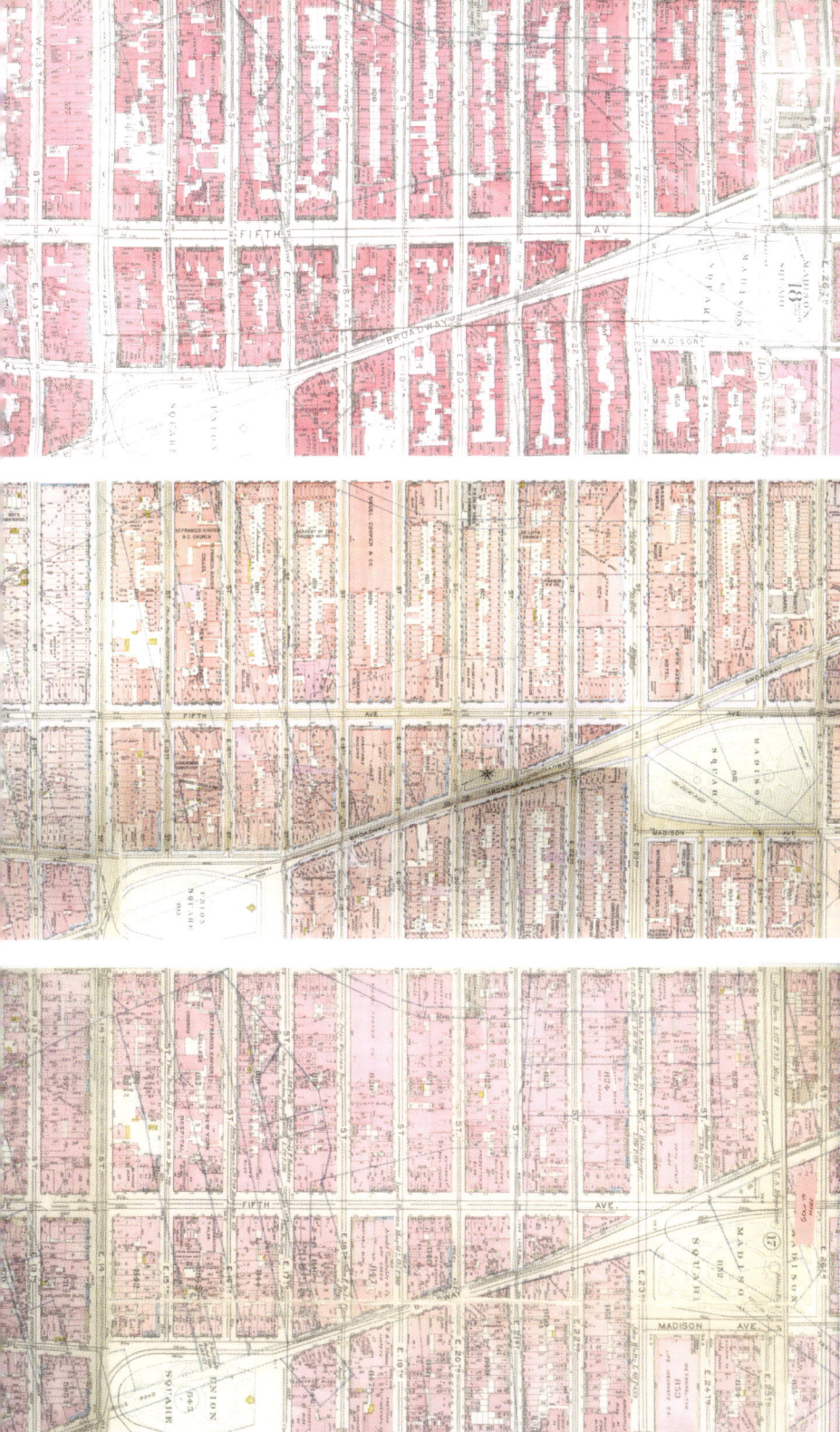

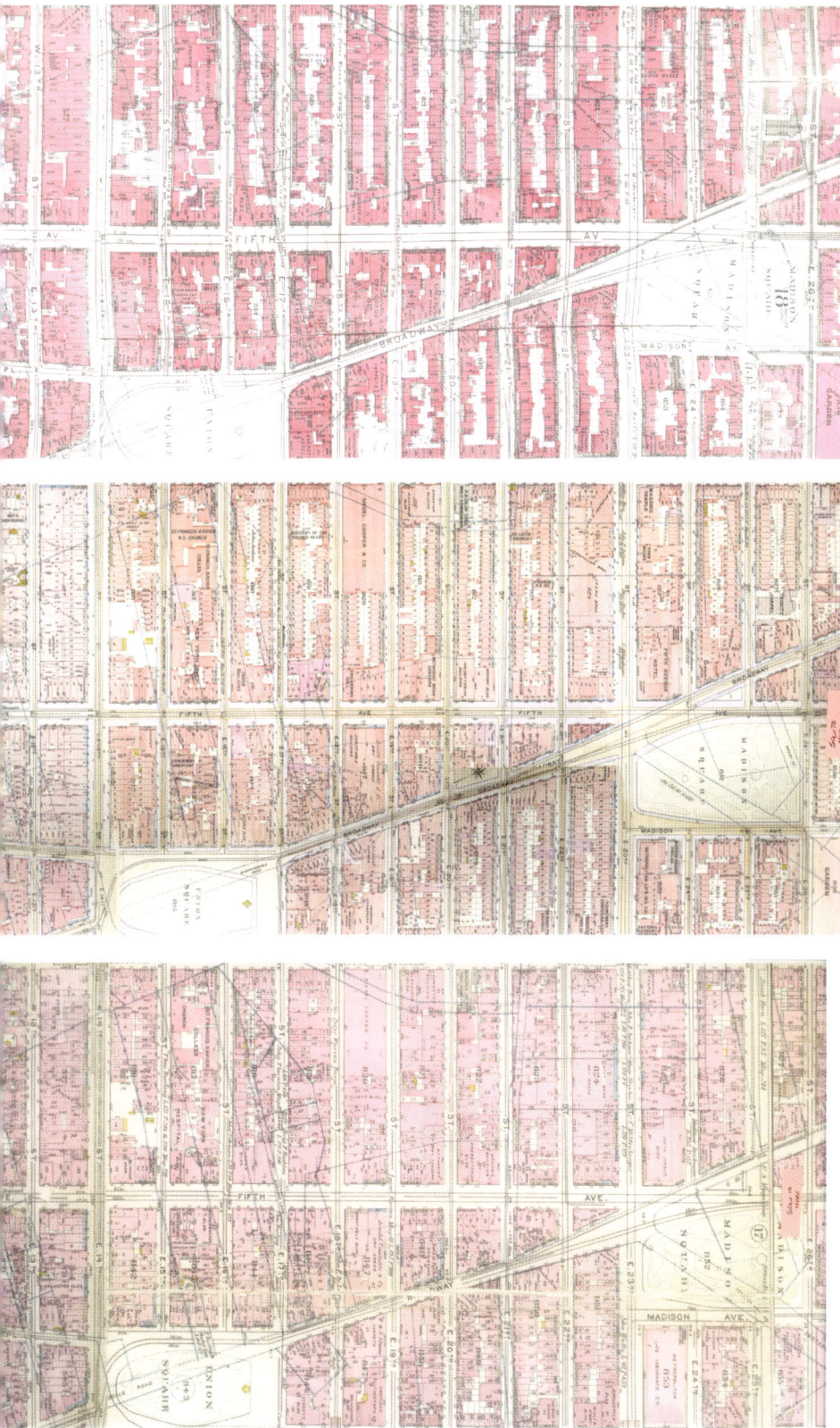